I0896380

BATTLE *of* BRITAIN
REMEMBERED

BATTLE *of* BRITAIN REMEMBERED

DILIP SARKAR
MBE, FRHistS, FRAeS

AIR WORLD

THE BATTLE OF BRITAIN MEMORIAL TRUST CIO
incorporating the
BATTLE OF BRITAIN
FIGHTER ASSOCIATION

AIR WORLD

BATTLE OF BRITAIN REMEMBERED

First published in Great Britain in 2025 by
Air World
An imprint of
Pen & Sword Books Ltd
Yorkshire – Philadelphia

ISBN: 978 1 39905 811 7

Typeset by SJmagic DESIGN SERVICES, India.

Printed and bound in the UK by CPI Group (UK) Ltd.

The Publisher's authorised representative in the EU for product safety is Authorised Rep Compliance Ltd., Ground Floor, 71 Lower Baggot Street,
Dublin D02 P593, Ireland.
www.arccompliance.com

For a complete list of Pen & Sword titles please contact:

PEN & SWORD BOOKS LTD
George House, Units 12 & 13, Beevor Street, Off Pontefract Road,
Barnsley, South Yorkshire, S71 1HN, England
E-mail: enquiries@pen-and-sword.co.uk
Website: www.pen-and-sword.co.uk

or

PEN AND SWORD BOOKS,
1950 Lawrence Road, Havertown, PA 19083, USA
E-mail: uspen-and-sword@casematepublishers.com
Website: www.penandswordbooks.com

FSC www.fsc.org
MIX
Paper | Supporting responsible forestry
FSC® C013604

Contents

Acknowledgements

This unique series of eight books has arisen from over forty years of research into and study of the Battle of Britain, throughout which time I enjoyed a privileged relationship with survivors and the relatives of casualties – too many to thank individually, but all have my sincere appreciation.

Suffice it to say, it has been an absolute privilege to produce this work for the Battle of Britain Memorial Trust and National Memorial to 'The Few', and I must thank our Chairman, Richard Hunting CBE, Honorary Secretary, Group Captain Patrick Tootal OBE DL RAF, Trustee, Wing Commander Andrew Simpson RAFVR(T), Major (Ret'd) Jules Gomez, Site Manager, National Memorial to 'The Few', and Audrey Gomez; both Malcolm Triggs and Becca Collier-Cook for their help in promoting the work. I would also acknowledge kind assistance from Edward McManus of the Battle of Britain London Monument.

In relation to this special project, I must thank Charles Hewitt, Martin Mace and Matthew Potts of Pen & Sword, and the production and marketing teams, who are always a pleasure to work with and collectively do a first-class job. Martin, of course, deserves a special mention for his sterling work on my behalf at The National Archives, and for being a very good friend and kindred spirit, always helpful and sharing my passion for making history both accessible and inclusive.

Regarding the recognition of Air Chief Marshal Sir Keith Park as one of 'The Few', I would like to thank the great man's great-nephews, Stephen and Brian Park, MOD AHB, Simon Moody of the RNZAF Museum, and Gail Romano of the Auckland War Memorial Museum.

Also helpful in various ways have been Andy Long; Chris Wiseman; Geoff Zuber, President of the Australian Spitfire Association; John Parker, Public Officer of the Hunter Fighter Collection Inc and Curator of Hunter Warbirds; Ross Pay and Vintage Fighter Restorations; Steve Vizard, Airframe Assemblies; Squadron Leader Ian Smith MBE RAF (Ret'd); Jarrod Cotter; Geoff Nutkins of the Shoreham Aviation Museum; David

Brocklehurst MBE, Chairman of The Kent Battle of Britain Museum; Linda Duffield and friends of The Kenley Revival Project; Robert Westbrook and Howard Wilton of the Manston Spitfire and Hurricane Memorial Museum; Joe Hill, former Curator, Battle of Britain Bunker; Anthony Philpott and Julia Williams of the RAF Hornchurch Heritage Centre; Paul Heys; Andy Saunders; Darren Priday, RAF Museum, Cosford; Philip Harvey; Amy Seadon, Aerospace Bristol; Glen Gelder; Mary Bean; Richard Hutchinson; Kate Ashby; Tony and Trish Osmand; Angela and Tim Lodge; Philip Harvey; Matthew Whiteman; Sam Heughan; Jarrod Cotter; Scott Booth and the Laguna Spitfire Legacy Project; Jan Leeming; Mark Donegain, Fowlmere Airfield Museum.

This particular eight-volume project is an unprecedent investigation into the Battle of Britain, from many angles, and the process has been both intense and time consuming. The forbearance of my family, especially my wife, Sue, and friends, therefore, is essential. I am also grateful for the interest and encouragement reflected by my social media followings. Thanks to all, team effort!

Author's Note and Glossary

The aviation-minded reader will notice that I have referred to German Messerschmitt fighters by the abbreviation 'Me' (not 'Bf', which is more technically correct), or simply by their numeric designation, such as '109' or '110'. This not only reads better but is authentic: during the Battle of Britain, Keith Lawrence, a New Zealander, flew Spitfires and once said to me 'To us they were just "Me's", "109s" or "110s", simple, never "Bf".'

In another attempt to preserve accuracy, I have also used the original German, wherever possible, regarding terms associated with the Luftwaffe and *Regia Aeronautica* (the Italian Air Force), such as:

Bundeswehr	The armed forces of the Federal Republic of Germany.
Geschwader	The whole group, usually of three *Gruppen*.
Gruppe	A wing, usually of three squadrons.
Gruppen	Wings.
Gruppenkommandeur	Wing commander.
Jagdbomber ('*Jabo*')	Fighter bomber.
Jagdflieger	Fighter pilot.
Jagdgeschwader	Fighter group, abbreviated to JG.
Jagdwaffe	The fighter force.
Jäger	Hunter, in this context a fighter pilot or aircraft.
Kampfgeschwadern	Bomber group, abbreviated to KG.
Lehrgeschwader	Literally a training group but actually a precision bombing unit, abbreviated LG.
Luftflotte	Air Fleet.
Oberkommando der Wehrmacht (OKW)	German armed forces high command.
Schwarm	A section of four fighters.
Seelöwe	Sealion, the codename for Adolf Hitler's proposed seaborne invasion of England.

Stab	Staff.
Stabschwarm	Unit of fighters.
Staffel	Squadron.
Staffeln	Squadrons.
Stuka	The Ju 87 dive bomber.
Wehrmacht	Armed forces.
Zerstörer	Literally 'destroyer', the term used for the Me 110.
Zerstörergeschwader	Destroyer group, abbreviated to ZG.

Each *Geschwader* generally comprised three *Gruppen*, each of three *Staffeln*. Each *Gruppe* is designated by Roman numerals, i.e. III/JG 26 refers to the third *Gruppe* of Fighter Group (abbreviated 'JG') 26. *Staffeln* are identified by numbers, so 7/JG 26 is the 7th *Staffel* and belongs to III/JG 26.

Rank comparisons may also be useful:

Adjutant	Adjutant
Feldwebel	Sergeant
Fähnrich	Officer Cadet
Gefreiter	Private 1st Class
General	General
Generalfeldmarschall	General Field Marshal
Generalleutnant	Lieutenant General
Hauptmann	Squadron Leader
Leutnant	Pilot Officer
Major	Wing Commander
Oberfeldwebel	Flight Sergeant
Oberleutnant	Flight Lieutenant
Oberst	Group Captain
Reichsmarschall	Marshal of the *Reich* (German Empire)
Unteroffizier	Corporal, no aircrew equivalent in Fighter Command

RAF Abbreviations:

AAF	Auxiliary Air Force
AC2	Aircraftman 2nd Class
AFDU	Air Fighting Development Unit

AHB	Air Historical Branch
AMO	Air Ministry Order
ARP	Air Raid Precautions
BBMF	Battle of Britain Memorial Flight
BEF	British Expeditionary Force
BoBFA	Battle of Britain Fighter Association
CO	Commanding Officer
CWGC	Commonwealth War Graves Commission
DFC	Distinguished Flying Cross
DFM	Distinguished Flying Medal
DSO	Distinguished Service Order
E/A	Enemy Aircraft
ENSA	Entertainments National Service Association
FAA	Fleet Air Arm
GPC	Guinea Pig Club
HQ	Headquarters
LAC	Leading Aircraftman
LAM	London Air Musuem
MC	Military Cross
MOD	Ministry of Defence
MRAF	Marshal of the Royal Air Force
NATO	North Atlantic Treaty Organization
NCO	Non-Commissioned Officer
OC	Officer Commanding
OR	Other Ranks
ORB	Operations Record Book
OTU	Operational Training Unit
P/O	Pilot Officer
PDU	Photographic Development Unit
PRU	Photographic Reconnaissance Unit
RAAF	Royal Australian Air Force
RAF	Royal Air Force
RAFVR	Royal Air Force Volunteer Reserve
RCAF	Royal Canadian Air Force
RDF	Radio Direction Finding
RFS	Reserve Flying School
RN	Royal Navy
R/T	Radio Telephone
SASO	Senior Air Staff Officer

SHAEF	Supreme Headquarters Allied Expeditionary Force
SSC	Short Service Commission
UAS	University Air Squadron
USAF	United States Air Force
WAAF	Women's Auxiliary Air Force
WAAG	Wealdon Aviation Archaeology Group

Also, 'Angels' refers to height measured in thousands of feet; hence 'Angles 15' means 15,000ft. A 'vector' is a compass course, measured in degrees, a 'bandit' is a confirmed enemy aircraft whilst a 'bogey' and an 'X-Raid' are, as yet, unidentified but potentially hostile radar plots. 'Tally Ho!' was shouted when the enemy were sighted and the leader was ordering an attack. To the Germans, hostile aircraft were 'Indians' and the German fighter pilot's victory cry was 'Horrido'.

BUCKINGHAM PALACE

The Battle of Britain's significance can be summed up, quite simply: it was Hitler's first reversal of the war at a time when German military might appeared invincible'.

Britain, alone, was consequently able to hold out as the only base in western Europe from which war against Hitler could continue to be waged, and, ultimately, with American help, from where the liberation of enemy occupied Europe was successfully launched. The Battle of Britain, therefore, deserves its place in history alongside such turning points as Waterloo and Trafalgar, the young airmen who made this victory possible immortalised by Churchill as 'The Few'. Of those near 3,000 aircrew, 544 lost their lives in action during the Battle of Britain, and over 700 more would perish before the Second World War ended. It is right, therefore, that we remember the Battle of Britain and those who fought for the freedoms we enjoy today.

In his eight-volume official history for the Battle of Britain Memorial Trust CIO and National Memorial to The Few, the historian Dilip Sarkar has produced the most detailed narrative ever likely to be produced on this epic air battle. This final volume, 'Battle of Britain Remembered', chronicles how the Battle has been memorialised and commemorated, exploring its place in popular culture, acknowledging the work of the Commonwealth War Graves Commission and other organisations, and the key memorials, monuments and museums dedicated to honouring The Few. This is an appropriate conclusion to this seminal work, which supports the Trust's invaluable contribution to commemorating The Few – who must never be forgotten.

Anne

Introduction

The living, including survivors, have commemorated wars for centuries, and this became especially important after the huge casualties of the American Civil War, which was the world's first head-on collision with mass death caused by industrial warfare. Indeed, it was during that hellish conflict that for the first time, in 1862, casualties were buried in individual, named graves, in war cemeteries, thus making their sacrifice somehow special. Previously, the dead of battle had historically been interred in mass graves marked, perhaps but far from always, by a generic memorial to the battle concerned, perhaps mentioning by name the victorious commander only. The First World War, similarly, was Europe's first experience of this bestial level of violence, generating unprecedented casualties, and afterwards, with so many bereaved, the sacrifice involved was elevated to a sacred-like status. During the First World War 1.1 million men and women lost their lives in the service of the former British Empire, and this enormous scale of loss led to creation of the Imperial War Graves Commission in May 1917 (which became the Commonwealth War Graves Commission in 1960), to provide permanent care for casualties graves and to commemorate the missing. In those days, international travel was not what it is today, overseas journeys being literally foreign to ordinary people, and so innumerable relatives were unable to visit the immaculately tended, often vast, war cemeteries in which their loved ones lay, far away. Consequently, for them, and the families of the missing, without a focal point or closure for their grief, countless local war memorials, inscribed with the names of the fallen, appeared all over the United Kingdom and beyond. The same was the case after the Second World War, in which a further 600,000 from all parts of the Commonwealth, and the names of that conflict's fallen were not only added to existing local war memorials, but commemorated on certain specific monuments. This, of course, included the Battle of Britain.

That the Battle of Britain has been commemorated is beyond doubt – but how that has changed over time, and the diverse nature of that remembrance is complex, not least because of how very much society and the world has changed since 1940. Naturally, general enthusiasm was at its peak in the immediate post-war years, but the more distanced in time we become from 1940, the understanding of and, therefore, relevance of that tumultuous and desperate year, and, indeed, victory in the Battle of Britain, fades. Fortunately, there remain certain 'agents of remembrance', official and unofficial, not least the Battle of Britain Memorial Trust, which maintains the National Memorial to 'The Few' at Capel-le-Ferne, the RAF itself and Commonwealth War Graves Commission, and those of us to whom the Battle of Britain and those who fought, and in 544 cases died, in it, still mean something. It is hoped, therefore, that although the memory will inevitably dim and fade as the years pass, the evidence confirms that it will never evaporate completely.

This book seeks to mark in time where we are today with regard to remembering and commemorating the Battle of Britain, and how we arrived at this point.

Dilip Sarkar MBE FRHistS FRAeS, BA(Hons)
June 2025

Chapter One

How Relevant is the Battle of Britain Today?

Beyond doubt, Britain's contribution to the Allies' total victory during the Second World War is arguably the proudest moment in modern British history, a lynchpin of post-war national identity and pride. That being so, then Britain's victory in the Battle of Britain, Nazi Germany's first military reversal and failure of the war, must surely be the most epic but unexpected success in what was perceived – then and now – as a 'good war', a 'people's war', with a clear-cut divide between good and evil. In 1945, when Europe was liberated by the Allied forces, the true extent of Nazi bestiality was revealed for all to see, so there is no ambiguity, despite German army belt buckles proclaiming '*Gott Mitt Uns*' ('God with us'), about whose side God must have been on. Indeed, after the disastrous Fall of France and the Dunkirk evacuation it seemed that only divine intervention would save Britain. The popular narrative, however, speaks to us of 'Britain alone', railed faithfully behind its bulldog prime minister, the day being saved only by a mere handful of dashing Hurricane and Spitfire pilots, fighting against overwhelming odds and who, therefore, paved the way for that ultimate total victory. But how true is that narrative?

On 7 June 1940, in the wake of the BEF's evacuation from north-west France, the *Evening Standard* published David Low's famous cartoon of a British soldier standing on the fabled white cliffs of Dover, shaking a fist at the Germans – who were in France, just 22 miles away across the English Channel. 'Very well, alone!', the tin-hatted 'Tommy' shouted. Although the current trend amongst academic historians appears to be diluting the significance of the Battle of Britain, and challenging whether Britain really was 'alone', the fact remains that, whilst accepting that the popular Battle of Britain narrative is heavily myth-laden, Low had a valid point: first Poland, then the continental Western democracies had fallen to Nazi Germany in quick succession; of those belligerent nations, only island Britain remained free. British Prime Minister Winston Churchill knew as an historian that states that go down without a fight are destined to disappear, whilst those that fight on, even if defeated, are destined to rise again. Whatever the odds, therefore, however hopeless the outlook appeared, surrender was never an option – and in a practical and immediate sense, Britain – as opposed to the British – really was alone. But what does that mean?

Certainly, Britain enjoyed the huge resources of the British Empire and Commonwealth, but this aid was far away, across hazardous oceans infested with German submarines, and took time to assemble and transport. The United States was neutral, after the First World War pursuing isolationism from events in Europe, and the Soviets had signed an unholy alliance with Adolf Hitler. Whilst Britain hoped for American intervention against Germany, and collapse of the Nazi-Soviet Non-Aggression Pact, also bringing Joseph Stalin into the Allied camp, so far as the immediate future

VERY WELL, ALONE

David Low's cartoon, published in the *Evening Standard* on 7 June 1940.

was concerned, Britain really was alone – and it was only the British people, not those far away in countries of the British Empire and Commonwealth, who were threatened by German air attacks. In that sense, then, let us be clear: Britain – and everyone in the country – was alone and fighting on.

Considering Germany's military record to date in the Second World War, and following Dunkirk, surrender did seem to some to be Britain's only realistic option. Indeed, the truth was that the Fall of France and Hitler's lightning-fast Blitzkrieg across Western Europe to the Channel ports had changed everything strategically – and despite British propaganda spinning the Dunkirk evacuation into a victory arising from defeat, the unpalatable truth was that it was a catastrophe of immeasurable proportions, the immensity of which is, perhaps, difficult for us to truly comprehend today. What lay ahead for Britain? Nobody knew. Between the wars, the fear of aerial bombing, emphasised by the fate of the Basque town of Guernica in the Spanish Civil War, and the bombing of Chongqing in China by Japan, was comparable to the post-war hysteria concerning the new, devastating atomic weapons. In the event, destructive though German bombing would be, it would not be the predicted Armageddon – but the situation in which Britain found itself in June 1940 was infinitely worse than even the most pessimistic predictions: a disaster indeed.

The background concerning the development of air power, from the First World War onwards, the details and strengths of the RAF and Luftwaffe, and, of course, Britain's system of air defence, were well-covered in Volume I, *The Gathering Storm: Prelude to the Spitfire Summer of 1940*, so will not be duplicated here. In sum, however, the RAF comprised a comparatively small core of professional airmen, the ranks of which were bolstered in 1939 when the part-time territorials of the AAF and RAFVR's 'Citizen Volunteers' were mobilised and called to full-time service. Collectively, this strength, and that of numbers of aircraft, were roughly equal by the time the Battle of Britain was fought – but the Luftwaffe exclusively comprised professionals, many of whom had learned their violent trade during the Spanish Civil War, working out modern tactics, and had since fought their way victoriously from Poland to the Pas-de-Calais. The RAF, conversely, had yet to fight in their monoplane fighters when the storm broke on 3 September 1939, and, indeed, before the war Fighter Command tacticians assumed that air attacks would come from Germany itself, approaching Britain's east coast across the North Sea, and because such flights exceeded the range of single-engined fighters, Air Ministry's tacticians foresaw only interceptions of unescorted bombers. This is another reason why the Fall of France changed everything, providing Hitler with bases in north-west France, putting even London within the range of the Me 109 fighter, albeit only for a limited period of time. Offset against this, Britain's defences included radar – more accurately RDF – providing Fighter Command with early warning of enemy aircraft assembling and approaching, which would prove an essential bonus in the battle ahead.

The Luftwaffe was equipped with modern monoplanes, and the Me 109 'Emil' was, at the time, a more advanced design than even the Supermarine Spitfire, enjoying the advantages of fuel injection, an automatic constant speed propeller, and two 20mm cannon. The 109 and Spitfire were both superior in performance to the Hawker Hurricane, which was Fighter Command's primary fighter, equipping more squadrons – two-thirds – than the much-needed Spitfire, with its high-altitude performance comparable to that of its Teutonic adversary. Whereas the Me 109E equipped the entire enemy single-engined fighter force, Fighter Command's single-seaters were divided between the more modern, all metal, Supermarine Spitfire, and the less advanced Hawker Hurricane, which although inferior in performance was available in greater numbers. Then there were and the Boulton Paul Defiant turret-fighter, which proved under-powered and unsuitable for daylight fighter combat, and even the Gloster Gladiator biplane. The RAF fighters, though, were doing the job for which they were designed and intended as short-range defensive interceptors – whereas the 109s were pressed into service as long-range escort or offensive fighters, roles for which they were neither designed or best-suited suited. Both sides also had twin-engined fighters, the RAF's Bristol Blenheim and the Luftwaffe's Me 110, both of which had longer range than the single-engined types but which ultimately proved vulnerable to attack by the latter, more manoeuvrable, fighters. Fast and well-armed though the German twin-engined bombers were, however, they lacked the bombload necessary for strategic bombing, the Luftwaffe having really been created to provide close air support, flying artillery, effectively, for advancing ground troops. So far, this had worked perfectly, and the unprecedented German victory over Allied forces in France owed much to the Me 109 achieving total aerial superiority over the battlefield, enabling the panzers to operate beneath this protective aerial umbrella. And that, in fact, was what the Battle of Britain was about: aerial superiority over southern England, as a prelude to a German seaborne invasion.

Prior to his astonishing, lightning-swift victory over France and the Low Countries, Hitler had never planned either the strategic bombing or a seaborne invasion of Britain. This was simply not his original strategy. Hitler was certainly driven, so far as the West was concerned, by a deep-rooted desire to avenge the ignominy of the 1919 Versailles peace treaty, and to expunge this humiliation by defeating the French, but Britain, with the British Empire and Commonwealth, not to mention legendary RN, however, he much admired, even feared, and knew full-well that any war against Britain was unlikely to be swiftly prosecuted – and it was quick wins that the *Führer* needed. Politically, Nazism and Communism were ideologically opposed, and Hitler's aim was to expand the Reich territory eastwards, defeating the Soviets in the process and taking advantage of this huge living space and its vast resources. Indeed, Hitler's generals were confident of another Blitzkrieg victory against the ill-prepared Russians – but not against the British. So, when Hitler danced his victory jig at Valenciennes, when France signed the Armistice in the very railway carriage that Germany had surrendered in 1918, and then went sight-seeing in Paris, a seaborne invasion of Britain was not at the forefront of the *Führer*'s mind. The BEF, however, had left behind its armour and heavy weapons in France, so Britain's land defences in southern England were consequently and substantially weakened – so much so, in fact, that without the support of either America or the Soviet Union, it seemed there was no hope. Britain, Hitler therefore believed, could easily be persuaded, through blockade, the fear of bombing, threats and diplomacy, to accept Germany's surrender terms. With Britain thus subdued, Hitler could then roll up Russia.

After a lull following Dunkirk, some seventy He 111 bombers ranged far and wide over eastern England on the night of 18/19 June 1940, heralding the start of a new onslaught. Hitler, however, was reluctant to order an all-out air attack on Britain, preferring instead to rely upon the brinkmanship which had served him so well when dealing with Neville Chamberlain and Édouard Deladier in the late 1930s. The Luftwaffe, therefore, focused upon attacking convoys in the Channel, and not coastal or inland targets. This hostile activity began on 2 July 1940, on which day the OKW first announced that preparations were to be made for a seaborne invasion of southern England, the plan soon to become Operation *Seelöwe*. The service chiefs, however, had no experience of such a huge, combined operation, and the RN was a major deterrent to such a hazardous undertaking, which Hitler fully appreciated. Whilst the three services drew up plans, which became Operation *Seelöwe*, and Hitler played 'air fleet diplomacy' over Channel-bound convoys, emphasising the aerial might that could be deployed against Britain if necessary, the *Führer* focused his mind on making a 'last appeal to reason', a deluded expectation that Britain would accept terms (covered in detail by Volume 2, *The Breaking Storm: 10 July 1940–12 August 1940*). Following a further bluff on 16 July 1940, when Hitler's infamous *Führer* Directive 16 proclaimed that preparations to invade England would now be made, and 'if necessary carried out', his offer of terms was eventually made in a speech on 19 July 1940 – and, unsurprisingly, firmly rejected by the British. Whilst Churchill mobilised the English language, offering nothing but 'blood, sweat and tears', announcing that Britain would fight and repel any invader 'on the beaches', and anywhere else if necessary, Hitler now faced a dilemma: his terms having been rejected, he either had to go ahead and fulfil his threats – or back down and lose face. There was only ever going to be one option: Hitler now had to entrust his deputy and Luftwaffe chief, *Reichsmarschall* Hermann Göring, with achieving aerial supremacy over southern England as a prelude to the sailing of Operation *Seelöwe*. So far undefeated, Göring was sublimely confident and predicted that the RAF could be defeated in just a four or five days of good weather.

Ironically, bad weather would confound the *Adler Angriff*, the 'Attack of the Eagles', which was not launched until 13 August 1940, and was rather a damp squib – although three days later saw the greatest German attack of any day during the Battle of Britain, which, so far as the British Air Ministry was concerned, had begun not on 2 July 1940 but eight days later, on 10 July 1940. On 15 August 1940, attacks were made on a huge front, from St Eval in Cornwall to Newcastle and Sunderland in the north-east – and saw *Luftflotte* 5, based in Norway, defeated by 12 and 13 Groups of Fighter Command in a single day (see Volume 3, *Attack of the Eagles, 13 August 1940–18 August 1940*). Effort was being concentrated on coastal targets and airfields, but too little emphasis given to the destruction of RDF stations, the importance of which the Germans did not fully understand. The weather continued to frustrate raids, which soon primarily targeted RAF airfields (see Volume 4, *Airfields Under Attack: 19 August 1940–6 September 1940*). Although clearly a sensible strategy, especially attacking the all-important sector stations, accommodating vital operations rooms, the effect of these raids, successful though some were, was reduced through poor intelligence – something which the Luftwaffe suffered from throughout the Battle of Britain. Consequently, too much effort was expended attacking airfields unconnected with Fighter Command, such as RAF Eastchurch and RAF Lympne, and insufficient effort directed at the sector stations around London, namely RAF Kenley, RAF Northolt, RAF Biggin Hill, RAF Hornchurch and RAF North Weald. Indeed, the Luftwaffe simply failed to understand how Fighter Command was organised and controlled. There was also another problem by early September 1940: time was running out. The 15 September 1940 had been set for the date on which Operation *Seelöwe* must go ahead, but the Luftwaffe was no further forward in achieving its objective. On the contrary, it was abundantly clear that Fighter Command was far from defeated – and nor would it be by the due date.

It was now that Göring changed tack once more, turning the Luftwaffe's attention to the destruction of London, the intention being not only to disrupt the capital but also lure Fighter Command to battle, for destruction en masse. So the popular legend has it, this diversion to bomb London saved Fighter Command's airfields, which were on their knees. This is not true: although some had been hurt, badly on occasion, all remained operational – but it is fair to say that had those heavy attacks continued, the airfields could have been knocked out. That, though, was also unlikely, and not only because of often questionable target selection due to poor intelligence: the Luftwaffe, through changing tack and not concentrating effort, ignored the principles of war – and would pay the price for that.

Rising losses led to arguments in the German camp, the bombers demanding closer fighter escort, something the Me 109, with its limited range, was ill-suited to, and also ignored the lessons of the First World War, which confirmed that the fighter is at its most lethal when allowed to road freely, seeking out and destroying the enemy. The great attack on London began on 7 September 1940 (see Volume 5, *Target London: 7 September 1940–17 September 1940*), but this meant that the German bombers had further inland to penetrate, providing Fighter Command more opportunities to intercept, and the effectiveness of the Me 109 was reduced by the greater burden of providing close escort, burning up more fuel and reducing flying time over southern England. Indeed, many 109 pilots would run out of petrol before regaining the French coast, or forced-land on French beaches. On 15 September 1940, *Luftflotte* 2 threw all it could at London, having been advised that Fighter Command was reliant purely upon its last handful of Spitfires and Hurricanes. No. 11 Group, defending London and the south-east, reacted to both heavy raids that day in strength, which were reinforced over the capital by the five-squadron-strong 12 Group Duxford Wing. The sight of so many RAF fighters was shattering to the German aircrews on what has gone down in history as 'Battle of Britain Day', and it was abundantly clear that the boastful *Reichsmarschall* was unable to deliver. Two days later, Hitler made his decision: Operation *Seelöwe* was postponed indefinitely.

Despite this, Göring remained convinced that his Luftwaffe alone could defeat Britain, daylight attacks continuing whilst the main emphasis switched to night bombing. With Britain's nocturnal defences in their infancy, this enabled to German bombers to intrude over Britain with impunity – the trade-off being that bombing was less accurate. Consequently, being unable to precisely attack military targets by night, this heralded, in fact, the start of the nocturnal area bombing of cities (later, RAF Bomber Command would devastate German cities after dark, its chief, Air Marshal Sir Arthur 'Bomber' Harris chillingly commentating in March 1942 that the Germans had 'sowed the wind and now they are going to reap the whirlwind'). The Germans' target priorities changed again, focusing upon the British aircraft industry, and there were some successes, such as the devasting raid on the Bristol Aeroplane Works at RAF Filton on 25 September 1940, and the even more destructive raid on Supermarine at Woolston the following day. This was all too little too late, however. The Me 109s, though, were enjoying greater success, being unshackled from their close escort role and sweeping over southern England at heights of up to 31,000ft or more. Had these been pure fighter sweeps, such incursions could have been ignored by the defenders, but the inclusion of fighter bombers in these formations from 20 September 1940 onwards meant that all such raids needed intercepting, and their very high altitude stretched 11 Group, which had to mount standing patrols, virtually dawn until dusk. By 30 September 1940, nonetheless, the German twin-engined bombers had reached the point that their losses were unsustainable, so all types but the Ju 88 were switched to night operations (see Volume 6, *Daylight Defeat: 18 September 1940–30 September 1940*).

Going forward into October 1940, by day lone Ju 88s continued to target the British aircraft factories, the last major raid being flown by Ju 88s at *Gruppe* strength against Westlands at Yeovil on the 7th of that month. Elsewhere, the high-altitude fighter sweeps and fighter-bomber raids continued, but such light, random, daylight bombing was mainly of nuisance value and so, again, these operations were largely intended to bring Fighter Command to battle. Clearly, such attacks could never bomb Britain into submission or effect the circumstances necessary for *Seelöwe* to sail, however. Moreover, the unpredictable British autumn weather, Channel tides and conditions, were now firmly in the defenders' favour: on 12 October 1940, Hitler cancelled *Seelöwe* completely, unless, miraculously, the situation changed. Arguably, therefore, the Battle of Britain, if we are to understand that it was fought to prevent the seaborne invasion of southern England, actually ended on that day and not, as the British Air Ministry decided, 31 October 1940 (see Volume 7, *The Final Curtain: 1 October 1940–31 October 1940*).

The Luftwaffe, though, was not destroyed, leading some to argue that there was, therefore, no victory at all. This is nonsense because that outcome was not the objective – Britain's survival was. And survive it had. Because of Fighter Command's robust and unwavering defence, denying the Luftwaffe aerial superiority, *Seelöwe* had been abandoned and with it the threat of invasion passed. Indeed, as the weather deteriorated, as autumn wore on, it was clear to everyone that the immediate likelihood of invasion had been staved off – but with the opposing fighter forces continuing to clash until the weather closed right in during February 1941, and the night blitz of British cities in full swing throughout the winter of 1940/1941, the defenders naturally assumed that the spectre of invasion would reappear the following spring. But it did not: *Seelöwe* was a dead duck, so, beyond any doubt, there was most certainly a British victory. In recognition of this, operational Fighter Command aircrews were honoured by being awarded the coveted Battle of Britain Clasp to the 1939–1945 Star (see Chapter Two) – but contrary to the popular myth and narrative, Fighter Command did not, in fact, fight or win this essential victory alone.

Concurrently with Fighter Command's defence, there was a forgotten battle ongoing, that fought by Bomber Command and Coastal Command, the FAA and PDU. Bomber Command's responsibilities included relentlessly attacking the invasion ports and disrupting assembly of the German invasion fleet, and enemy airfields, by day and night, in addition to attacking naval, military and industrial targets in Germany itself – even Berlin. Coastal Command flew countless convoy protection and anti-invasion patrols, attacking enemy shipping and the Channel ports, carrying out crucial reconnaissance and the mining of German waters. Similarly, the FAA also sowed mines, attacked ports and shipping, and the unarmed pilots of the PDU (later PRU) returned from their unarmed sorties, often deep into enemy territory, with vital intelligence. Whilst the battles fought by Fighter Command were over England itself, and watched by those on the ground, the war being fought elsewhere was invisible – but no less important. It is right, therefore, that we should have a better understanding of that today.

Having suffered his first reversal of the Second World War, Hitler, as we all know, turned his attention to Russia. The surprise invasion of the Soviet Union on 22 June 1941, though, also included a strategy against Britain – which is far less widely known and understood. Churchill's two great hopes, as already explained, were for America to abandon its policy of isolationism from Europe and join the war against Germany, and for the

Soviet-Non-Aggression Pact to fail so that the Russians would also join the Allied cause. By quickly defeating Russia, however, Hitler reasoned that this would extend Japanese influence in the Far East, thereby fully occupying the Americans – and with no hope of American or Russian support, Britain would then have no choice but to surrender. Fortunately, the German advance floundered at the gates of Moscow, and was smashed at Stalingrad, and the Japanese attack on the American Pacific Fleet at Pearl Harbor on 7 December 1941 at last brought the United States into the war. Hitler's initial strategy against Britain had failed, as had the attempt to wrest aerial superiority from the RAF to facilitate *Seelöwe*; Hitler's revised plan, to conquer Russia, also failed, so on 7 December 1941, both of Churchill's high hopes were realised – Britain was no longer 'alone'. In addition to its own resources and those of the British Empire and Commonwealth, the immense resources of both America and Russia were now arraigned against Nazi Germany. For Hitler, now fighting on two fronts, this was a disaster which ultimately ended in the unconditional surrender of Germany on 8 May 1945. And so now we come to why victory in the Battle of Britain was – and still is – so immeasurably significant.

The most obvious significance of victory in the Battle of Britain is, of course, that Britain remained free as base from which, with American help and in due course, the Allied strategic bombing campaign could be unleashed on Germany, and the liberation of enemy occupied Europe eventually effected. Britain became, therefore, a unique and vital base from which war against Hitler could still be waged. Had Britain fallen, with the rest of the Western democracies already under the Nazi yoke, this could never have happened because there was no other such geographic base. We know how perilous was the subsequent Battle of the Atlantic, the U-boat menace plundering Allied merchant shipping, and the courageous story of the Allies' response – but the fact is without victory in the Battle of Britain, there would have been no other battles: no Battle of the Atlantic, no victories in the Mediterranean theatre, or in the Far East. The Axis Powers – Germany and Italy in Europe and Japan in the Far East – would have controlled everything, including Russia, the resource-rich Ukraine and the countries of Britain's former Empire and Commonwealth, and Russia. With such vast resources controlled by the fascists, America, alone, which in any case was too far away to physically intervene in Europe, is very unlikely to have defeated or arguably even challenged the all-powerful Axis. There is, however, much more to it than the obvious and inevitable 'what ifs' of history.

Victory in the Battle of Britain preserved the democratic British way of life, upon which countless nations have modelled their societies and political systems. The Second World War itself accelerated social change, the hierarchical social barriers of the past not entirely dismantled but certainly reduced, heralding and making possible changes ahead for the better in British society – a greater equality between the sexes, professionally, politically and socially, being a foremost case in point.

Back then, in 1940, it was also the age of imperialism, the Western industrial nations having embarked upon journeys of discovery and colonising nations of the Middle East and Far East. An age of empire, today it is widely acknowledged, fortunately, that the subjugation of nations and exploitation of their wealth, peoples and resources, was wrong, leading to the claim that all victory in the Battle of Britain did was preserve this injustice. Again, this misses the essential point: the dismantling of Britain's Empire was not something that could be achieved, legally, administratively, politically or logistically overnight – and first Nazism had to be defeated. Ultimately, the British Empire was dismantled – but had Britain not remained free in 1940, that would never have happened – and Britain's commitment to a better world post-war is surely indicated by India, that enormous, glittering, jewel in the Crown, being granted independence just two years after the war against Japan had been won. In a Nazi, fascist, dominated world, the return of such freedoms would never have been possible, and nor would the multi-cultural diversity of today.

So, victory in the Battle of Britain was not just something of its time, eighty-five years ago, no, the consequences of it resonate and still have currency today. Indeed, everything that Britain is and will become, for good or bad, arises from the fact that Britain did not falter, fail or fall in 1940. However much people may complain about the Britain of today, we still have freedom of speech, political freedom, freedom of choice – all a world away from Nazi murder, sadism, mayhem and oppression. Although 'The Few' officially refers to a specific group of airmen, those of Fighter Command, as we have seen as the volumes of this unprecedented narrative progressed, a forgotten battle was being fought concurrently by the aircrews of Bomber Command and Coastal Command, the FAA and small PDU; in this context, therefore, 'The Few', to me, refers to all of those RAF servicemen and women who played their part during the Battle of Britain. Victory belongs to them all.

That victory remains just as relevant today – and always will be – as will the sacrifice of those who achieved it: 'The Few' and the many.

Chapter Two

The Battle of Britain Clasp and 'The Few'

The 'Battle of Britain' is possibly unique in that it was named even before it began. On 18 June 1940, British Prime Minister Winston Churchill spoke in the House of Commons and told members that 'What *General* [Maxime] Weygand called the Battle of France is over. I expect that the Battle of Britain is about to begin.' He was right, and the Air Ministry would later decide that the Battle of Britain was fought between 10 July 1940 and 31 October 1940.

Churchill actually said a great deal more in what was a lengthy speech, briefing members of Parliament on the tumultuous events of the previous few days, during which, on 16 June 1940, *Marshal* Philippe Pétain had retired to Vichy in southern France and set up a new, puppet, government; the following day, France had sued for peace. Churchill's intention was to reaffirm, in the light of this 'colossal military disaster', to both the domestic and international audience, that Britain was resolved to fight on – alone. The prime minister spoke of the 'great question of invasion from the air, and of the impending struggle between the British and German Air Forces', emphasising that no invasion could take place 'until our Air Force has been definitely overpowered'.

That Britain's fate would now be decided in the air was clear, and, in what is the best-remembered part of this speech, the prime minister concluded,

> Upon this battle depends the survival of Christian civilisation. Upon it depends our own British life, and the long continuity of our institutions and our Empire. The whole fury and might of the enemy must very soon be turned on us. Hitler knows that he will have to break us in this Island or lose the war. If we can stand up to him, all Europe may be free and the life of the world may move forward into broad, sunlit uplands. But if

> we fail, then the whole world, including the United States, including all that we have known and cared for, will sink into the abyss of a new Dark Age made more sinister, and perhaps more protracted, by the lights of perverted science. Let us therefore brace ourselves to our duties, and so bear ourselves that, if the British Empire and its Commonwealth last for a thousand years, men will still say, 'This was their finest hour.'

The battle ahead now named, this was also the start of the forthcoming sixteen-week conflict achieving a special place in the hearts and minds of the free world, which saw a David and Goliath scale conflict in what was a clear-cut struggle between good and evil. Four hours after Churchill addressed the House of Commons, a version of the same speech was broadcast by the BBC to several million listeners. Although not considered Churchill's best performance, nonetheless this, of all his speeches, remains foremost amongst them. 'Rhetoric', though, Churchill wrote, 'was no guarantee of survival' – but there was nothing else on offer, and this gifted orator had now mobilised the English language, making it too a weapon of war.

On 'Eagle Day', 15 August 1940 (see *Attack of the Eagles*, Volume 3) the British Prime Minister, Winston Churchill, had personally watched the high tension and drama unfolding from the observation gallery of Air Vice-Marshal Keith Park's underground Operations Room at 11 Group's RAF Uxbridge HQ. The prime minister was in company with his chief staff officer, General Hastings Ismay, and afterwards was deep in thought as the pair were driven back to Chequers, the prime minister's country house in Buckinghamshire. 'Don't speak to me', Churchill told Ismay, 'I have never been so moved'. Churchill then said, spontaneously, 'Never in the field of human conflict was so much owed by so many to so few.'

On 20 August 1940, with the Second World War nearly a year old, Churchill addressed the House of Commons at length, an appropriate moment at which, he said, 'to pause on our journey at this milestone and survey the dark, wide field'. The prime minister began by comparing 'German aggression with its forerunner a quarter century ago', opining that 'this war is in fact only a continuation of the last' but 'very great differences in its character are apparent'. In identifying differences between 1914 and 1940, because of air power, Churchill rightly observed,

> The whole of the warring nations are engaged, not only soldiers, but the entire population, men, women and children.

> The fronts are everywhere. The trenches are dug in the towns and streets. Every village is fortified. Every road is barred. The front line runs through the factories. The workmen are soldiers with different weapons and the same courage. These are great and distinctive changes from what many of us saw in the struggle of a quarter of a century ago. There seems to be every reason to believe that this new kind of war is well suited to the genius and the resources of the British nation and the British Empire … If it is a case of the whole nation fighting and suffering together, that ought to suit us, because we are the most united of nations, because we entered the war upon the national will and with our eyes open, and because we have been nurtured in freedom …

Churchill's introductory sentiments were clear enough, and he went on, at length, to discuss war aims and review Britain's defences and fighting forces. 'The whole British Army is at home … The whole island', he said,

> bristles against invaders, from the sea or from the air … As in Nelson's day, the maxim holds, 'Our first line of defence is the enemy's ports.' Now air reconnaissance and photography have brought to an old principle a new and potent aid … Or Navy is far stronger than at the beginning of the war … The seas and oceans are open … I said in the very dark hour two months ago, of continuing the war 'if necessary alone, if necessary for years'. I say it also because the fact that the British Empire stands invincible, and that Nazidom is still being resisted, will kindle again the spark of hope in the breasts of hundreds of millions of down-trodden or despairing men and women throughout Europe, and far beyond its bounds, and that from these sparks there will presently come a cleansing and devouring flame.

The everlasting impact of this significant speech, however, concerned 'The great air battle which has been in progress over this Island', which, 'for the last few weeks has recently attained a high intensity':

> The gratitude of every home in our Island, in our Empire, and indeed throughout the world, except in the abodes of the

> guilty, goes out to the British airmen who, undaunted by odds, unwearied in their constant challenge and mortal danger, are turning the tide of the world war by their prowess and by their devotion. Never in the field of human conflict was so much owed by so many to so few.

This was the rhetoric of genius, because here Churchill paid tribute to the RAF aircrews, arguably connecting the current struggle and those fighting in the air with King Henry V's eve of battle speech in William Shakespeare's play: 'We few, we happy few, we band of brothers'.

On 25 October 1415, St Crispin's Day, Henry V's disease-ravaged and comparatively small army defeated the flower of French nobility at the Battle of Agincourt – a victory no one, least of all the bowmen of England and Wales, expected Henry to win. And now, in 1940, was a direct parallel, clearly not lost on Churchill – whose lines 'Never in the field of human conflict was so much owed by so many to so few' has gone down in history to define the Battle of Britain. With these words, Churchill immortalised the RAF aircrews – but, as we have seen, these brave men were not exclusively 'British'. The RAF now fighting against Hitler's Germany was, in fact, a multi-national force: men from the Commonwealth: Canadians, New Zealanders, Australians, and even volunteers from still neutral America, and, of course, free airmen from the occupied lands: Poles, Czechs, Belgians, French and Dutchmen.

Significantly, Churchill continued,

> All hearts go out to the fighter pilots, whose brilliant actions we see with our own eyes day after day; but we must never forget that all the time, night after night, month after month, our bomber squadrons travel far into Germany, find their targets in the darkness by the highest navigational skill, aim their attacks, often under the heaviest fire, often with serious loss, with deliberate careful discrimination, and inflict shattering blows upon the whole of the technical and war-making structure of the Nazi power. On no part of the Royal Air Force does the weight of the war fall more heavily than on the daylight bombers who will play an invaluable part in the case of invasion and whose unflinching zeal it has been necessary in the meanwhile on numerous occasions to restrain.

In popular culture, Churchill's speech and reference to the 'few' is assumed to have referred exclusively to fighter pilots – but clearly that was not at all the case. In this narrative we have seen, day by day, how Bomber Command and Coastal Command heavily contributed to air operations throughout the Battle of Britain, and Churchill actually paid a greater tribute to 'our bomber squadrons' attacking Germany by night, concluding that 'On no part of the Royal Air Force does the weight of the war fall more heavily than on the daylight bombers …' Clearly, then, the prime minister fully acknowledged the contributions of Bomber Command, and especially the daylight bombers of 2 Group, and reference to 'so few' concerned the RAF as a whole. The Battle of Britain, though, was essentially a defensive battle, much of which was fought over England by Fighter Command and within sight of those on the ground. Consequently, those combats and the fighter aircrew involved epitomised the Battle of Britain, eclipsing, so far as the public was concerned, the less visible efforts of Bomber Command. This is why, no matter what Churchill actually said and meant, his speech and reference to 'the few' immortalised Fighter Command's aircrews in the Battle of Britain – ever since known as 'The Few'.

The abridged version of Churchill's speech broadcast by the BBC was, we know from Daily Home Intelligence Reports, well-received by the public:

> Morale continues high. The Prime Minister's speech was received extremely well, according to all reports. From Northern Ireland comes the comment that it is the most forceful and heartening he has yet made. Newcastle reports that it has created a strong feeling of confidence. Two Bristol verbatim reports are as follows:
>
> 'Everyone feels now, come what will, we are top dogs; the past week has shown that we shall win no matter what the slight doubts there were before.'
>
> 'Bristol has implicit trust in Churchill. If he says things are all right Bristol people know they are all right; if he says they are bad, they know they are bad.'

Londoners were as confident in Churchill as Bristolians: 'Churchill's speech yesterday, particularly his reference to the RAF, thought to be completely right – epitomizes the feeling of the country.'

The aircrew themselves, modest as ever regarding their august achievements, were irreverent, however; in his memoir, *Spitfire! The Experiences of a Fighter Pilot*, published in 1942 and writing under the pseudonym 'B.J. Ellan', Squadron Leader Brian John Edward Lane DFC remarked,

> 'So few', Mr Churchill said – but no debt as he would have you believe; rather so few so lucky to be able to get on with the job whilst less fortunate folk looked on and awaited their chance. I think he was really referring to our mess bills, anyway!

Nonetheless, on 20 August 1940, in the House of Commons and via the subsequent BBC broadcast, a legend was born: that of a handful of dashing fighter pilots, heavily outnumbered, winning the day. This fight at odds, and the defenders' courage in what appeared, to all intents and purposes, a hopeless struggle, was certainly a message Churchill intended to be received, loud and clear, by the United States – and it was. On 24 March 1941, the American *Life* magazine headlined 'Fighter Command RAF Heroes Save England', describing 'The Few' as 'England's most important young men today … youths who fly the Hurricane and Spitfire fighters in the Battle of Britain. They undoubtedly saved England last fall from a Nazi invasion.' And there we have it: no mention of the other commands, or, indeed, Defiant or Blenheim fighters. *Life*, with 13.5 million copies sold a week, and many more readers than that figure, had cemented the myth with a clatter of type-writer keys.

Propaganda in war is crucial, of course, not least to demonise the enemy and heroicise one's own warriors, something the Air Ministry was swift to exploit, commissioning a successful novelist, Hilary St George Saunders, to produce a pamphlet on the Battle of Britain. Published on 29 March 1941, it became a global best-seller, effectively, at a time when Britain remained alone, without American or Russian allies, and when war news was grim, Saunders comparing the Battle of Britain to such great historical battles as 'Marathon, Trafalgar and the Marne'. By the end of 1941, 4.8 million copies had sold in Britain, and by 1942 the publication appeared in forty-two editions and no less than twenty-four languages; it is estimated that worldwide as many as 15 million copies were sold, not least, importantly, in America.

It was, though, an odd little booklet. Deliberately, it was decided not to name any individuals beyond Luftwaffe chief *Reichsmarschall* Hermann

Göring – with no mention whatsoever of the two architects of victory, namely Air Chief Marshal Sir Hugh Dowding, commander-in-chief of Fighter Command, and Air Vice-Marshal Keith Park, commanding 11 Group. Both men, of course, had fallen foul of their ambitious service rivals and their political supporters, who had used the 'Big Wing Controversy' as a means of ousting them (see *The Final Curtain*, Volume 7). This was, really, an incalculable insult, the omission lost on neither the press or, indeed, Churchill, who took the matter up with Secretary of State for Air Sir Archibald Sinclair:

> The jealousies and cliquism which have led to the committing of this offence are a discredit to the Air Ministry and I do not think any other service department would have been guilty of such a piece of work. What would have been said if the War Office had produced the story of the Battle of Libya and had

Air Chief Marshal Hugh Dowding with Their Majesties King George VI and Queen Elizabeth (future Queen Mother) at Bentley Priory, his Fighter Command HQ, during the Battle of Britain.

> managed to exclude General [Archibald] Wavell's name, or if the Admiralty had told the tale of Trafalgar and left Lord [Horatio] Nelson out of it! It grieves me very much that you should associate yourself with such behaviour.

The Minister, who had not personally been involved in the project, received an explanation from his minions, responding to Churchill that the intention was to publish a simple tale unfettered by a who's who, which in itself could cause internal problems, sweetening the pill by emphasising the enormous distribution achieved. Churchill was nonplussed. With damage limitation in mind, Sinclair had Dowding sent a copy with an explanation as to why he was not mentioned. Typically, Dowding's concern was not for himself but that the Hurricane was actually 30 mph slower than the pamphlet stated, and Fighter Command was not, as Saunders claimed, stronger after the battle than before it beforehand. Lord Dowding, however, went on to write and publish his own important despatch on the Battle of Britain, using the Air Ministry's 'admirable account' as a source; what the great man really thought of Saunders's pamphlet is unrecorded.

The official Air Ministry accounts of the Battle of Britain.

On 26 October 1941, an article on the Battle of Britain, written by Dowding, was published in the *Sunday Chronicle*, giving Park full credit for 'his initiative and resource in countering each new move on the part of the enemy, and his leadership of the gallant men he commanded, were beyond all praise.' Dowding sent Park a copy, with a note about publication of his forthcoming Despatch, saying 'I think I will do you justice'. Clearly, for the leaders of 'The Few', it was a case of 'if you want something doing properly, do it yourself'. Submitted to the Air Ministry in 1941, the *London Gazette* published Dowding's Despatch, which remains amongst the most important primary sources concerning the Battle of Britain, in September 1946. By that time the Second World War had been won – and 'The Few', specifically in an official context the aircrew of Fighter Command, had been officially recognised and honoured, although this remains the subject of debate even today.

The reader will be aware, considering the various detailed explanations throughout this narrative, that I challenge the official dates of the Battle of Britain, those being 10 July 1940 to 31 October 1940. When the Battle of Britain was fought, and why, is important and a point to labour, especially given its relevance here. The Battle of Britain, we are told, was fought to deny Germany the aerial superiority necessary to facilitate a seaborne invasion of southern England. Nothing more or less. That being so, the enemy must set the date, not the defender, because the Battle of Britain proper could only be considered started when German air operations were directly appended to a stated intention to invade. This happened on 2 July 1940, when the OKW announced that aim, and air battles over the Channel began. In his Despatch, Lord Dowding 'arbitarily' chose 10 July 1940 as the start date because the fighting was heavier that than on previous days. That choice, however, was made by Dowding in 1941, when the war remained ongoing and obviously there had yet to be any opportunity to interrogate surviving German commanders or scrutinise enemy documents. Consequently, when Dowding chose 10 July 1940, the significance of 2 July 1940 was unknown. Similarly, although Dowding considered the day battle over by 31 October 1940, it was equally unknown that Hitler had cancelled Operation *Seelöwe* on 12 October 1940. Consequently, the fact is that any air fighting over and attacks on Britain outside of the period 2 July 1940 to 12 October 1940, even the terrible night blitz on British cities, must, therefore, be considered as part of the wider war and not the actual Battle of Britain, because these operations were not appended to an intention to invade. There can be no other argument. Nonetheless, for the reasons explained, the Air Ministry

Lieutenant Commander Richard John 'Dickie' Cork DSO DSC (left), a FAA pilot who fought in the Battle of Britain with 242 Squadron, in conversation with Air Vice-Marshal Sir Trafford Leigh-Mallory, who commanded 12 Group during the Battle of Britain, at a wartime reunion – both men would be killed in flying accidents before hostilities concluded. *(Kate Ashby)*

accepted and decreed that the Battle of Britain was fought between 10 July 1940 and 31 October 1940, and this remains the case today.

By early 1944, with D-Day fast approaching and with the Russians advancing westward, although a long road still lay ahead, the ultimate Allied victory was in sight. Indeed, in July 1943, award of the Africa Star was announced for those officers and other ranks of the British and Colonial forces who had served after 23 October 1942, and fought in the second, but not first, Battle of El Alamein; minds, therefore, were already focused upon recognising the victors' contributions. A 1939–1943 Star was concurrently being mooted in Parliament and elsewhere for those of the same personnel criteria who did not qualify for the Africa Star but had served overseas, elsewhere, or in 'dangerous waters', for a minimum of six months and including time spent in captivity. Although both the WAAF and

Voluntary Aid Detachment were included, there was great debate over the Star and recognition generally. On 22 March 1944, Churchill spoke on the matter in the House of Commons, making clear the difficulties involved: what about the steadfast British police, National Fire Service, the Home Guard, men of Dover's coastal batteries, and many more besides? Other members expressed their views, significantly amongst them Sir Ronald Ross, Londonderry's MP, who, in part, said,

> We have acknowledged that those who won the great victory of North Africa shall have upon the ribbon of their Africa medal a particular distinction. Now that battle was undoubtedly one of the turning points of the war but, on the other hand, there was another battle which was an even more significant turning point in the war, and the men who were the spearhead which won that battle have never received the slightest recognition in the shape on an award as a separate body. I refer to the fighter pilots of the Battle of Britain. They have had from the Prime Minister the most unexampled tribute that any body [*sic*] of fighting men have ever had, but has that been translated into something which shall be visible to those who meet them in the street? No. In my submission, they should be entitled to wear some emblem upon their 1939–43 Star which would make it plain that they were the fighter pilots of the Battle of Britain.

Ross went on to acknowledge that certain awards concerned many thousands of recipients – but that in the case of 'The Few' this would not apply because 'There are very few survivors left of that gallant band'. Major Sir Jocelyn Lucas MC, MP for Portsmouth South, suggested that there were 'About 100' survivors of the Battle of Britain, but Ross did not 'suppose' there were even that many. Ross's suggestion received great support, Commander Peter Agnew, MP for Camborne, pointing out that 'The suggestion has been made that fighter pilots should have a special rosette to be added to their 1939–43 ribbons'; Ross agreed and wrote accordingly to Secretary of State for Air Archibald Sinclair.

The fact is, though, that just under 3,000 aircrew of Fighter Command flew operationally during the Battle of Britain, 544 of whom lost their lives between 10 July 1940 and 31 October 1940, and 795 more before the war ended. There were, therefore, many more survivors than either Ross or Lucas believed – not least because it was not simply a case of 'fighter pilots' – navigator-observers and air-gunners of Blenheim squadrons, and air-gunners of the two Defiant-equipped units also played their part. This, then, was the start of something more complex than any member in the House of Commons that day could ever have imagined.

On 2 April 1944, Sinclair responded to Ross and agreed that 'eventually' the Battle of Britain ought to be especially commemorated by the award of a star or clasp', and put the matter to the committee of civil servants concerned.

As the war went on, finally ending in Europe on 8 May 1945, and in the Far East on 15 August 1945, plans for a 1939–1943 Star changed to cover 1939–1945. Most significantly, on 24 May 1945, AMO A.532/1945 confirmed that a clasp to the 1939–1945 Star would be awarded to 'aircrew of fighter aircraft engaged in the Battle of Britain between 10 July and 31 October 1940'. From the outset, therefore, the intention was only to recognise fighter aircrew, and not even Fighter Command's support staff; indeed, Churchill argued that groundcrews faced no more danger than civilians, and the Committee on the Institution of Honours, Decorations and Medals in Time of War declined to argue the point. It is a matter of fact that the air fighting began on 2 July 1940, but given this criteria those aircrew only involved between 2 and 9 July 1940, and not beyond, were also excluded – which included the eight fighter pilots either killed or reported missing, or the seven others wounded during that period, and two more who later died of wounds sustained.

According to the MOD AHB (letter to Dilip Sarkar, 3 October 2023):

> subsequent AMOs, starting with AMO741/45 on 22 July 1945, re-frame the Clasp as for: 'air crew personnel who flew in fighter aircraft engaged in the Battle of Britain between 10th July 1940 and 31st October 1940', within the squadrons which are then listed'. It concluded that 'The Clasp is not available for personnel who flew in aircraft other than fighters, notwithstanding that they may have been engaged in the air during the qualifying period.'

This, then, made it clear: there would be no Battle of Britain honour for aircrew of Bomber Command and Coastal Command, or the PDU.

MOD AHB:

> This wording then remains consistent up to the final 1960 re-issue (AMO850/60). This reframes the award slightly as

> for: 'Aircrew who flew at least one operational sortie in fighter aircraft of these units.'
>
> AMO532/45 contained several errors that were quickly noted and corrected – not only the vague wording about units, but also the dates. The issue of AMO741/45 makes it clear that this AMO is 'issued to implement that new scheme for campaign stars and the Defence Medal announced in AMO A532/45'. Therefore, AMO532/45 can only be considered as a broad intent, while AMO741/45 lays out the detailed instructions on implementation. It even states that 'All action taken under [previous AMOs] is to be regarded as cancelled and the claims of all personnel are to be reviewed in the light of the new instructions.'
>
> Therefore, it is clear that AMO532/45 was never intended as more than a broad 'holding AMO'. This is proven by the declaration in AMO741/45 and by the fact that the wording, notably the dates, was quickly changed. The subsequent AMOs make it quite clear that the spirit of the Clasp was that it would apply to members of RAF Fighter Command during the established dates of the Battle of Britain. The list of squadrons also confirms this, containing, with one exception, only member units of RAF Fighter Command. No Ferry or Maintenance units are listed. It is important to note that No. 59 Squadron was included in AMO741/45, but removed by AMO850/60. This was because it was not a squadron in RAF Fighter Command.

This is not, however, entirely accurate.

For the avoidance of doubt, the following RAF Fighter Command squadrons were accredited as having flown in the Battle of Britain:

> 1, 3, 17, 19, 23, 25, 29, 32, 41, 43, 46, 54, 56, 64, 65, 66, 72, 73, 74, 79, 85, 87, 92, 111, 141, 145, 151, 152, 213, 219, 222, 229, 232, 234, 238, 242, 245, 247, 249, 253, 257, 263, 264, 266, in addition to 421 and 422 Flights, and the Fighter Interception Unit.

The following AAF fighter squadrons:

> 501, 504, 600, 601, 602, 603, 604, 605, 607, 609, 610, 611, 615 and 616.

The following Commonwealth and foreign squadrons:

> 1 (RCAF), 302 and 303 Polish squadrons, and 310 and 312 Czech squadrons.

The Bristol Blenheim Mk I-equipped 235 Squadron, and 236 Squadron of Coastal Command was also included. No. 235 Squadron flew convoy protection patrols and reconnoitred the North Sea; 236 Squadron undertook anti-shipping patrols over the Channel and Irish Sea, but 248 Squadron, operating the Blenheim Mk IV light-bomber and based in the Shetlands was also included. The two former squadrons flew fighters, but why the latter, a bomber-equipped squadron, was included is difficult to understand. AHB mentions the removal of 59 Squadron from the list by AMO850/60, this being because the unit flew the Blenheim Mk IV bomber, so the fact that 248 Squadron remained listed can only have been an oversight.

Also accredited were two FAA squadrons, 804 and 808, the former flying Sea Gladiators at Hatston in Orkney, the latter Fairey Fulmars

The medals of Flight Lieutenant Alexander Gordon Osmand, a Hurricane pilot with 213 Squadron during the Battle of Britain but later killed in action fighting the Japanese. The coveted Battle of Britain Clasp can be seen on the 1939–1945 Star's ribbon.

from the Isle of Man, then Wick, before joining the aircraft carrier HMS *Ark Royal* in August 1940 and serving in the Mediterranean. No. 808 Squadron had, in fact, been temporarily seconded to Fighter Command (and is, therefore, the non-Fighter Command unit referred to above by the AHB).

Only award of the coveted Clasp entitled a member of RAF aircrew to join the ranks of 'The Few', those men who flew at least one operational sortie with one of the officially accredited squadrons or other units. Now that sounds simple – but is it?

Whilst many of the aircrew concerned fought a long and hard battle, it is a fact that many replacement pilots arriving on squadrons towards the official end of the Battle of Britain, or posted to squadrons away from the combat area, made an operational patrol, thereby qualifying for the Clasp, but saw no action. Indeed, amongst the seven station commanders and even a controller at Dyce, who were not actually serving with any of the accredited units but flew at least one operational patrol with one of them, thereby qualifying for the Clasp, not all saw action. Pilot Officer Alec Bird and Pilot Officer Richard Manlove, however, of 4 Ferry Pilots' Pool at RAF Kemble, flying Hurricanes, intercepted a Ju 88 over Stroud on 25 July 1940, Bird either colliding with or deliberately ramming the bomber, bringing it down and losing his life in the process. It seems unfair, therefore, that although Bird gave his life in the defence of this country during the Battle of Britain, his name, or that of Manlove, is not listed amongst 'The Few', something which deeply upset his now late widow, Marjorie. On 3 October 2023, the AHB explained why:

> No. 4 FPP is not a listed unit within AMO741/45 or AMO850/60. It was part of RAF Maintenance Command.
>
> The AMOs make clear that engagement with the enemy is not enough justification in and of itself.
>
> Operating as a fighter does not necessarily qualify the sortie as being an 'operational sortie on a fighter aircraft' as defined in the AMO. For example, in the context of the Bomber Command Clasp, heavy bombers in the Middle East/ Mediterranean may have bombed targets in Italy and Germany, but they were not part of RAF Bomber Command. They may have been carrying out the same role, but they did not come within the correct command structure. The inclusion of a list of squadrons in AMO741/45 onwards clearly shows the intent

> that the Battle of Britain Clasp should only apply to units of RAF Fighter Command.
>
> While nobody can doubt the courage and contribution of both P/O Bird and P/O Manlove, unfortunately they fall outside the established criteria for the Battle of Britain Clasp.

Whilst the Clasp only applying to units of RAF Fighter Command is not entirely accurate, considering the inclusion of Coastal Command and FAA squadrons, it is clear that 4 FPP was not a fighter unit, and that is a matter of fact. Similarly, Sergeant Bruce Hancock, who was undergoing night-flying training on Ansons and lost his life when he either collided with or rammed a He 111 attacking his airfield at Windrush on 18 August 1940, cannot be named amongst 'The Few' given that he was not flying a fighter or serving with one of the accredited units.

Another bone of contention amongst some is that certain pilots flying with OTUs during the Battle of Britain and who were actually flying under the direction of Fighter Command, saw action, claiming victories, but are similarly not listed amongst 'The Few' – a case in point being Flight Lieutenant Peter Prosser Hanks DFC, an instructor at 5 OTU, Aston Down, who also attacked the Ju 88 over Stroud on 25 July 1940, but withdrew his claim when he heard about Pilot Officer Alec Bird's gallantry and demise.

Why is the Clasp so important, that key to being recorded in history as being one of 'The Few'? That harks back, surely, to the significance of and pride in the Battle of Britain as a defining moment in history that preserved this country. Over the years, various scoundrels have masqueraded as being legitimate recipients of the Clasp, only to be exposed, and I can think of at least two 'Walter Mitty' types whose claims to be related to certain famous Battle of Britain pilots have no basis in truth. All of this odd behavior actually adds to the aura surrounding Churchill's fabled few, in a strange sort of way.

There have, however, been recent additions to the number of Clasp holders. For example, in March 2019, the AHB and Battle of Britain Memorial Trust accepted evidence that Sergeant Donald Brown, a pilot on 604 Squadron, qualified for the Clasp, although sadly having died in 1993, this new recipient did not live to receive the award. One of the problems is that there is no actual official list of 'The Few', the main sources being unofficial and those researched by Flight Lieutenant John Holloway, for the book of remembrance in Westminster Abbey, published in Derek Wood and Derek Dempster's *Narrow Margin* in 1961, and the late New Zealander,

Kenneth Wynn, for his 'Men of the Battle of Britain', first published in 1989, updated in 2015, then bolstered by a supplementary volume in 2020. Online, the Battle of Britain London Monument website also lists biographical details of 'The Few', and unlike the actual bronze cast monument on Westminster's embankment, which also records names of 'The Few', can easily be updated with any additions. At the National Memorial to 'The Few', at Capel-le-Ferne, high on the white cliffs overlooking Folkestone, the Christopher Foxley-Norris Memorial Wall also lists the names – and, fortunately, blank space was included when the wall was built for any, inevitable, additions required. At the time of writing, some six more names await being added – included a very special man indeed: Air Chief Marshal Keith Park. How this came about is quite a tale.

When visiting the War Memorial Museum in Auckland, New Zealand, during April 2023, I was delighted to see Park's medals and uniform displayed. The intriguing thing was that the medal group included the Battle of Britain Clasp to the 1939–1945 Star, and the Rosette denoting same appeared on his uniform's medal ribbons. But why, as Park's name did not appear on any list of 'The Few'? As a group commander, Park had not actually served in one of the fighter squadrons or other accredited units – but it was, however, widely known that Air Vice-Marshal Keith Park, as he then was, flew himself about 11 Group in his personal Hurricane, 'OK1'. Nowhere, though, had I ever seen reference, officially or otherwise, to him having made an operational flight during the Battle of Britain. Here was something to investigate.

Gail Romano, the Second World War curator at Auckland War Memorial Museum, could offer no explanation regarding the Clasp's inclusion in Keith Park's medal group. Had a mistake been made, I wondered, when the medals were displayed? No, researching post-war photographs clearly showed the great man wearing the Clasp or Rosette, so clearly Park knew this. Via Gail Romano, I then contacted Stephen Park, Park's great-nephew, but the family could shed no light on the mater either, except to say,

> We got to know Uncle Keith quite well as youngsters. While we knew he was something of an air ace and helped lead the air defence of Britain during the Second World War, we were more aware of his personal characteristics, including his strong moral compass. He was driven to do the right thing. During the Battle of Britain, for example, he believed passionately in the British response to the odious Nazi regime and its allies,

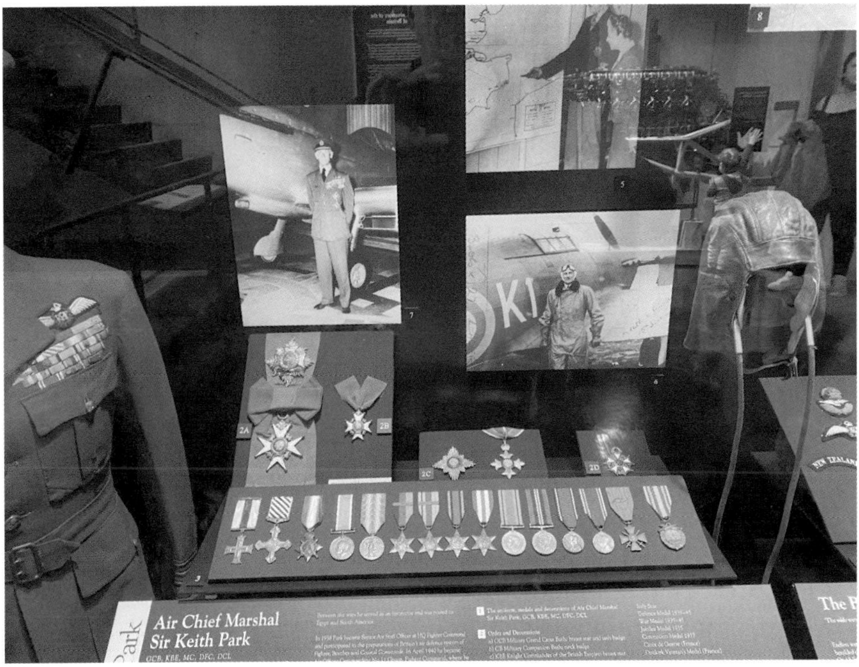

Above: The medals of Air Chief Marshal Keith Park at the Auckland War Memorial Museum, which include the Battle of Britain Clasp.

Right: Air Chief Marshal Keith Park, wearing the 'Battle of Britain Rosette' on his 1939–1945 Star's medal ribbon, indicating that he is a Clasp holder, the actual Clasp or 'Bar' only being worn on the full-size medal ribbon.

> and was in a position to take the fight to them. At the same time he was acutely aware of the tragic human cost, and we know that to his dying day he grieved for and held dear the memory of 'his boys' (as he called his pilots) who died during the Battle of Britain.
>
> In later civilian life he directed the same clear-eyed focus on helping his home country and city, especially those less fortunate.

The AHB, however, found no record of Air Chief Marshal Keith Park having been officially awarded the Clasp. Indeed, his medal card, listing his entitlement, was missing, leading Stephen Park to comment that

> He was, fundamentally, an honest operator. There is no way he would have worn the Clasp to the 1939–1945 Star (as evidenced) unless it had been awarded to him. We are more certain of that than we are of any ambiguity implied because of a lost RAF Officer's Medal Card.

Further intrigued, next stop was the Air Force Museum of New Zealand in Christchurch. Although the research curator, Simon Moody, had no explanation either, Simon very helpfully provided an all-important copy of Park's flying log book (Form 414). And therein was the essential evidence…

On 10 July 1940 – the Battle of Britain's official start date – Park had recorded in his log having flown in his Hurricane from Northolt on the following sortie: 'Lympne. Convoy. West Malling.' Now this was the opening of the air battles over Channel-bound convoys, and clearly whilst visiting the coastal airfield of Lympne, on the southern Kentish coast, Park had seen a convoy out to see and flown over it. Two days later he recorded having flown his famous Hurricane 'To Kenley to meet PM and escort back to Northolt'.

Clearly, these were operational flights which, to my mind, qualified Keith Park as one of 'The Few' and, therefore, justified his wearing of the Clasp. The possible issue, as I saw it, was that as a group commander he had not actually been a member of one of the officially accredited squadrons, or flown with any of them given that he flew himself around 11 Group solo. Be that as it may, further research identified, as previously mentioned, seven station commanders and even a sector controller from Dyce who held the Clasp, having made at least one operational patrol with an accredited squadron on their stations between the relevant dates. It seemed to me, then, that the name of Air Chief Marshal Keith Park must also now be included amongst 'The Few'.

On 9 May 2023, the matter was put to the AHB, which, on 6 July 2023 responded, formally: 'We agree that AVM [Keith] Park was a legitimate recipient of the Battle of Britain Clasp because of the sorties he flew. So, there it was: official acceptance, without argument, that Air Chief Marshal Keith Park was – and is – one of 'The Few'. On 31 July 2023, AHB clarified in writing that until I raised the matter there had been 'no serious questions over his eligibility' and that 'The only *de facto* (Nominal) Roll is contained within the Medal Cards held by the MoD Medals Office, although … the card for AVM Park is unfortunately missing' (in point of fact, there is also the '*de facto*' roll compiled by Flight Lieutenant John Holloway, and which the BoBFA (see Chapter Three) used as its basis for admitting members).

So there we have it: because, as Stephen and Brian Park suspected, of a missing MOD medal card, the name of Air Chief Marshal Keith Park – a legitimate recipient of the Battle of Britain Clasp – was omitted from the Christopher Foxley-Norris Memorial Wall and Battle of Britain London Monument.

Stephen and Brian Park, great-nephews of Keith Park, said,

> We are, of course, delighted that our old Uncle Keith has now been formally acknowledged as being one of The Few. While we appreciate that recognition of his vital role during the Battle of Britain secures his place in history anyway, that wasn't always a certain thing. So, we are very grateful to Dilip Sarkar for alerting the Air Historical Branch to the evidence of why he qualified as one of The Few. We think this matters. When those of us who knew Keith Park personally are no longer around, all that's left of certainty is his record of service, which speaks for itself to future generations.

Group Captain Patrick Tootal OBE DL, honorary secretary of the Battle of Britain Memorial Trust, which maintains the National Memorial to 'The Few', including the Christopher Foxley-Norris Memorial Wall, said,

> Following research by Dilip Sarkar connected with his eight-volume history for the Battle of Britain Memorial Trust, the Trust has verified Sir Keith Park's entitlement to

> the Battle of Britain Clasp. The Trust, in conjunction with the Air Historical Branch, stringently maintains the criteria for entitlement and the evidence provided has shown that Sir Keith completed two operational flights in a fighter aircraft within the defined period of the Battle. Sir Keith Park's name, therefore, will be added to the database and appear on the Memorial Wall in due course. A bust of Sir Keith Park is already in situ at the National Memorial to the Few at Capel-le-Ferne.

Edward McManus of The Battle of Britain London Monument: 'It has long been accepted that Keith Park's leadership of 11 Group Fighter Command was instrumental in securing victory in 1940. This acknowledgment, that he also flew operationally aged 48, can only enhance his reputation and increase our debt to him.'

Gail Romano, associate curator of war history at Auckland War Memorial Museum said,

> We have never questioned the validity of Sir Keith Park's Battle of Britain Clasp and were surprised when Dilip [Sarkar] asked about the provenance. His medal array is as received, since it isn't museum practice to modify medals which come into the collection and, having knowledge of Sir Keith's Second World War significance, we saw no reason to question the clasp. Although these days he is perhaps less well-known to our growing population, many New Zealanders do remember the role he played in the Battle of Britain and later during the siege of Malta. His name is honoured in several public spaces and during the recent unveiling of a new statue of Park, former Defence Minister Ron Mark said, 'No other New Zealand-born military figure has had a greater impact on history …' But by all accounts, Sir Keith was not a flamboyant man or one who made a fuss or otherwise courted notice. He was quiet, humble and a true gentleman. Life consistently shows how easy it is to overlook such people. I'm very glad Dilip realised Sir Keith wasn't officially recognised as one of 'The Few' and took on the project to have that omission corrected. He has achieved justice for a man who deserves the respect of official acknowledgement.

Joe Hill, curator of military history at the Battle of Britain Bunker, Uxbridge, said,

> I am delighted to see efforts made to formally recognise Air Chief Marshal Sir Keith Park as one of 'The Few'. At the Battle of Britain Bunker we proudly display a large bronze statue of Sir Keith, as well as preserving and displaying the door and brick wall of a property inhabited by him, during the Battle of Britain. Sir Keith directed the Battle from our Operations Room, where Bunker visitors learn about his contribution to the war on our daily tours.

From a personal perspective, Keith Park has been a hero of mine since watching the 1969 film *Battle of Britain*, aged 8, and having since spent a lifetime researching and writing about the 1940 aerial conflict, suffice it to say the satisfaction felt at having proved him to be one of 'The Few' was, and is, immense. After the Battle of Britain, Air Chief Marshal Hugh Dowding and Air Vice-Marshal Keith Park, the two primary architects of victory, were poorly treated by the authorities – which both men remained bitter about until their dying day. Hopefully, then, this recognition in some small way makes up for that.

So, 'The Few' are, rightly or wrongly, a very specific set of RAF Fighter Command aircrew, whose deeds are not forgotten, even in this rapidly changing world increasingly distanced in time for the tempestuous events of summer 1940. As Squadron Leader Geoffrey Harry Augustus Wellum DFC, an 18-year-old Spitfire pilot on 92 Squadron at Biggin Hill during the Battle of Britain famously said, 'We don't want a medal, we just want to be remembered'. In our next chapter, we will explore exactly how 'The Few' are remembered.

Chapter Three

The Battle of Britain – Memorialisation and Remembrance

With the Second World War at its height, the United States still neutral and since 22 June 1941 Hitler's forces rampaging eastwards, into Russia, on 4 July 1941, a particular plaque was unveiled in Westminster Abbey. This modest, understated, memorial, perhaps surprisingly reads 'An American citizen who died that England might live'. At the unveiling, Secretary of State for Air Archibald Sinclair said, 'Here was a you man for whom life held so much. Under no compulsion he came to fight for Britain. He came and he fought, and he died.' Here, then, was a memorial not to the Battle of Britain itself – but to an individual.

The wealthy American international banker, Olympian and Anglophile, William Meade Lindley Fiske III, of Chicago. More commonly known as 'Billy' Fiske, read economics and history at the University of Cambridge before joining London's exclusive White's Club, an unofficial recruiting ground for the so-called 'Millionaire's Mob', 601 (County of London) Squadron at the socio-economic elite AAF. Having met and married Rose Bingham, Countess of Warwick, despite America's neutrality, Fiske joined 601 Squadron, and by 20 July 1940 he was a fully trained fighter pilot, a pilot officer, and flew his first operational sortie in a Hawker Hurricane from Tangmere. In less than a month, Pilot Officer 'Billy' Fiske flew forty-two such sorties, destroying a Ju 88 on 'Eagle Day', 13 August 1940. Three days later, 601 Squadron intercepted a formation of Ju 87s heading for Tangmere, Fiske's Hurricane being damaged in the ensuing combat. With a dead engine, Fiske – who was an excellent pilot – glided back to the aerodrome to make a wheels-up forced-landing. As the fighter touched down, however, the petrol tank exploded – Corporal G.W. Jones and AC2 C.G. Faulkner dashed to the scene in their ambulance and managed to get the pilot out of the blazing wreck. The bottom half of Fiske's body, however, was grievously burned, the gallant American volunteer succumbing to his injuries in Chichester Hospital the following day.

With such wealthy and powerful friends, and Churchill's interest, the memorial was arranged at Westminster Abbey – a most prestigious venue indeed – highlighting that despite the United States' isolation from events in Europe, there were American volunteers fighting and giving their lives for Britain. Fiske was the first of them to die on active service in the RAF – and his fitting tribute is very likely the first Battle of Britain related memorial of any kind. Buried at Boxgrove Priory, near Chichester, in a high-profile funeral on 20 August 1940, many years later, on 17 September 2008, a stained-glass window by Mel Howse, dedicated to Fiske, was unveiled in the priory. This was commissioned by the 601 Squadron Association, including the now late Squadron Leader Jack Riddle, one of 'The Few' who had actually flown with Fiske. Given that the Fiske memorial in Westminster Abbey was very likely the first such tribute to one of 'The Few', that his memory should be so honoured at Boxgrove nearly seventy years after his death indicates that the Battle of Britain's memory, and that of 'The Few', collectively and individually, endures.

The plaque commemorating the American volunteer Pilot Officer William Meade Lindley Fiske III in Westminster Abbey. *(Paul Heys)*

Pilot Officer William Meade Lindley Fiske III's grave at Boxgrove Priory.

Certainly, there was both dramatic and visual evidence of this on 15 September 1945, the fifth anniversary of 'Battle of Britain Day' and the first post-war, when Group Captain Sir Douglas Bader, the famous legless fighter ace, led the huge Battle of Britain commemorative fly past over London. No less than 300 RAF fighters, many flown by Battle of

The stained-glass window dedicated to Pilot Officer William Meade Lindley Fiske III at Boxgrove Priory.

Britain pilots, led the aerial procession, which lasted a full ninety minutes. Squadrons of Fighter Command and Coastal Command contributed aircraft, including the RAF's first jet-propelled fighter, the Gloster Meteor, heralding a new age in British aviation. For the first time since the old pre-war Empire air days, ninety RAF bases opened their gates to the public that day, these 'Battle of Britain at Home' days, which also became an annual event.

Without doubt, even before the Battle of Britain Clasp was promulgated and awarded to 'The Few', having fought in the Battle of Britain set an airman aside, as special, and equally a brotherhood existed between them. Even whilst the Second World War still raged, 15 September 1940 was celebrated and commemorated annually as 'Battle of Britain Day', the turning point and indicator that the Luftwaffe had failed in its endeavour, and reunions of 'The Few', sometimes attended by Lord Dowding, took place. No record, however, was kept of these informal gatherings, but post-war, in 1946, Lord Dowding was guest of honour at a meeting of 'The Few' in London, and at the following year's occasion both his Lordship and Air Chief Marshal Keith Park attended. That year also saw the unveiling of the Battle of Britain Memorial in Westminster Abbey, unveiled by His Majesty King George VI on 10 July 1947, the seventh anniversary of the official start-date – there could be no more prestigious location, firmly indicating the high regard in which the nation held 'The Few'.

In the iconic abbey, the last resting place of so many English kings and queens, and, of course the unknown soldier, the chevet of Henry VII Chapel was dedicated to those of 'The Few' who made the ultimate sacrifice during the Battle of Britain. This particular chapel was an appropriate location,

Air Chief Marshal Hugh Dowding and Air Chief Marshal Keith Park at the 1947 Battle of Britain reunion dinner.

given that a shard of shrapnel from a German bomb had pierced the chapel's east wall, the hole caused by which being preserved beneath glass. The chapel featured an impressive memorial window, designed and painted by the stained-glass artist Hugh Easton, which included the heraldic crests of sixty-three of the combatant squadrons. The roll of honour researched by

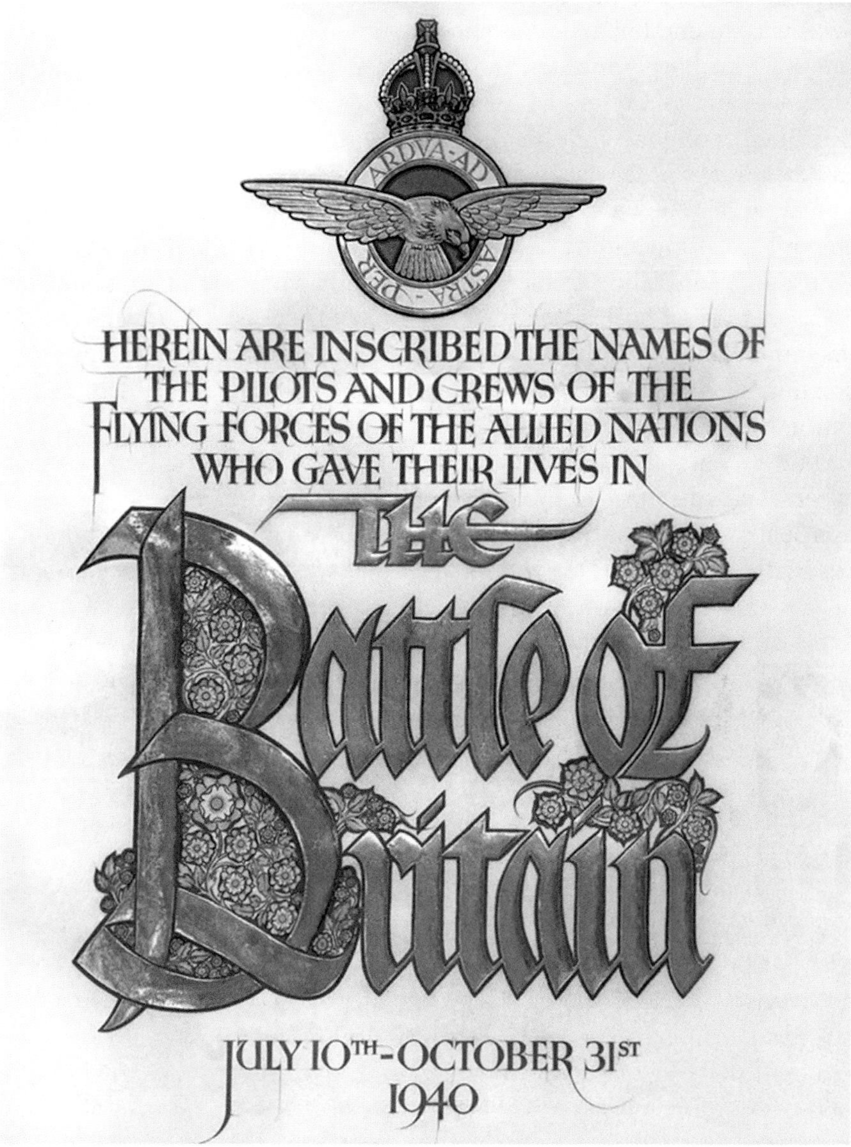

The illuminated Battle of Britain roll of honour. *(Dean and Chapter Westminster Abbey)*

Wing Commander Lord Derek Dowding, who flew Spitfires with 74 Squadron in the Battle of Britain, unveiling his late father's memorial tablet in Westminster Abbey's Battle of Britain Chapel in 1972.

Flight Lieutenant John Holloway and produced on parchment, bound in blue leather, was brought to the chapel from its original position on a lectern north of the chapel – significantly, and entirely appropriately, this *de facto* roll includes RAF aircrew losses from Fighter, Bomber, Coastal, Training and Maintenance commands, and the FAA, suffered between 10 July 1940 and 31 October 1940, and is therefore an inclusive list, not one just focused upon 'The Few'.

After the First World War, the RAF Memorial was designed by Sir Reginald Blomfield, dedicated to the service's casualties to date, and located on London's Victoria Embankment, to the east of Whitehall. Unveiled by the Prince of Wales (later Edward VIII) on 16 July 1923, and by extension since 1945, Second World War losses are also commemorated by this monument – on which, since 15 September 1946, the serving Chief of the Air Staff places a wreath annually on 'Battle of Britain Day', and every Remembrance Day, the RAF Benevolent Fund does likewise. Arguably, this 1946 act of remembrance could well have been the first post-war commemoration of the Battle of Britain – but the Battle of Britain

Chapel in Westminster Abbey was the first specific memorial to the Battle of Britain, and as such remains an important shrine.

On 2 November 1948 – All Souls' Day – the Polish Air Force Memorial, created by Mieczysław Lubelski, was unveiled on Western Avenue, Northolt, close to RAF Northolt, with which the Poles had a long and august association, by MRAF Lord Tedder. This impressive memorial commemorated the Polish Air Force contribution in the Second World War generally, which, of course, included the Battle of Britain, during which the 145 Poles serving with Fighter Command represented the largest number of foreigners fighting with the RAF. Twenty-nine Poles were killed during the Battle of Britain, but, due to a lack of space, not all of their names are recorded on the Memorial, which lists just 1,241 by name of the 2,408 Polish airmen who made the ultimate sacrifice. Although, with the passing of both time and members, the Polish Air Force Association in Great Britain was wound up some years ago, the more recently forced Polish Air Force Memorial Committee and Polish Airmen's Association UK still holds an annual services of remembrance at the site every September. Around the Memorial's base are inscribed these moving and appropriate words: 'I have

The Polish Air Force Memorial at Northolt.

Infographic at the adjacent Polish Air Force Memorial Remembrance Garden.

fought a good fight. I have finished my course. I have kept my faith' – and never could truer words be spoken. In more recent times, the Polish Air Force Memorial Remembrance Garden has been created behind the actual memorial.

Hugh Easton, who had created the chapel's stained glass, also created the second specific memorial, the Battle of Britain memorial window commissioned by Rolls-Royce commemorating 'The Few' and the company's contribution to their victory. Unveiled at Rolls-Royce's Osmaston Works in Derby on 11 January 1949 by MRAF Lord Tedder, public viewing was permitted on Sundays, and during the first month alone some 50,000 visitors viewed the tribute. Later, this impressive, 6.5m high and 4.5m wide, window was moved to the Rolls-Royce Learning and Development Centre, also in Derby, where it can be seen today, illuminated by no less than 5,184 LEDs.

The next memorial to be unveiled was a significant one indeed: on 17 October 1953, the now late Her Majesty Queen Elizabeth II inaugurated

The Rolls-Royce Battle of Britain memorial window.

the Air Forces' Memorial on Cooper's Hill, Runnymede, commemorating, by name, over 20,000 aircrew from Britain, its Commonwealth and Empire, Belgium and Czechoslovakia who operated from bases in Britain, and North and West Europe, and who have no known grave. Designed by Sir Edward Maufe and built of Portland stone, using sculpture by Vernon Hill, the cloisters bearing the names engraved into panels feed into a building with a viewing platform overlooking the fields of Magna Carta, reminiscent of an airfield control tower. Throughout, the painted ceilings were designed by John Hutton, and the poem etched into the gallery window was written by Paul H. Scott:

> If I climb up into Heaven, Thou art there;
> If I go to Hell, though art there also.
> If I take the wings of the morning
> And remain in the uttermost parts of the sea,
> Even there also They hand lead me,
> And they right hand shall hold me.

In Her Majesty's address, the queen spoke these solemn and truthful words: 'As only free men can, they knew the value of that for which they fought, and that the price was worth paying.'

The names of 150 of 'The Few' are commemorated at Runnymede, although this has been a dynamic entity, given that the remains of a number of pilots have been recovered, identified and buried appropriately post-war (see Chapter Six). Also included is Pilot Officer Denis Ashton of 266 Squadron, whose remains were recovered by the RN the month after he was shot down, and buried at sea. The six FAA pilots reported missing flying with Fighter Command during the Battle of Britain (including the Canadian Sub-Lieutenant Jack Carpenter, who was also buried at sea) are commemorated on the Lee-on-the-Solent Memorial, dedicated to FAA aircrew with no known grave, which was unveiled by the Duchess of Kent on 20 May 1953 (FAA personnel were also commemorated more recently by the FAA Memorial designed by James Butler and unveiled by the former His Royal Highness Charles, Prince of Wales (now His Majesty King Charles III) on 1 June 2000, in Victoria Embankment Gardens).

The CWGC is responsible for maintaining both the Air Forces' Memorial and the Lee-on-Solent Memorial – and, of course, the other memorials around the globe on which are recorded those of 'The Few' who were lost in other theatres and have no known grave, such as the Singapore and Malta

Above and below: The RAF's Memorial at Runnymede, commemorating over 20,000 aircrew with no known grave – including 147 of 'The Few'.

Memorials. The CWGC also maintains the many war graves and British war cemeteries around the world in which the always immaculate graves of 'The Few' who perished either during the Battle of Britain or afterwards, whilst still serving, can be found. Some lie in vast fields of stone, others in isolation, in civilian cemeteries and churchyards. The civilian resting places, however, can be problematic, especially nowadays when many churchyards have been left to go wild, graves becoming overgrown. In these cases, although churches are paid a small annuity to ensure that service graves are respectfully tended and maintained, this duty, it is sad to say, is not always discharged. Consequently, with so very many graves to care for, the CWGC relies heavily upon information from the public concerning graves falling into a poor state, and in recent years has mobilised the like-minded through its 'Eyes On, Hands On' volunteering programme, which in part formalises and harnesses what many people have done off their own back over the years through taking ownership of graves locally, restoring, cleaning and ensuring they are kept in a good condition. This is especially important with regard to private memorials provided by families, which eighty-five years may have moved away or even died out. Nonetheless, the CWGC still has a responsibility to these private graves, if only to ensure that the casualties' names are legible. Overall, then, today we can be sure that most of the graves of 'The Few' are likely to be watched over and in the main well maintained.

Returning to the survivors and the backdrop of major memorials being unveiled in the immediate post-war period, by the early 1950s, survivors' reunion dinners, remained informal and were still not appended to any organisation, were held at Dowding's former HQ, Bentley Priory. In 1954, Gieves, the well-known society tailor, was commissioned to produce a tie for Clasp holders: a gold silhouette of the British Isles and the Battle of Britain Rosette on a dark blue background – which remains the tie of what formally became the BoBFA. With membership limited to 'The Few' themselves, this was an exclusive club indeed. The last known member of 'The Few', Captain John 'Paddy' Hemmingway DFC, sadly passed away on 17 March 2025, aged 105. That any member should achieve such longevity was doubtless far from anyone's mind when the first newsletter was distributed to members on 27 March 1958. This document, distributed by a serving officer, Air Commodore Charles Widdows CB DFC, a pre-war Cranwellian who had flown Blenheims with 29 Squadron during the Battle of Britain, clearly set out the new association's objectives:

- To look after the welfare of members of the Association and their dependents, in co-operation with the Royal Air Force Benevolent Fund and other charitable and advisory institutions, according to their needs.
- To preserve the memory of fighter aircrew who died in the Battle of Britain.
- To foster good fellowship amongst members of the Association in perpetuating the comradeship which existed during the Battle of Britain.
- To perform the functions and ceremonies in furtherance of the objects of the Association, and to arrange representation at other appropriate functions and ceremonies to which the Association might be invited.

Lord Dowding accepted the new association's invitation to become president, and Air Chief Marshal Keith Park became life vice-president, with ex officio vice-presidents MRAF Sir Dermot Boyle, the chief of the

The heraldic crest of the exulted BoBFA.

Air Staff, and the commander-in-chief of Fighter Command, Air Chief Marshal Sir Thomas Pike. Squadron Leader Don Higgin, who was not one of 'The Few' himself, became honorary secretary, and Widdows the chairman. Most importantly, Her Majesty Queen Elizabeth, The Queen Mother, Britain's wartime queen, graciously agreed to become patron.

A year later, the second newsletter was published, announcing Widdows's retirement from the service and the news that Air Vice-Marshal John 'Baron' Worrall, who had first commanded 32 Squadron in the Battle of Britain before serving as Biggin Hill's senior controller, was the new chairman, and Wing Commander Bob Oxspring, a flight commander on 66 Squadron in the Battle of Britain, succeeded Higgin as secretary. So began this most exulted of all brotherhoods: the BoBFA.

Over the years, naturally, there were many changes to the committee, and all involved served with pride. For many years Air Commodore Don MacDonell, the Laird of Glengarry, served as chairman, and Wing Commander Pat Hancock was a most dedicated secretary (and extremely helpful to this author over many years); Group Captain Tom Gleave, of Guinea Pig Club fame, served for many years as deputy chairman and Historian, succeeded in the later role by Wing Commander John Young. Air Chief Marshal Sir Christopher Foxley-Norris as chairman, and

Members of the BoBFA in 2000, the Battle of Britain's sixtieth anniversary year.

Members of the BoBFA with wartime sweetheart, Dame Vera Lynn – all pictured are sadly now deceased.

Air Commodore Peter Brothers as his deputy were quite a double-act, and so it went on – until the survivors were literally too few or infirm to continue, and at which time, 1995, Malcolm Smith, the senior lecturer and chair of history at the University of Wales, Lampeter, became secretary, serving for eleven years when the role went to the current secretary, Group Captain Patrick Tootal, who also fulfils the role of honorary secretary to the Battle of Britain Memorial Trust.

During the course of its existence in pursuit of its stated aims, the BoBFA enjoyed annual reunions at Bentley Priory and elsewhere, for many years being entertained by the USAF at RAF Alconbury. In terms of remembrance, the Battle of Britain service at Westminster Abbey was always an annual highlight, and members provided historical advice to such films as the 1969 epic *Battle of Britain* – out of which arose a particular dilemma: that of reconciliation.

At this time, the Cold War remained ongoing, and post-war West Germany had joined NATO in 1955, so was an important ally of democracy. In the immediate wake of the Second World War, German military aviation had been substantially restricted by the victorious Allies, the Allied Control Commission winding up the wartime Luftwaffe in 1946. When West Germany joined NATO, however, a new Luftwaffe was created as part of the *Bundeswehr*. Many former German wartime aircrew joined the new service and re-trained in America to fly the Republic F-84 Thunderstreak jet. By 1966, the Luftwaffe was equipped with Lockheed F-104 Starfighter jets, and General Johannes 'Macky' Steinhoff, a 176-victory wartime ace, was chief inspector of the new Luftwaffe, his deputy being *Generalleutnant* Günther Rall, the third most successful fighter pilot in the history of aerial warfare with 275 victories. Naturally, the new Luftwaffe cooperated on exercises with the RAF, and consequently former wartime adversaries found themselves allies.

There are numerous examples of downed Allied, particularly RAF, airmen being entertained in German messes whilst awaiting transport into captivity, most famously amongst them the legless Wing Commander Douglas Bader, who was brought down over France, most likely the victim of 'friendly fire' in a particularly confused combat over Saint-Omer on 9 August 1941, and who was a guest of *Oberst* Adolf Galland, another great German ace and *Kommodore* of JG 26, and his *Stabschwarm* for high tea

The best of friends: *General* Adolf Galland and Group Captain Douglas Bader at a post-war function.

at Wissant. When the tables were turned and Galland was a prisoner of the Allies, and Bader had been released from Colditz, the pair communicated again, and became friends post-war. *Generalleutnant* Galland, as he had become, was the chief German advisor to the *Battle of Britain* film, and also became friends with Wing Commander Robert Stanford Tuck, another former prisoner and prominent Battle of Britain ace. The promotion and release of the film caused much interest, and led to a request from the Luftwaffe for a meeting of survivors from both sides.

Flight Lieutenant Richard Jones, a Spitfire pilot on 19 Squadron during the Battle of Britain, recalled to me that

> The matter was considered by the BoBFA's committee but ultimately declined. This was because it was felt that the events of 1940 were still too close, too raw, especially for the widows, children and other family members of those who died. It was a pity, because many of us were interested in meeting our old foes, but perfectly understood and respected the decision. Some years later, in 1988, I was a guest at RAF Abingdon dinner where I met *Major* Günther Domaschk, who had expressed a wish to meet a Spitfire pilot. During the Battle of Britain he told me that he was an *Oberleutnant*, the Technical Officer of II/JG 2 and flew Me 109s. We had a good old chat and I was pleased to meet him, as I was various other former wartime Luftwaffe airmen at your many events.

A fellow diner, apparently, overhead Jones and Domaschk deep in conversation, 'like long-lost brothers'; anyone who knew Richard Jones, who died in 2009, with his kind and gentle manner, would not be surprised. 1969, however, was too early for a wider demonstration of reconciliation.

Despite the Cold War, by 1971 the RAF had been considerably reduced, there being just seven stations holding Battle of Britain at Home Days that year, and in 1978 only Abingdon and St Athan participated. Indeed, the annual flypast had been long discontinued by then, the last successive sortie having being flown on 17 September 1961 and reduced to those aircraft of the RAF Historic Aircraft Flight. The Flight had formed at Biggin Hill on 11 July 1957 with the three former Temperature & Humidity Testing Flight's Spitfire PR Mk XIXs, which had flown the Spitfire's last operational sortie in what was now the jet age, and the service's last airworthy Hurricane. Later renamed simply the Battle of Britain Flight, between 1959 and 1965

Air Chief Marshal Lord Hugh Dowding at North Weald with Group Captain Douglas Bader and the pilots the legless fighter ace had just led over London on the first post-war Battle of Britain flypast.

just one Spitfire PRXIX and the Hurricane remained on strength, until in 1968, when the Flight's sole Battle of Britain survivor, Spitfire Mk IIA, P7350, arrived – complete with Battle of Britain combat damage (see *The Final Curtain*, Volume 7) – joining Spitfire Mk VB, AB910, which had been gifted to the Flight by Vickers Armstrong Limited and delivered by Jeffrey Quill, formerly Supermarine's chief test pilot, on 15 September 1965. In 1969, the Flight was renamed the 'Battle of Britain Memorial Flight', in which guise we still know it today. Based at RAF Coningsby, the Flight's mission is to

> maintain the priceless artefacts of our national heritage in airworthy condition in order to commemorate those who have fallen in the service of this country. The RAF BBMF also serves to promote the modern-day Air Force and to inspire the future generations.

In 1973, the impressive Avro Lancaster, PA474, joined the Flight, the aircrew of which are all serving RAF personnel, the aircraft served by a

In 2010, for the seventh anniversary, BBMF Spitfire and Battle of Britain P7350 was painted to represent the machine flown by Squadron Leader Geoffrey Harry Augustus Wellum in 1940, when a pilot officer on 92 Squadron, and Hurricane R4118 appeared in the markings of Wing Commander Bob Foster DFC of 605 Squadron – who had actually flown this aircraft during the Battle of Britain. On 19 August 2010, the two veterans were flown out of RAF Coningsby in Aztec G-LIZZ, formatting with P7350, flown by Squadron Leader Tony Parkinson MBE, and R4118, piloted by a former OC BBMF, Squadron Leader Al Pinner MBE. This incredible tribute was organised by the then current OC, Squadron Leader Ian Smith MBE. *(Jarrod Cotter)*

dedicated ground team, which now operates the 'Lanc', a C-47 Dakota, six Spitfires, two Hurricanes and two de-Havilland Chipmunk training aircraft. These irreplaceable aircraft are flown to celebrate and delight crowds at state events and celebrations, including royal coronations and Trooping the Colour, major air shows and other public events. Like the RAF world-famous RAF aerobatic team, the Red Arrows, BBMF is very much part of the fabric of British national pride – and long may that be the case.

Squadron Leader Ian Smith MBE RAF (Ret'd):

> As a child I was fascinated with the Battle of Britain. My bedroom ceiling was adorned with numerous Airfix models, Spitfires and Hurricanes chasing Messerschmitt 109s and Heinkels! Fast forward forty-years and my lifelong ambition to fly both a Spitfire and Hurricane was achieved with the Battle of Britain Memorial Flight. My good fortune was not

Squadron Leader Geoffrey Harry Augustus Wellum with Spitfire P7350. *(Jarrod Cotter)*

Wing Commander Bob Foster DFC with Hurricane R4118. *(Jarrod Cotter)*

limited to just flying these wonderful aircraft, though, as for three years I had the privilege of commanding the Flight.

The Battle of Britain can rightly be considered to be the Royal Air Force's greatest Battle Honour. I spent thirty-two years in the Royal Air Force as a fighter pilo, and was involved in quite a few conflicts during those years – although none of the magnitude of those dark days in 1940. I often wonder how I would have fared as an eighteen-year-old Spitfire or Hurricane pilot.

The Flight are custodians of the Britain's aviation heritage. Its mantra remains the same after more than sixty-years of flying these iconic aeroplanes: to honour those who paid the ultimate sacrifice in the freedom of our country. Whilst we now honour all those who 'gave their all' in the service of the Royal Air Force, one only has to look skyward to see and hear a Spitfire and Hurricane and automatically acknowledge our 'Finest Hour' – with which those fighters are synonymous.

Winston Churchill made many historic speeches during the Second World War: 'A Nation that forgets its past has no future', is the one that resonated most with me during my time commanding the Flight. It remains extremely important that we continue to educate today's generations of the sacrifices that have been made by those before us. The world would be a very different place had the whole country not risen to the challenge in the summer of 1940.

Lest We Forget…

One especially important aerial pageant commemorating the Battle of Britain which BBMF contributed to was the incredibly impressive RAF flypast celebrating the fiftieth anniversary, on 15 September 1990. In what was the biggest RAF aerial pageant since the 1953 coronation of Her Majesty Queen Elizabeth II, a total of 166 (just 2 less than in 1953) aircraft over-flew The Mall and Buckingham Palace at noon. Hundreds of thousands turned out to watch the spectacle – prominent amongst them members of the BoBFA, which marched into the palace grounds led by its chairman, Air Chief Marshal Christopher Foxley-Norris. The queen and the royal family watched the streams of aircraft from the palace's famous balcony, and there was very much an air of celebration concluded by a huge firework display

Squadron Leader Ian Smith MBE when OC BBMF. *(Jarrod Cotter)*

that night. It was an awe-inspiring occasion and an appropriate one with which to mark the fiftieth.

Although the 1969 *Battle of Britain* had inspired a new wave of interest in the events of 1940, from 1990 and the fiftieth anniversary of the Battle of Britain onwards an enthusiast cult built up around wartime survivors, especially 'The Few', devotees following their heroes around to various events, avidly collecting their signatures on books, not least my own, and aviation prints. This was an interesting development, because in the winter of their lives, many of 'The Few' engaged with this phenomenon, looking forward to these meetings and the attention, a chance to meet old friends and reminisce, and – most importantly – inspire younger generations. This was, perhaps, the last survivors' final sortie in terms of preserving and promoting the memory of those who died, and, indeed, promoting that sense of Battle of Britain brotherhood that actually touches people worldwide. For me personally, these were halcyon days, surrounded by 'The Few', and my events, although we did operate at air shows on occasion, were really about bringing the Battle of Britain story to the

From 1990 onwards, a cult built up around 'The Few', enthusiasts avidly collecting their heroes signatures on prints of books. Dilip Sarkar's signing events become world famous, the author providing a unique opportunity for the general – not just aviation – public to meet 'The Few'. Dilip is pictured here at the launch of *Through Peril to the Stars* in 1993. Those of 'The Few' pictured are Wing Commander Bernard Jennings, Wing Commander George Unwin, Flight Lieutenant William Walker, Squadron Leader Iain Hutchinson, Group Captain Christopher Currant, Flight Lieutenant Richard Jones and Group Captain Gerry Edge.

Another popular guest at Dilip Sarkar's events was Lady Bader, pictured here with the author at the launch of *Missing in Action: Resting in Peace?*, in 1998, together with Flight Lieutenant Richard Jones, Flight Lieutenant Gordon Batt, Flight Lieutenant Ron Rayner (not one of 'The Few'), Geoffrey Stevens and Keith Lawrence.

high street, as it were, and to the attention of people who were not necessarily aviation enthusiasts but who would nonetheless be inspired by these wonderful men – and women, given the WAAF survivors we were also proud to host, alongside other supporting staff, from engine fitters and armourers to Ops 'B' controllers and the relatives of casualties. The Honourable Lady Odette Dowding, Lord Dowding's daughter-in-law and widow of his son, Derek, who was one of 'The Few', and Lady Bader were a frequent guest, as was Air Vice-Marshal Johnnie E. Johnson, the RAF's officially top-scoring fighter pilot of the war, and a host of other august personalities, from famous aces to what Peter Fox, formerly a 19-year-old Hurricane pilot in the Battle of Britain, taking about himself and friends, famously described as 'Also rans'. It was the 'Also rans', though, that interested me personally much more, and the exercise was all about providing the public a unique, and often unexpected, opportunity to meet these wonderful people from the pages of history.

Lord Dowding, the BoBFA's original president, however, was never made MRAF, unlike his counterpart, the commander of Bomber Command, Arthur Harris – a matter, along with the treatment of Dowding and Park after the Battle of Britain, which rankled 'The Few'. Made 1st Baron of Bentley Priory on 2 June 1943, this came not close to redressing the injustice that Dowding was never elevated beyond air chief marshal. The great man ultimately died at home, in Tunbridge Wells, on 15 February 1970, his ashes being interred a month later beneath the Battle of Britain memorial window in Westminster Abbey; a simple tablet states, succinctly, 'He led The Few in the Battle of Britain'. It was eight years later that Air Chief Marshal Christopher Foxley-Norris became chairman of the BoBFA and determined to rectify the fact that nearly fifty years after the Battle of Britain there was no substantial memorial to Lord Dowding – which he considered 'a matter of surprise and concern, or even shame'. Certainly, the Scottish town of Moffat had paid tribute to its most famous son when a bronze plaque created by Scott Sutherland, commemorating Lord Dowding was unveiled in the town on 9 September 1972, and a memorial plaque graced a slab of Moffat granite erected in Calverly Park, Tunbridge Wells, where Dowding spent the last years of his life, but to Foxley-Norris – more commonly known in BoBFA circles as 'CFN' – it was unthinkable that there was no public tribute to the great man in London. The pathway to the BoBFA achieving this long overdue recognition for their chief, however, was far from straightforward.

In 1978, Foxley-Norris, who had flown Hurricanes with 615 Squadron during the Battle of Britain, launched a campaign for the international BoBFA membership to raise funds for and awareness of the need for a London monument to Dowding. Between March and October 1987, the subject was discussed by the House of Lords, but there was no support forthcoming from government concerning funding, and Environment Minister Willian Waldegrave, confirmed that it was 'the policy of successive governments since 1956 not to sponsor further memorials to leaders of the Second World War'. The lords, however, were overwhelmingly supportive and as exasperated as Foxley-Norris and the BoBFA at the government's unhelpful attitude. Other obstacles included planning permission included the environment minister's approval, Westminster Council's planning permission, discussions with the Royal Fine Art Commission over the site, and church authorities. After no mean amount of discussion, it was decided that the tribute would take the form of a 9ft-high bronze statue by the sculptor Faith Winter, located outside the Central Church of the

RAF, St Clement Danes, in London's Strand. All approvals were eventually obtained, the £50,000 required being the BoBFA's responsibility to raise, and the association's royal patron, who was aware of her late husband's desire to see Dowding made MRAF (see *The Final Curtain*, Volume 7) accepted an invitation to eventually unveil the work.

Suffice it to say, the money was raised, and at 10.35 hrs on Sunday, 30 October 1988, Her Majesty Queen Elizabeth, The Queen Mother unveiled the huge statue. That, against the backdrop of governmental disinterest, this had been achieved by 'The Few' themselves, would doubtless have pleased Lord Dowding very much. Considered by many to have been a remote and austere figure, the evidence does not entirely support this: during the Battle of Britain, Dowding actually flew himself around in a communications aircraft, visiting certain airfields – most notably Fowlmere, where he listed to 19 Squadron's complaints about the problematic cannon-armed Spitfire Mk IBs; 'Stuffy' reacted decisively, immediately ordering their replacement with machine-gun-armed Spitfire Mk IAs, much to the pilots' delight. One of those young men was Pilot Officer Wallace' Jock' Cunningham DFC, who rather summed things up:

> Lord Dowding's is the big success story here – a strong man who had resisted political pressure to throw away a lot more fighters in France for a battle already lost. He was preserving Fighter Command for the battle to come. Again, a success story in the Battle of Britain. Clearly, his was the credit for the strategy. He listened, said little but acted decisively. I had direct experience of his quick and clear thinking when our 20 mm cannons were performing badly; he visited the Squadron, heard what we had to say, and within hours we were re-equipping with machine-gun Spitfires. So, treasure the memory of 'Stuffy' Dowding – do not sell him short. His was the victory in directing and sustaining his 'Twelve Legions of Angels'.

During the early part of the Second World War, that the RAF had a legless fighter ace was great propaganda, and after the war, in 1956, Group Captain Douglas Bader's story became a global best seller, *Reach for the Sky*, by the Australian former Spitfire pilot and author Paul Brickhill (see Chapter Four), and Daniel 'Danny' Angel's film of the same name, starring Kenneth More, was a similar international success, cementing Bader as the most

The Douglas Bader Statue at Goodwood, created by sculptor Kenneth Potts. *(Kenneth Potts)*

famous of 'The Few' – rightly or wrongly. Knighted in 1976 for 'services to disabled people', Douglas Bader died suddenly, aged 72, on 5 September 1982. Later that year, Bader's family and friends founded the Douglas Bader Foundation, offering support to the disabled amputee community, upholding his story as an inspiration to this very day. There are tributes to Bader on a worldwide basis, from roads and buildings in his name – to what was the first statue to a specific member of 'The Few'. This life and a quarter scale bronze by the sculptor Kenneth Potts, based upon a photograph of Bader in my archive, was commissioned by Lord March and situated outside Goodwood Flying Club on what is the former Westhampnett airfield, the Tangmere satellite where Bader based himself with 616 Squadron when leading the Tangmere Wing in 1941. Appropriately, the sadly now late Lady Bader unveiled the statue on 9 August 2001 – the sixtieth anniversary of Bader's last operational wartime flight, made from that very airfield.

On 15 September 2007, an article on the lack of recognition in the UK for Air Chief Marshal Keith Park was published in the 'Mrs Moneypenny' column of *The Financial Times*, charging that this omission was 'A Collective memory failure'. A week later, the London financier Terry Smith offered fiscal support to an appropriate memorial to Park in London – and so the 'Sir Keith Park Memorial Campaign' was born, which was officially launched on 7 March 2008. The campaign rapidly gathered momentum here and in New Zealand, the sculptor Lee Johnson was chosen to create a statue 9ft high. Having been through similar processes to that involving Dowding's statue, on 30 September 2008 the maquette was unveiled at City Hall with members of the BoBFA, the Park family, the high commissioner for New Zealand and other VIPs in attendance. On 7 May 2009, Westminster Council approved placing a temporary fibre-glass cast of the Park statue on Trafalgar Square's empty fourth plinth, which was unveiled on 4 November 2009. Since removed and now exhibited in the car park of the Battle of Britain Bunker, Uxbridge, the permanent bronze was unveiled in Waterloo Place, off Pall Mall, on 15 September 2010. Like the Dowding statue this is an impressive tribute indeed, and rightly so in Central London.

Arguably, Keith Park is New Zealand's greatest war hero, who returned to Auckland post-war and contributed to public life as a city councillor until his death in 1975. In the War Memorial Museum in Auckland, his uniform and medals are displayed (see Chapter Two), and a cast of Lee Johnson's huge state appears outside Auckland's Museum of Transport and Technology, where there is a memorial and life-size replica of Park's

The huge statue of Keith Park at the Battle of Britain Bunker, Uxbridge.

Hurricane 'OK1'. In 2019, the Sir Keith Park Memorial Airfield Inc was established to cooperate with the Thames-Coromandel District Council to, amongst other things, raise awareness of Park's achievement and service in Thames, his place of birth. At the airfield, a more accurately painted 'OK1' replica than that at MOTAT has been installed, and plans are afoot for another large-scale statue. So, Air Chief Marshal Sir Keith Park – now officially one of 'The Few' himself – is no longer forgotten, either in the UK or his native land.

Another important shrine at which both Dowding and Park are remembered, is, of course, The Battle of Britain Memorial, achieved, managed and maintained by The Battle of Britain Memorial Trust CIO, at Capel-le-Ferne, high on the cliffs overlooking Folkestone.

Visitors to the cliff-top site are first welcomed by 'The Beaverbrook Wall', on which are inscribed Churchill's immortal words: 'Never in the field of human conflict was so much owed, by so many, to so few.' At the heart of this hallowed site is The National Memorial to 'The Few', a seated airman, carved by Harry Gray, gazing out across the Channel, over which so many battles were fought. The airman – whose rank is indistinguishable – looks towards Boulogne, the French coast clearly visible in good weather and a reminder of just how close the Germans were in summer 1940.

The replica of OK-1 outside Auckland's MOTAT.

Above: A recent aerial view of the National Battle of Britain Museum at Capel-le-Ferne, near Folkestone. *(BoBMT)*

Right: Wing Commander Geoffrey Page, instigator of the National Memorial, speaking at the memorial's unveiling in 1993. *(BoBMT)*

A BBMF Spitfire flies over the airman memorial at a recent Memorial Day. *(Jarrod Cotter)*

The National Battle of Britain Memorial was unveiled by Her Majesty Queen Elizabeth, The Queen Mother, wartime Queen of England and patron of the BoBFA, pictured here with, from left, the then chief of the Air Staff, Air Chief Marshal Sir Michael Graydon; Wing Commander Geoffrey Page and Air Chief Marshal Christopher Foxley-Norris, chairman of the BoBFA. *(BoBMT)*

The figure sits upon a propeller boss, surrounded by the heraldic crests of those units that fought in the Battle of Britain, the three propeller blades cut out of the chalk, also making this large memorial site impressive from the air. It is entirely appropriate that the vision for this exemplary tribute was that on one of 'The Few', namely Wing Commander Geoffrey Page, who had been shot down and horrendously burned whilst flying Hurricanes during the Battle of Britain with 56 Squadron. Opened by Her Majesty Queen Elizabeth, The Queen Mother on 9 July 1993, over the years this inspirational, open, space has been substantially added to.

In such high esteem was former BoBFA chairman and president of the Battle of Britain Memorial Trust Sir Christopher Foxley-Norris held, that after his death in 2003, it was decided to name the proposed wall listing 'The Few' at the National Memorial site in his honour. With echoes of America's Vietnam Wall, the fifteen black panel record all the names in alphabetical order – with a section wisely left blank for any future additions, which will soon include the name of Keith Park. The 'Christopher Foxley-Norris Memorial Wall' was unveiled by His Royal Highness Prince Michael of Kent on 3 July 2005.

After the death of Flight Lieutenant William Walker, a Spitfire pilot on 616 Squadron during the Battle of Britain, in 2012, his ashes were interred

Above, below and opposite above: Memorial Day, held every July, is an important annual event in the National Battle of Britain Memorial's calendar. *(BoBMT)*

Patron of The Battle of Britain Memorial Trust, His Royal Highness Prince Michael of Kent at the Christopher Foxley-Norris Memorial Wall. *(BoBMT)*

Battle of Britain Spitfire pilot William Walker's poem at the Christopher Foxley-Noris Memorial Wall – where his ashes were interred in 2012.

there. Furthermore, a gifted poet who used verse as a means of rationalising his wartime experience, a separate panel was erected bearing the text of his 'Our Wall':

> Here inscribed the names of friends we knew
> Young men with whom we often flew.
> Scrambled to many angels high,
> They knew that they or friends might die.
> Many were very scarcely trained
> And many badly burnt or maimed.
> Behind each name a story lies
> Of bravery in summer skies;
> Though many brave unwritten tales
> Were simply told in vapour trails.
> Outnumbered every day they flew,
> Remembered here as just 'The Few'.

The Christopher Foxley-Norris Wall, recording individual names of 'The Few'.

The bust of Lord Dowding at the National Battle of Britain Memorial.

Over the years, further tributes have been added to the site, and adjacent to the wall, on 28 October 2010, the then Her Royal Highness Camilla, Duchess of Cornwall (now Queen Camilla) unveiled a bust of Air Chief Marshal Keith Park by the sculptor Will Davies, who later produced a bust of Lord Dowding, unveiled on 31 May 2017 by His Royal Highness Prince Michael of Kent, Patron of the Battle of Britain Memorial Trust.

The bust of Air Chief Marshal Keith Park.

Most importantly, 'The Wing' visitor centre, in the shape of a Spitfire's wing, opened by Her Majesty Queen Elizabeth II on 26 March 2015, accommodates the 'Scramble Experience', providing an overview of the Battle of Britain, which being 'hands on', harnessing modern audio and visual technology, is equally popular with and appealing to younger

On 26 March 2015, the now late Queen Elizabeth II opened the 'Wing' visitor centre, accommodating the 'Scramble' experience at the National Battle of Britain Memorial, and is seen here on that occasion with Group Captain Patrick Tootal OBE, honorary secretary of both the Battle of Britain Memorial Trust and the BoBMT. *(BoBMT)*

The 'airman', behind which can be seen 'The Wing' visitor centre and 'Cockpit Café', and Christopher Foxley-Norris Memorial Wall.

audiences; a classroom – the 'Geoffrey Page Centre', shop and 'Cockpit Café' are all included in the visitor centre. Elsewhere, the site includes Hunting Lodge, providing a space for a library and meetings (which can be hired out). A replica Spitfire and Hurricane are displayed at the site, along with a controversial, life-size, stainless steel replica of a crashed Ju 87 *Stuka* dive bomber, created by German artist Mister Hex, intended to promote reconciliation.

The National Memorial site also hosts the annual Battle of Britain Memorial Day, which at one time was a highlight of the diaries of 'The Few'. Although, sadly, not the case today, the occasion remains an important diary date and act of remembrance, a colourful spectacle supported by the RAF, various other organisations, and featuring a BBMF flypast. As a charity, the Battle of Britain Memorial Trust is largely reliant upon fund raising and public donations, and faces a constant challenge in maintaining this vitally important site. We can all help by becoming a 'Friend of "The Few"' and helping raise awareness of the trust's mission, which, like the

National Memorial itself, is 'dedicated to the heroic and selfless deeds of the men who won the Battle of Britain'.

Recently, a new appeal was launched by the forward-thinking trustees, the 'Blade of Honour' project, to honour the many, all of those who howsoever supported 'The Few' or in some way contributed to victory in the Battle of Britain. Non-Clasp holders such as Pilot Officer Alec Bird and Sergeant Bruce Hancock immediately come to mind (see Chapter Two), and this initiative seeks to go far wider, including, for example, RAF ground crews and other support staff, ARP wardens, the emergency services, the Observer Corps, and many more, as the trust's chairman, Richard Hunting CBE, explained,

> We don't have a set list of organisations or professions that we feel qualify but are inviting people to nominate the person they think should be commemorated – probably but not necessarily, a relative – and produce evidence that they played a part in this historic victory. They can be military or civilian, so long as they have contributed.

The named tributes will be in the form of engraved tiles, which will be aligned along the leading edge of one of the three propeller blades emanating from the boss atop which sits the airman figure. It is entirely right that this tribute should be included on this primary site.

Another major initiative is 'The Next Sortie: Bringing the Battle of Britain to Life', launched in January 2024 and looking forward to the thirtieth anniversary of the National Memorial's opening, as the trust's website explains:

> In support of its twin aims of commemorating the bravery and sacrifice of The Few and inspiring and educating future generations, the Trust has unveiled ambitious plans to add to the resources at the popular clifftop site.
>
> A £1m appeal has been launched to extend Hunting Lodge to create more space for an exciting new aerial dog fight simulator experience and for displaying Battle of Britain artefacts.
>
> Two high-tech simulators will allow visitors to experience the thrill – and fear – of an aerial duel against a determined enemy, highlighting the challenges facing the aircrew of the RAF in 1940.

> Visitors will take the controls of a Supermarine Spitfire or a Messerschmitt Bf109, allowing them to compete in the kind of aerial battle that would have been a common sight in this part of the country as the Battle was at its height.
>
> As well as housing the simulators, the extension to Hunting Lodge will provide the Trust with space to display more of the artefacts it has been gifted over the years, again helping to bring the battle to life for this and future generations.
>
> As a charity with no public funding, the Trust can only make a reality of this dream with the help of supporters. It is looking for public help to raise the £1m needed and take the Memorial forward into the next 30 years.

So the National Memorial site is not a one-off tribute, but an ongoing, evolving memorial, moving with the times – and long may that remain the case.

Westminster is also home to an imposing tribute, namely the Battle of Britain London Monument, situated on the Victoria Embankment, between

On 18 September 2005, the Battle of Britain London Monument was unveiled by the then Prince Charles, Prince of Wales, and Camilla, the Duchess of Cornwall, seen here with members of the BoBFA. *(Edward McManus)*

the RAF Memorial and Westminster Bridge. Taking the form of bronze sculpted relief panels by Paul Day, cladding what was an existing 25m long plinth, the friezes depict an inclusive range of human experience, from fighter pilots to civilians, and includes the individual names of 'The Few', or at least those known to have been eligible for the Battle of Britain Clasp when the monument was created and unveiled on 18 September 2005 by the then Prince Charles, the Price of Wales, and Camilla, the Duchess of Cornwall. It really is a superb tribute in an absolutely prime capital location – and the Battle of Britain Historical Society is to be congratulated for having initiated this project. The London Monument, namely Edward McManus, also hosts an online resource, which can be updated as more information is discovered, providing individual biographical details of 'The Few' (see Bibliography).

In 1945, it was decided that a number of Pacific steam locomotives – originally known as the West Country Class – would collectively be known as the 'Battle of Britain Class', to commemorate the RAF victory of 1940. Forty-four locomotives comprised the class, individually named after personalities, airfields and organisations involved with the Battle of Britain, 21C153 being named 'Sir Keith Park' and so-named by the great

The then Prince Charles unveiling Paul Day's Battle of Britain London Monument at Westminster. *(Edward McManus)*

Above and below: Two views of the Battle of Britain London Monument, which also records names of 'The Few'.

New Zealander at Brighton Station on 19 September 1947. Twenty years later, the Class was completely withdrawn from service, 'Sir Keith Park' having been towed to Barry scrapyard in March 1966, where it languished until 1979, when it was purchased by Charles Timms and restoration began. Over the years, the locomotive changed hands several times until eventually purchased and fully restored to steam by Southern Locomotives Limited, entering service with the Severn Valley Railway in August 2012. The following year, on 31 August 2013, the locomotive was re-dedicated in memory of Keith Park, and in 2020 'SKP' moved to the Spa Valley Railway, which runs from Tunbridge Wells West to High Rocks, Groombridge, in Kent. In May 2021, moved to the Swanage Railway for maintenance, and was withdrawn from service in February 2022 when its boiler ticket expired. With a new boiler, 'SKP' moved to Herston in February 2024, and at the time of writing work remains ongoing to get the locomotive running again – and what an impressive sight that will be.

Unusually, four large physical memorials exist to individual Battle of Britain airmen.

Flying Officer Richard Demetriadi of 601 Squadron was killed in action on 11 August 1940, and his father, Sir Stephen Demetriadi, a wealthy senior civil servant, businessman and Sussex landowner, decided he wanted a permanent and living memorial to his son – so donated land at Ditchling Beacon, the highest point in Sussex, to The National Trust. A modest sign records the gift and commemorates Flying Officer Richard Demetriadi by name, and must be seen by countless people annually enjoying the East Sussex countryside and panoramic views.

In 1953, a 2.4km square lake in Manitoba, Canada, was named in memory of Pilot Officer John Benzie, of Winnipeg, who flew Hurricanes with 242 Squadron in both the Fall of France and Battle of Britain, until reported missing on 7 September 1940, during the Duxford Wing's first action. Believed to have crashed into the Thames Estuary, Benzie was commemorated on the Runnymede Memorial – but in 1980, the former London Air Museum recovered the burnt-out wreckage of a Hurricane, and its pilot, at Blackacre, Theydon Bois, Essex. Nothing was found to confirm the aircraft's identity, or that of the pilot, beyond the fact that the crash was known to have happened on 7 September 1940. Three Hurricane pilots were reported missing on that day, one of whom, Flight Lieutenant Hugh Beresford of 257 Squadron, had been recovered from his Hurricane's crash site on the Isle of Sheppey in 1979. It cannot, though, be ascertained whether the Theydon Bois crash was that of Benzie or the other outstanding

The plaque commemorating Flying Officer Richard Demetriadi at Ditchling Beacon.

pilot, namely Flying Officer Lancelot Mitchell of 257 Squadron, and so the remains were buried at Brookwood as an unknown airman. Nonetheless, Lake Benzie is an impressive expanse of water a fitting memorial to Pilot Officer John Benzie – who may, or may not, still be missing.

Salem-Leckrone Airport, in Salem, Illinois, commemorates the American volunteer Pilot Officer Phillip 'Uncle Sam' Leckrone, who was from Salem and flew Spitfires with 616 Squadron in the Battle of Britain – which he survived, only to be killed in a flying accident during a training flight on 5 January 1941. The other physical tribute is, unusually, in Antarctica: the Lewis Chain of four rock nunataks on the western side of the Shackleton Range's Gordon Glacier commemorates LAC John Lewis, a radar operator on 25 Squadron during the Battle of Britain and who survived the war, dying in 1990.

There are, in fact, virtually countless memorials associated with the Battle of Britain, official and otherwise, either commemorating 'The Few' collectively or individually. Indeed, as we have already seen, the types of memorials and monuments are diverse indeed – Group Captain Douglas Bader even having a public house named in his honour, and an English Heritage 'blue plaque'. English Heritage has administered the London blue plaque scheme in 1986, the circular blue plaques commemorating prominent individuals, and has since erected 360. On 31 May 2009, Sir Richard Branson and David Bickers, chairman of the Douglas Bader Foundation, unveiled the blue plaque commemorating Bader at his former London home, 5 Petersham Mews in the Royal Borough of Kensington and Chelsea, SW7.

English Heritage would not, however, agree to the erection of such a plaque at 19 Barrow Point Avenue, Pinner, Middlesex, where Squadron Leader Brian Lane, the 23-year-old commander of 19 Squadron during most of the Battle of Britain, grew up, the reason given being that Lane was just one of many who lost their lives during the Second World War, having been reported missing on 13 December 1942. That, however, missed the point, because all the evidence indicates that Lane was a truly exceptional fighter pilot, leader and human being. Paul Baderman, the Pinner resident who made the application, was unprepared to accept this decicion and consequently commissioned an independent blue plaque, which was ultimately funded by the 19(F) Squadron Association. On 25 September 2011, I was delighted to speak on the occasion of the plaque's unveiling, the honour performed by 19 Squadron's last surviving Battle of Britain pilot, Flight Lieutenant Ken Wilkinson, and Lane's flight rigger, John Milne.

The English Heritage blue plaque at 5 Petersham Mews. (*Douglas Bader Foundation*)

Commemorative plaques, in fact, these days abound, dedicated to individual members of 'The Few' and erected in associated churches, schools attended and, in certain cases, their crash sites. In 1987, for example, our former Malvern Spitfire Team erected a small roadside cairn in Madresfield, Worcestershire, dedicated to the memory of Polish Flying Officer Franciszek Surma, who flew Hurricanes during the Battle of Britain with various squadrons before being reported missing on 8 November 1941, when flying Spitfires with 308 'City of Kraków' Squadron. This was perhaps an unusual commemoration given that Surma was not killed at Madresfield – on 11 May 1941, he baled out of Spitfire R6644 owing to an engine fire, the aircraft crashing beside Jennet Tree Lane, near where the Polish ace landed safely by parachute. That Surma was later reported missing, however, touched our hearts, and hence why the tribute was decided. Unveiled by two of 'The Polish Few', namely Squadron Leader Boleslaw 'Gandy' Drobinski DFC and Squadron Leader Ludwik Martel VM KW, on 11 September 1987, at the time it was the only memorial to an individual fighter pilot in the UK. Back then, two of Surma's sisters were still alive, who much appreciated the gesture; a Catholic family, to them our

The former Malvern Spitfire Team's modest memorial to Flying Officer Franciszek Surma at Madresfield, Worcestershire. When unveiled in 1987, this was the first and only commemoration of an individual Polish airman.

modest memorial was a symbolic grave at which their beloved could at last find peace and rest for eternity.

Certain crash sites where Battle of Britain aircrew were killed have also been marked, most commendably in recent times by the Shoreham Aircraft Museum near Sevenoaks in Kent, which, in 2006, decided to so honour all those pilots who lost their lives within a 10-mile radius of the premises. So far, twelve such memorial stones have been unveiled, most recently, at the time of writing, one to Pilot Officer Colin Dunstan Francis of 253 Squadron. Shot down on 30 August 1940 and reported missing, the pilot's remains were not recovered until 1981 from his Hurricane's crash site at Stansted; buried at Brookwood, the Shoreham tribute was unveiled on 12 March 2024. As the museum's website states, the list of pilots within this 10-mile radius is long, and this worthy initiative relies entirely upon voluntary efforts and donations.

Another, now long-standing, initiative continues to be undertaken by the Battle of Britain Historical Society, through the erection of memorial plaques at schools attended by The Few. The idea, of course, is to connect past with present through raising awareness with current students of the sacrifices made by their forbears – who were often only a little older. Moreover, whilst the marking of heritage sites with blue plaques is widely known,

The memorials erected by Shoreham Aircraft Museum in Kent. *(Geoff Nutkins)*

green plaques are less so, which recognise the connection of a person with a location. For example, Leicestershire County Council has so far unveiled thirty-six green plaques in the county, following nominations from members of the public, including one at The Wagon & Horses public house in Curzon Street, Ibstock, on 13 October 2022, dedicated to and a former home of Hurricane pilot Sergeant Herbert Black, killed in action on 29 October 1940.

'The Last of "The Few"' statue, depicting Group Captain John Hemmingway, the last known member of 'The Few' (who sadly died in 2025, aged 105), at The Kent Battle of Britain Museum.

The most recent, substantial, memorial to 'The Few' is the 'Spirit of The Few' sculpture at the exemplary Kent Battle of Britain Museum at Hawkinge (see Chapter Seven). Envisioned by the museum's chairman, David Brocklehurst, whose inspiration was the famous photograph taken at Hawkinge airfield on 29 July 1940, of seven Hurricane pilots of 32 Squadron relaxing on the grass before the next scramble: Flying Officer Rupert Smythe, Flight Lieutenant John Proctor, Pilot Officer Keith Gillman, Flight Lieutenant Peter Brothers, Flight Lieutenant Peter Gardner, Flying Officer Douglas Hamilton Grice DFC and Flying Officer Alan Eckford. The life-size statues were made by the Ramsgate art studio SPACER, sculpted by Stephen Melton, and the substantial cost was raised through public donations. On 29 July 2022 – the eighty-second anniversary of the photograph being taken, the 'Spirit of The Few' was unveiled by Squadron Leader Woods, the current OC 32 Squadron, at an event attended by relatives of the seven pilots concerned, after which four Hurricanes over-flew the site. More recently, in February 2023, the museum took delivery of a statue, also created by Stephen Melton and SPACER, based on a photograph of 'The Last of "The Few"', Group Captain John Hemmingway, which is another fitting artwork and tribute.

A recent development in memorialisation is the restoration of historic aircraft to airworthiness. Considering that certain of these aircraft crashed from great heights, their wreckage recovered from their crash sites many years later, it could be considered remarkable that such restorations are even contemplated. Nonetheless, substantial amounts of wreckage with irrefutable identification, such as a maker's plate and serial number, or other definite provenance, can be registered with the Civilian Aircraft Authority in the UK as restoration projects. The fact is, however, that only a small amount of original parts may be used in what are often virtually complete reconstructions and not exactly 're-builds'.

One current restoration project concerns Spitfire X4009, the aircraft in which the Australian Flight Lieutenant Pat Hughes DFC of 234 Squadron recorded ten aerial victories before his death in action on 7 September 1940. On that day, Hughes shot down a Do 17, exploding with such force that X4009 was also badly damaged, forcing the pilot to abandon ship. Sadly, Hughes's parachute failed and his body was found in the garden of a bungalow 100 yards away from where his Spitfire crashed at Sundridge in Kent. A married man, Hughes was buried near his widow's home in Hull, and was the most successful Australian fighter pilot of the Battle of

Britain, with fourteen, and three shared destroyed, one shared destroyed unconfirmed and a probable; Hughes was also the third most successful ace from 'Down Under' of the entire Second World War.

In 1969, the crash site of X4009 at Darks Farm, Bessels Green, was excavated by the former Halstead War Museum, substantial remains being recovered, with other parts held by the Kent Battle of Britain Museum, Hawkinge, and privately by aviation archaeologist Steve Vizard of Airframe Assemblies.

Nearly eighty years after the Battle of Britain, the engine and other wreckage of X4009, amounting to 500kg, was acquired by Ross and Ann-Maree Pay, of the Scone, New South Wales-based Pay's Group, a vintage aircraft restoration concern. The Spitfire was then donated by Pay's Group to the not-for-profit Hunter Fighter Collection Inc, also based in Scone, where X4009 will be returned to flying condition as 'The Pat Hughes Flying Memorial'. In January 2021, the project received a grant of $150,000 from the 'Saluting Their Service' initiative by the Commonwealth Department of Veterans' Affairs, this enabling work to be completed by Airframe Assemblies on longitudinal structural members and fuselage frames. Stage two is now underway at Vintage Fighter Restoration, also in Scone, with more fund raising ongoing, to complete the fuselage, begin wing and tail assemblies, and start sourcing the necessary mechanical and electrical components required in addition to the engine and propeller cores. Naturally this is very expensive work, and Hunter Fighter Collection Inc has appealed for donations of at least $2 a piece, tax deductible, in Australia. It is hoped that sufficient financial support will be forthcoming to see this Spitfire soar aloft again – a flying memorial to Flight Lieutenant Pat Hughes.

John Parker, Hunter Fighter Collection Inc's public officer and curator of Hunter Warbirds:

> Our efforts in restoring Pat Hughes' aircraft, X4009, are as much about the man and his life as they are about the actual Spitfire. Pat was a man whose legacy deserves to be celebrated and elevated in the consciousness of all Australians.
>
> The restoration is progressing well, and we are making great progress in promoting the work being done and Pat's place in history. Pat was, as you may know, little known in Australia as a Battle of Britain ace, and we are working hard to raise his profile and place in our history. We are very fortunate to have access to the facilities of Vintage Fighter

> Restorations at Scone NSW – the premier Spitfire restoration facility in Australia. Ross Pay and his team at Vintage Fighter Restorations are doing a magnificent job in the restoration and working with various sub-contractors in the UK to complete the task.
>
> As with any publicly funded restoration project funds are always at a premium and Hunter Fighter Collection Incorporated (a registered Australian charity) are working very hard to raise the necessary finance to complete and operate the Spitfire. Once complete it will remain with us at our large state of the art museum in Scone and be flown at events and ceremonies across the country as a flying memorial to Pat and all the Australians who flew in the Battle of Britain.

The project, then, is clearly an important one, deserved of support, and it is hoped that before too long the sound of the re-born X4009 will be roaring across Australian skies – a living memorial to Flight Lieutenant Pat Hughes.

A similar initiative is the 'Laguna's Spitfire Legacy' project, which although not focused on an actual Battle of Britain aircraft, that concerned being a later Mk IIB, P8331, does honour one of 'The Polish Few', namely Wing Commander Piotr Laguna, who flew Hurricanes with 302 Squadron during the summer of 1940. Laguna, who was shot down in P8331 on 27 June 1941, and killed in the resulting crash near Calais, provides a central focus whilst the project also seeks to recognise 'all the brave fighter pilots of the Second World War … and the 18,000 Polish pilots and ground crews of the Polish Air Force.' Entirely run by volunteers, the objective, through fund raising, partnerships and sponsorship is to re-build P8331, again as a living memorial, as it were, which will then be operated by the BBMF. Hopefully, this aircraft too will soon grace European skies and be a regular fixture on the air show circuit.

Today, though, the gates of so many RAF stations have long been closed, and those remaining open no longer hold Battle of Britain at home days. The air shows that do occur largely tend to be focused upon the aircraft themselves, rather than the Battle of Britain or other specific wartime battles, although a notable exception is the enormously popular annual Battle of Britain Air Show held every September by the Imperial War Museum (IWM) at Duxford, its working airfield near Cambridge. Home to various vintage aircraft operators, this former Battle of Britain 12 Group Sector Station, once home to the 'Big Wing', reverberates on a virtual daily basis with the roar of

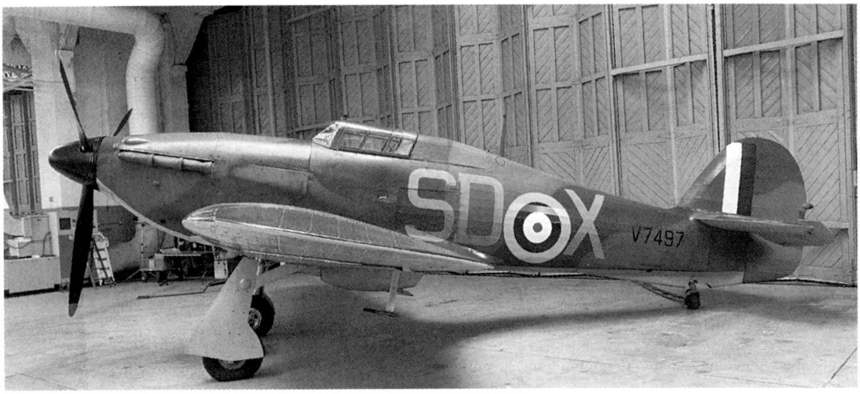

Hurricane V7497, which saw action flying with 501 Squadron during the Battle of Britain and now restored to flying condition, pictured at Duxford in 2024.

Hurricanes and Spitfires, and the annual Battle of Britain Air Show remains the high-spot of many an enthusiast's calendar. Beyond doubt, Duxford has become the central focus for the warbird movement in the UK, and in addition to the Battle of Britain Air Show its other shows, commemorate other historic occasions, such as Operation Market Garden and D-Day, and regular 'Flying Days' throughout the season have paid tribute to 19 Squadron, which famously received the RAF's first Spitfire at Duxford in August 1938.

Nowadays, there are, in fact, a whole wave of events pedalling nostalgia, harking back to the 1940s, which are promoted, somewhat astonishingly considering the actual privations and death toll, as 'the good old days', making, in some ways, this glorification and romanticisation of war difficult to comprehend. Nonetheless, from 1940s hangar dances, with 'vintage' singers and jitterbugging GIs, to full-on military themed festivals, the public flock in droves. Amongst them are Second World War re-enactors, and various groups bring Battle of Britain history to life as fighter pilots, groundcrews, WAAFs, even an authentically reproduced operations room, and more. Today, it seems, there are specialist suppliers producing every conceivable item of Second World War military uniform and equipment, enabling alter egos from the Home Guard to the *Waffen*-SS, and much effort, not to mention cash, is invested in sourcing exactly the right, historically accurate, 'kit'. Indeed, Second World War re-enactment, which first revolved around vintage military vehicles, has since burgeoned into a popular pastime, supported by a substantial cottage and wider industry. At Duxford, for example, whole squadrons of young, and not so young, men and women provide displays to the public and join the crowds,

A happy visitor to the Battle of Britain Bunker, Uxbridge, Trish Driver, with living history enthusiasts Larry McHale and Daniel Richards. *(Martin Driver)*

portraying the wartime Allied air forces, or may civilians, gleefully posing with Spitfires, Hurricanes, Mustangs and the B-17 'Sally B'. Such 'living history' certainly has a place, and is a fairly recent phenomenon – never seen, or perceived, at the post-war RAF Battle of Britain at home days. Arguably, this is indicative of the Second World War's status as a 'good war', a 'people's war', promoting the myth of a united nation aligned behind its bulldog prime minster, a utopian society far removed from the Britain of today. To some extent, then, in this context, the past is very much viewed through rose-tinted glasses, presenting an oft distorted image of the wartime years – but those serious about presenting Battle of Britain 'living history' are to be commended.

The situation in Germany, of course, is very different, the country still coming to terms with 'Hitler's War' and guilt over the Holocaust especially. The swastika is a banned symbol in Germany, and memorials and museums lean towards memorialising the Nazis' victims; indeed, the Germans now see and present themselves as victims of Hitler, all of which is a vast debate in academia and an enormous subject all of its own. Certainly, in my experience, the majority of young Germans of today are keen to distance themselves from the Second World War, and prefer to conceal the fact that an ancestor fought, in whatever capacity, for Germany between 1939 and 1945. Unsurprisingly, no memorials will be found commemorating those Luftwaffe airmen who fought and died in the Battle of Britain. Later in the war, of course, the Allied strategic bombing campaign, by day and night, made the Battle of Britain pale into insignificance so far as the numbers of aircraft involved was concerned, the German defenders fighting a hopeless but protracted battle against overwhelming odds and an enemy with apparently infinite resources. After the war, incredibly, the German fighter pilots were blamed for not protecting German cities and shunned by many sections of society. The survivors often found it difficult to find work, leading to foundation of the *Geimeinschaft der Jagdflieger* (German Fighter Pilots' Association, GdJ), with its magazine *Jägerblatt* (Fighter Pages), and specific unit associations. Reunions were held, very low key, and members supported each other as a community of fighter pilots. On 17 October 1959, the GdJ unveiled a memorial at Geisenheim, near Frankfurt, to pilots of all nations killed on active service. The occasion was attended by service chiefs of the new Luftwaffe and Allied air forces, and many veterans, including *General* Adolf Galland, and so, in an unobtrusive way, leaning towards reconciliation, there is a memorial of sorts to the German dead of the Battle of Britain in the *Heimat* (homeland).

Suffice it to say, in sum, the memorialisation of the Battle of Britain, the way it is commemorated and remembered, has certainly changed with the passage of time – which is understandable: the world today is a much different place to either the wartime or immediate post-war years, and we are increasingly distanced in time from the events of 1940. Nonetheless, as evidenced by this chapter, the Battle of Britain is fortunate to have certain substantial and prominent memorials and monuments, and a diverse range of, and it appears ever-increasing, other more intimate commemorations. It is, therefore, in no danger of ever being actually forgotten – even if its post-war star shines not as brightly as once it did. This is why, collectively, all of the existing monuments, memorials and ongoing commemorative initiatives are so important and deserved of our support today, and forevermore.

Chapter Four

Battle of Britain Memoirs

During wartime, propaganda is as necessary and potent a weapon as any military hardware, and arguably the first published memories of the Battle of Britain were morale-boosting accounts in newspapers, news reel films and radio broadcasts, such as BBC newsman Charles Gardner's dramatic reporting of an air battle off Dover on 14 July 1940. The dashing young fighter pilots, the so-called 'Brylcream Boys', were heroes of the hour, their war seen as immensely exciting, glamourous, even, and the public's demand for their stories appeared insatiable. Immediately after the Battle of Britain, a number of 'The Few' set pen to paper, recording their experiences, their books arising being the start of a still burgeoning bibliography.

On 15 January 1942, *The Scotsman* included an article of 'RAF Authors', which began by saying that 'We shall have to wait until after the war for most of the "classic" stories of the exploits of the RAF. Conditions of active service do not permit the author-aviator the necessary leisure to write a "full-length" and considered book.' That was true, but at least two books by Battle of Britain pilots had already been published, both by MacMillan & Co. Limited of London. The first of these was reviewed in *The Scotsman*: *I Had a Row With a German*, by 'RAF Casualty', who, the journalist tells us, 'was one of the brilliant young pilots who took part in the Battle of Britain when it was at its fiercest'.

> [His book was] written simply, modestly, and earnestly. The author was wounded badly – his skin was almost entirely burnt off. He writes his book whilst convalescing, while waiting to return to flying duties. It seems to reflect admirably the faith of a thoughtful, intelligent, courageous pilot to whom the glamour and adventure of flying are secondary to the ideal for which we are fighting. His gratitude to those who have nursed him back to health preoccupies him far more than the thrilling combats in which he had taken part. The entire royalties of the book are to go to the RAF Benevolent Fund.

Left: 'RAF Casualty': Squadron Leader Thomas Percy Gleave of 253 Squadron.

Below: Group Captain Thomas Percy Gleave's published memoir, and other manuscripts.

Who, though, was 'RAF Casualty'? He was, in fact, Squadron Leader Thomas 'Tom' Percy Gleave CBE, born on 6 September 1908 in Liverpool, the second son of Arthur and Amy Gleave, and an exceptional individual by any standards.

Privately educated at Westminster High and Liverpool Collegiate schools, Gleave developed an early fascination for aeroplanes and in 1927 became a founder member of Merseyside Flying Club. On 6 July 1929, Tom was awarded his 'A' licence to fly civilian aircraft, his mother having funded the lessons necessary to convert his dreams of flight to reality. Although the young aviator wanted to become a full time pilot, he was persuaded to remain in the family tanning business, so spent six years 'making leather with flying as a side-line'. In the summer of 1929, the adventurous Gleave joined the Beardmore Tanning Company in Ontario, where he flew with the Toronto Flying Club. Although his father considered full time flying far too dangerous an occupation, Gleave was determined and applied to join the RCAF. Only then did his father relent but on condition Gleave came home and joined the RAF. So it was that in September 1930, Gleave accepted a SSC in the RAF, and after service flying training joined No. 1 (Fighter) Squadron at Tangmere.

Flying single-engined biplane fighters including the Siskin and Fury, Pilot Officer Thomas Percy Gleave excelled at aerobatics, joining the 1 Squadron aerobatic team. Ever intrepid, on 11 October 1933, Gleave attempted to become the first man to fly from England to Ceylon (modern-day Sri Lanka). Taking off from Lympne in a civilian Simmonds Spartan, four days later a down-draught forced him to 'land in a tree', in a Turkish ravine. The crash, Gleave recalled, 'modified' his nose. Back home, in 1934, with a rare 'exceptional' pilot rating, he became a flying instructor, and, in anticipation of war with Hitler's Germany, his commission changed to one of medium term. By December 1938, Gleave was a squadron leader at Fighter Command HQ Operations Room, serving as one of three bomber liaison officers. Anxious to see action once war broke out, eventually, on 2 June 1940, the day the Dunkirk evacuation successfully concluded, Gleave, by now a married man and a father, joined 253 Squadron as a 'supernumerary' officer to gain experience on the Hawker Hurricane monoplane fighter and current operational conditions.

What happened next was traumatic – and is the subject of his book. No. 253 Squadron was posted to Kenley during the Battle of Britain, suffering a number of casualties in the first few days, including the CO, Squadron Leader Harold Starr, who was shot down and killed on the morning of 31 August 1940. Having already temporarily commanded 253 Squadron previously, Gleave assumed command but was himself shot down in flames that afternoon. Escaping from the furnace that his cockpit rapidly became, and descending by parachute, the horrendously burned airman was taken in by the farming folk on whose land he had alighted – Gleave's main concern being the mess his wounds were making of Mrs Lewis's clean bed linen! Although the journey in an open-top car to Orpington Hospital seemed an eternity to Gleace, just fifteen minutes after departing the Lewis's farm he was admitted. On 3 September 1940, Gleave's wife, Beryl, received a telegram in error informing her that her gallant husband had been admitted but that his condition was 'not serious'. Nonetheless, Beryl rushed to her husband's bedside – finding him encased in dried Tannafax – and dangerously ill. Shocked and struggling to find words, Beryl laconically enquired 'What on earth have you been doing to yourself, darling?' Gleave's reply was priceless: 'Had a row with a German'.

So serious were Gleave's injuries that he required specialist treatment at the now world famous 'Ward 3', the Burns Unit of the Royal Victoria Hospital, East Grinstead. Under the care of the gifted surgeon Archibald 'Archie' McIndoe, Ward 3's patients were restored to good health in both mind and body, as Gleave later recalled,

> Archie [Archibald McIndoe] generated a bond of fellowship in which rank was forgotten. He believed that nothing could stand in the way of making terribly mutilated human beings whole again, and so we had much more freedom than was traditional in medical circles.

On the afternoon of 20 July 1941, after a typical Ward 3 Saturday night 'thrash', a number of patients, amongst them Squadron Leader Thomas Percy Gleave, decided to form a drinking club. So it was that the 'Guinea Pig Club' was formed, membership comprising wounded airmen treated by McIndoe. It would become far more than just a drinking club, however, and as Chief Guinea Pig, Gleave and his wife, Beryl, would devote much time and energy over the years to ensuring the welfare of its members.

The year 1941 also saw publication of *I Had A Row With a German*, which was well-received. That was not, however, the author's preferred title, which was *Eagles of Nemesis*, and, of course, the published version was heavily censored, with place names blanked out and personnel referred to by first or nicknames. The book's foreword was contributed by Air Vice-Marshal Trafford Leigh-Mallory, who wrote,

> It is a privilege to contribute a foreword to this modest story of gallantry and fortitude, told by a fighter pilot who fought and was badly wounded in the Battle of Britain.
>
> I commend this book to the great British public, who owe so much to those gallant gentlemen – the fighter pilots of the Royal Air Force.

Such words really captured the admiration of all for 'The Few', and Gleave's tale would be read by and inspire countless people, from school boys to air marshals.

Having returned to active duty, commanding RAF Manston, on 5 September 1942, Gleave was appointed 'Group Captain Air Plans' on the Special Planning Staff at Norfolk House, Portsmouth, working in Operation Round-Up – later to become Operation Overlord, the Allied invasion of Normandy. Group Captain Thomas Percy Gleave remained on the staff at what became SHAEF until Germany surrendered, after which he became SASO to the RAF delegation in France. Having subsequently served as group director at the RAF Staff College, Bracknell, Group Captain T.P. Gleave CBE was invalided out of the service in 1953 – as a direct consequence of his Battle of Britain injuries.

Thereafter, Gleave became a Cabinet Office historian, working on the Second World War in the Mediterranean and Middle East for thirty-five years. As a result of this endeavour he was elected to the Fellowship of the Royal Historical Society (FRHistS) and in 1974 became a consultant to the Cabinet Office's official history that he had spent so many years working on. He also became a committee member and later deputy chairman and historian to the BoBFA, and continued his good work for the Guinea Pig Club. On 12 June 1993, Tom Gleave died, aged 84, having led by any standards a full and extraordinary life – during which he became a quiet but compelling inspiration and did nothing but good. As Gleave himself said, 'I wouldn't have missed it for all the tea in China, to have taken part in the Battle of Britain and to have known Archibald McIndoe is more than many can achieve in one lifetime.' Amongst those achievements, then, was publication of what was the first memoir by an RAF fighter pilot who, in this case narrowly, survived the Battle of Britain. More recently, in 2022, I was pleased to contribute an introduction to a new edition of Gleave's excellent book, which includes much new information, especially concerning post-publication reviews and royalties. Re-visiting these wartime-published memoirs in this way is important, because it maintains their currency – although it is doubtful that their authors would have dreamed that there would be such interest eighty-five years later.

The other Battle of Britain memoir published in 1941, also by MacMillan & Co. Limited, was, perhaps surprisingly, by one of the nine volunteers from still neutral America: Pilot Officer Arthur 'Art' Gerald Donahue DFC, of St Charles, Minnesota, on 29 January 1913. Like Gleave's, Donahue's account is a modest one, according to the author just a 'tale of an ordinary American from a Midwest farm coming to a warring country, joining its fighting forces …' Why, though, did he do so? Donahue had learned to fly privately and aged 18 'went into commercial flying', and 'When the war started, I should have liked to volunteer at once for England. I felt that this was America's war as much as England's and France's because America was part of the world, which Hitler and his minions were so plainly out to conquer.' Concern for his parents prevented this, however, so Donahue applied for a commission in the United States Army Air Corps Reserve, but became 'frustrated for months by delays that were mostly hard to understand'. The Dunkirk evacuation, however, heightened this global American's concern – and having heard that American pilots were 'being hired for non-combatant jobs' in the RAF, he travelled to Canada and was 'promptly hired'. Just ten days later, Donhue sailed for England.

'It is hard', Donahue wrote,

> to give a specific reason why I became a combat pilot. Of course, I have always wanted to be one; and once I was in England the significance of the struggle seemed to carry me away. This was mid-July. France had fallen, and the invasion of England seemed imminent. Its success would open the world-up to a barbarian conquest. I had a growing admiration for the British people and a sincere desire to help them all I could. I could not help feeling that I would be fighting for my own country too. I felt drawn into the struggle like a moth to a candle.

Commissioned into the RAFVR as a pilot officer, on 18 July 1940, Donahue arrived at Aston Down, where he converted to Spitfires:

> This was the very height of my hopes. Of all England's superb fighting planes, the Supermarine Spitfires are generally considered masters of them all and the world's deadliest fighters. The pilots assigned to fly them consider themselves the luckiest of pilots.

Having previously flown low-performance aircraft, Donahue first had to get used to the Spitfire's comparatively great speed, feeling 'more like a passenger' on his first Spitfire flight. At Aston Down, he became friends with 20-year-old Pilot Officer Peter Kennard-Davis, referred to simply as 'Peter' in the book, the pair being posted together to join 64 Squadron at Kenley on 3 August 1940. In his new CO, Squadron Leader Don MacDonell, The Laird of Glengarry, who had also converted to Spitfires at Aston Down with the two friends, Donahue 'felt great confidence'. Air Commodore Don MacDonell, as he became, later wrote that the young American 'served me with great loyalty and gallantry. He became the "pet" of the Squadron. He was a little over five feet tall with close-cropped, blond hair and bright blue eyes.'

At what was a very busy time for 64 Squadron, Pilot Officer Arthur Donahue was in action almost immediately, being shot-up by a Me 109 he had chased back to France two days after arriving at Kenley, but returned his badly damaged Spitfire to safely land at Hawkinge. Just three days later, however, 'Peter' was shot down by a 109 over Dover, and baled out, badly wounded – succumbing to his injuries on 10 August 1940. A bitter personal blow for Donahue, the American was also shot down, two days after his friend's death, baling out of his Spitfire with burns, which saw him hospitalised until mid-September 1940. All of these events, and much more, Donahue describes in what is an extremely well written account. Late in 1941, however, Donahue was posted to Singapore, where the following year he was awarded the DFC and wounded fighting the Japanese – also publishing *Last Flight From Singapore*. Posted back to England, Donahue became a flight commander on 91 Squadron, but on 11 September 1942 he shot down a Ju 88 off Ostend – but the enemy rear gunner found his mark, damaging the Spitfire's coolant system, forcing Donahue to ditch off Gravelines. Sadly, this gallant 'Yankee in a Spitfire' was never seen again and is commemorated at Runnymede. Published so early on, his memoir, however, remains an important one in the propaganda campaign aimed squarely at encouraging America to join the Allied cause.

Books, of course, take time to write, and as *The Scotsman* observed, active service provides little time for recreational writing. Consequently,

Just three of the Battle of Britain memoirs published in 1942.

it would not be until 1942 that a number of Battle of Britain memoirs appeared in print.

Having already published the memoirs of Gleave and Donahue, MacMillan & Co. Limited was ahead of the game as the new year began, and soon the presses were rolling again, printing copies of what was destined to become a classic, not just as a Battle of Britain memoir but as a piece of English literature: *The Last Enemy*, by Richard Hillary (Richard Hope Hillary). Unlike the memoirs which followed in 1942, this was not just a tale of derring-do, written in the style of a schoolboy's adventure comic, but a seriously inward-looking and soul-searching document, the title of which was taken from Corinthians: 'The last enemy that shall be destroyed is death'. *The Times Literary Supplement*, however, thought it much more complex: 'The last enemy of his title is drawn from I Cor. XV. 26, but even that is not a very precise definition. It is not death, but rather the evil of negation, of life ingrown in self which engages Mr [Richard Hope] Hillary as he hunts himself through the fortunes of this striking discourse'. Why, though, was this particular memoir so 'striking'?

Hillary was one of those people who excelled at everything he did, blessed with complete self-confidence and belief. Educated at Shrewsbury, upon going up to Trinity College, Oxford, he became a prominent undergraduate student and member of a set which, in his own words, exemplified 'alert philistinism'. Popular, witty and clever, Hillary and his privileged friends perceived the world from on high, from the vantage point of 'Oxford's dreamy spires'. They were self-centred and aloof, considering themselves socially and intellectually superior – but the Second World War, and the Battle of Britain specifically, changed all that for Hillary, who joined the UAS and was then commissioned into the RAFVR. This, Hillary explained to a friend, was simply because in the RAF he would

> get paid and have good food. Secondly, I have none of your sentiments about killing, much as I admire them. In a fighter plane, I believe, we have found a way to return to war as it ought to be, war which is individual combat between two people, in which one either kills or is killed. It's exciting, it's individual and it's disinterested. I shan't be sitting behind a long-range gun working out how to kill people sixty miles away. I shan't get maimed: either I shall get killed or I shall get a few pleasant putty medals and enjoy being stared at in a night club.

But Hillary was wrong.

After advanced flying training, Pilot Officer Richard Hope Hillary converted to Spitfires at 5 OTU, Aston Down:

> The Spitfires stood in two lines outside 'A' Flight's pilots' room. The dull-grey-brown of their camouflage could not conceal their clear-cut beauty, the wicked simplicity of their lines. I hooked up my parachute and climbed awkwardly into the low cockpit. I noticed how small was my field of vision. Kilmartin swung himself onto a wing and started to run through the instruments. I was conscious of his voice but heard nothing of what he said. I was to fly a Spitfire. It was what I had most wanted through all the long, dreary, months of training. If I could fly a Spitfire, it would all be worth it. Well I was about to achieve my ambition and felt nothing. I was numb, neither exhilarated nor scared …
>
> I taxied slowly across the field, remembering suddenly what I had been told: that the Spitfire's prop was long

> and that it was therefore inadvisable to push the stick too far forward when taking off; that the Spitfire was not a Lysander and that any hard application of the brake when landing would result in a somersault and immediate transfer to a Battle squadron. Because of the Battle's lack of power and small armament, this was regarded by everyone as the ultimate disgrace.
>
> I ran quickly through my cockpit drill, swung the nose into wind, and took off. I had been flying automatically for several minutes before it dawned on me that I was actually in the air, undercarriage retracted and half way round the circuit without incident. I turned into wind and hauled up on my seat, at the same time pushing back the hood. I came in low, cut the engine, and floated down on all three points. I took off again. Three more times I came round for a perfect landing. It was too easy. I waited across wind for a minute and watched with satisfaction several machines bounce badly as they came in. Then I taxied rapidly back into the hangars and climbed out nonchalantly. Noel [Noël le Chevalier Agazarian], who had not yet soloed, met me. 'How was it?' he said. I made a circle of approval with my thumb and forefinger. 'Money for old rope', I said. I didn't make a good landing for a week.

Soon afterwards, Hillary and Pilot Officer Noël le Chevalier Agazarian 'Aga' ('Aggy') became aerial rivals, culminating in both flying a Spitfire between the arches of the Severn railway bridge – somehow typifying Hillary's attitude and outlook on life at the time. Hillary's closest friend was Pilot Officer Peter Pease, the son of Sir Richard and Lady Pease, formerly a Cambridge scholar, and the pair were posted together to fly Spitfires with 603 Squadron at Dyce. In his book, Hillary devotes a whole chapter to 'The World of Peter Pease', in which the author recounts an intellectual discussion between the pair on their bipolar views on life: self-centred Hillary and the more rounded Pease, who concluded,

> I can see that neither of us is going to convince the other. And I don't mind at all admitting that I am sure you will change your tune. It won't be long either. Something bigger than you and me is coming out of this, and as it grows you will grow with

> it. You are not entirely unfeeling, Richard [Hope Hillary]. I'm sure it needs only some psychological shock, some affront to your sensibility, to arouse your pity or your anger sufficiently to make you forget yourself.

Pease was right.

On 27 August 1940, 603 Squadron flew south, to Hornchurch, at the height of the Battle of Britain. Two days later Hillary destroyed a Me 109 and claimed a probable, but was shot down himself, crash-landing, unhurt, near Lympne. Another 109 was claimed destroyed on 31 August 1940, two destroyed, a probable and one damaged on 2 September 1940, so it seemed that Hillary was also set to become a brilliant fighter pilot – but then his luck ran out, and that life-changing moment predicted by Pease happened the following day.

Having been damaged when Hornchurch was bombed, Hillary's Spitfire had been fitted with a new canopy, but the hood would not slide to open and close smoothly. With three 'erks', the pilot frantically filed the grooves, but still jammed half-way. Then the inevitable happened: scramble. Within minutes, the Spitfires were fighting Me 109s over the Channel, off Margate – when Hillary was shot down by *Hauptmann* Erich Bode, the *Gruppenkommandeur* of II/JG 26. Having struggled to abandon his blazing machine due to the sticking hood, Hillary eventually got clear and deployed his parachute. Horrendously burned, after half an hour or so in the water, Hillary began suffering from shock and exposure: 'So I was going to die. It came to me like that – I was going to die and I was not afraid.' Indeed, Hillary tried to commit suicide and end his suffering by drowning, but failed, becoming delirious. 'Then, willing arms were dragging me over the side … and I was safe. I was neither relieved nor angry. I was past caring. It was to the Margate lifeboat that I owed my rescue.' Hillary would subsequently spend many months recovering from his burns, being treated, like Thomas Percy Gleave, at East Grinstead by Archibald McIndoe and becoming a 'Guinea Pig'. It was this experience that changed Hillary's whole outlook on life, as Pease had predicted – although Pease himself was dead, having been killed in action on 15 September 1940.

Hillary wrote, 'So Peter [Pease] had been right. It was impossible not to look only to oneself, to take from life and give except by accident, deliberately to look at humanity and then pass by on the other side. No longer could one say "The world's my oyster and the hell with the rest."'

But how to make sense of it all, that was now the question? And that is when Hillary, 'The last of the long-haired boys', decided to write, and concluded,

> I would write of these men, of Peter [Pease] and of the others. I would write for them and would write with them. They would be at my side. And to whom would I address this book, to whom would I be speaking when I wrote of these men? And that, too, I knew. To Humanity, for Humanity must be the public of any book. Yes, that despised Humanity which I had so scorned and ridiculed to Peter.
>
> If I could do this thing, could tell a little of the lives of these men, I would have justified, at least in some measure, my right to fellowship with my dead, and to the friendship of those with courage and steadfastness who were still living and who would go on fighting until the ideals for which their comrades had died were stamped for ever on the future of civilisation.

Richard Hope Hillary, author of the classic memoir, *The Last Enemy* – from a portrait by Eric Kennington.

In this, the *News Chronicle* decided that Hillary had found 'a reason for living'. Tragically, however, this much-changed young man would not live much longer: having returned to active duty, on 18 January 1943, whilst training to fly night fighters, Hillary's Blenheim crashed in bad weather, killing both pilot and navigator. It was a sad end indeed to this most gifted author, whose pen had so much more to offer; Richard Hope Hillary was 23 years old.

The *Sunday Times*: 'This book has quality. Most pilots, unfortunately, cannot write; most writers, unfortunately, cannot fly. The author of *The Last Enemy* can not only fly; he can also write.'

In *The Tatler*, Elizabeth Bowen wrote:

> A remarkable piece of literature … Every page shows that he would have been a writer under any circumstances … *The Last Enemy* is what I have deliberately called 'literature', because it contains not only the outer story of Mr [Richard Hope] Hillary's experiences, but the inner story of his adaptation to them … As a self-portrait, it has been executed with a detachment and lack of sentiment so rare that they cannot be admired enough.

By 1950, *The Last Enemy* had sold over 135,000 copies in England alone, and it had been translated into every European language. How many more have been sold to date is anyone's guess.

Unlike Richard Hope Hillary, Squadron Leader Brian Lane, who had led 19 Squadron in the air during most of the Dunkirk air fighting and Battle of Britain, was a rather reserved character, so it is perhaps surprising that his name appears amongst the list of RAF fighter pilot authors whose memoirs appeared in 1942. John Murray published Lane's book, *Spitfire! The Experiences of a Fighter Pilot*, covering the author's experience from the start of the Second World War to the night blitz. Typically, the work is subject to the usual censorship, with the names of personnel and places blanked out. Indeed, as with 'RAF Casualty', the author's name is concealed by a pseudonym: 'Squadron Leader B.J. Ellan'. What really shines through in Lane's account, the basis of which was notes recorded in his pilot's flying log book, is the camaraderie of a fighter squadron, the pilots' respect of and appreciation for their groundcrews, and, well, frankly, just how adrenalin-fuelled fighter combat is – and how these brave young pilots just considered that they were simply doing their duty and were the lucky ones, able to hit back. Lane's anonymity, though, could never last forever.

On 21 September 1940, Flying Officer Stanley Devon, and award-winning pressman turned official Air Ministry photographer, visited RAF Duxford and there photographed Squadron Leader Douglas Bader's 242 Squadron, and the Czechs of 310 Squadron. Afterwards, Devon went to Duxford's nearby satellite at Fowlmere, where the Duxford Wing's Spitfires were based, including Lane's famous 19 Squadron. There Devon shot a reel of film, showing Spitfires, their pilots and supporting personnel – including an iconic photograph of Lane, recently landed from a wing patrol over London, capturing a haunting image of concentration and fatigue. This photograph, in fact, was used to illustrate countless books and articles post-war – but the pilot was never identified. As a schoolboy I wanted to know who he was, what his story was – and then, in 1980, by chance I picked up a copy of *Spitfire! The Experiences of a Fighter Pilot*, realising that the author was the pilot whose image had so impressed me. Further research identified him as Squadron Leader Brian John Edward Lane – an ace – but I was deeply moved to discover that on 13 December 1942, he had been reported missing. Off the Dutch coast. What a journey then began for me personally, tracing and talking to survivors, piecing together the jigsaw that began looking into Lane's all-too short life and culminated in writing the history of 19 Squadron, 1938–1941. My first book, in fact, *Spitfire Squadron*, published in 1990, comprised a re-print of *Spitfire! The Experiences of a Fighter Pilot*, followed by my own account of the same period, written without censorship and with the benefit of survivors' first-hand accounts and access to official records. Since that time, various editions of Lane's text have been published, making it one of the most read first-hand accounts of the Battle of Britain.

Whereas only one edition of Lane's book was published during the war, a most successful memoir, in similar vein, was Flight Lieutenant David Moore Crook DFC's *Spitfire Pilot*. First published in June 1942, by Faber and Faber Limited, a second edition followed a month later, and a third in October 1942. Crook was an auxiliary airman, who flew Spitfires with 609 'West Riding' Squadron, seeing action at Dunkirk, and becoming an ace during the Battle of Britain, flying from RAF Middle Wallop and RAF Warmwell in 10 Group. The auxiliary squadrons were locally raised, on a territorial basis, and personnel were often friends or even related. Consequently, when casualties mounted, morale suffered accordingly, and Crook writes honestly about this, and how 609's Battle of Britain got off to a bad start. Interestingly, *Spitfire Pilot* is not as heavily censored as other accounts of the period, meaning that little detective work is required

Stanley Devon's iconic photograph of Squadron Leader Brian John Edward Lane, author of *Spitfire! The Experiences of a Fighter Pilot* and seen hereat Fowlmere with Flight Lieutenant Walter Lawson (left) and Flight Sergeant George Unwin.

to identify who is who and where is where. Like Donahue's memoir, Crook's is particularly well written, recorded in two blank A4 Air Ministry notebooks, and, also like the American, Crook wrote a second book, a thriller entitled *In Pursuit of Passey*. A married man and father, Crook did not survive the war: after the Battle of Britain he became a flying instructor, but on 18 December 1944, whilst serving with 8 (Coastal) OTU at Dyce, his Spitfire crashed from 20,000ft into the sea off Aberdeen; Crook was never found and is also commemorated at Runnymede. Crook's is another account we have recently published, following a promise I made to his widow, Dorothy, many years ago, using his original, unedited, text and photographs from the family archive.

Another interesting 1942 text by a 10 Group ace is Wing Commander Ian Gleed DFC's *Arise to Conquer*, published by Victor Gollancz and

Above: Flight Lieutenant David Moore Crook, author of *Spitfire Pilot*.

Left: Pictured by the Dilip Sarkar in 1990, David Moore Crook's widow, Dorothy – 'D' in the book.

dedicated to 'the ground staff of the RAF, without whose essential work the Battle of the air could never be fought'. Known as 'Widge', short for 'Wizard Midget', on account of his frequent use of the expression 'Wizard' and his diminutive stature, Gleed, a veteran of the Fall of France, flew Hurricanes with 87 Squadron at Exeter and Bibury throughout the Battle of Britain, during which he first commanded 'A' Flight, then the squadron. As Flight Lieutenant John Strachey wrote in his foreword to Gleed's book, 'I cannot but suppose that both the contemporary reader and the future historian will turn to this book when they wish to know what the pilots who did this thing were like.' In that, Strachey was surely right, because off of these first-hand accounts provide us rich and unique primary source material. Like Crook, Gleed writes, amongst other things, of the great air battles over Portland and Weymouth Bay in August 1940, which are an oft-neglected aspect of the Battle of Britain, but no less important that raids on southeastern targets. Defending the south-west, its aircraft factories and naval bases, 87 Squadron saw much action – Gleed survived, only to be shot down and killed when leading a Spitfire wing in Tunisia on 16 April 1943. Written in the typical jingoistic style of a *Boy's Own* adventure, this is the third memoir we have recently re-published, such is its quality, with more information about the author and some sixty snapshots of 87 Squadron's Battle of Britain taken by Gleed's friend, Sergeant (later Squadron Leader) Laurence 'Rubber' Thorogood. Consequently, the original text is enhanced and remains available for us 'to turn to', as Strachey rightly predicted.

Another text published in 1942, by Collins, was *Ten Fighter Boys*, compiled by Wing Commander Athol Forbes DFC and Squadron Leader Hubert 'Dizzy' Allen DFC, formerly commander and a flight commander respectively in 66 Squadron during the Battle of Britain. The book was Allen's idea, who felt that instead of waiting until after the war, 'People would be so much more enthralled to read first-hand about events that were going on all round at the time of reading.' Beginning in November 1940 – immediately after the Battle of Britain, ten 66 Squadron pilots, including both officers and sergeants, wrote their stories, each making up a separate chapter; by the time of publication, five were dead. No effort was made to edit out jargon, so the accounts are very much written in 'pilot speak'. Identities are concealed through the use of first or nicknames, the third chapter being written by a sergeant pilot called 'Jimmy' – who, sixty-years later, found himself the last living member of those 'ten fighter boys'.

Before training as a pilot, Jimmy 'Binder' Corbin was a teacher, a profession he resumed after the war, during which he fought in the Battle of Britain and in North Africa, being commissioned and decorated with the DFC. Written when aged 89, Corbin's 2007 memoir *Last of The Ten Fighter Boys*, is excellent, covering his whole war experience and more besides; a reflective piece, in which the author concluded,

> After the war I thought a lot about those poor men who were little more than boys and whose short lives had ended so violently and so abruptly. But it is now sixty years since the war ended. Much has happened to me in those intervening years and my experiences of combat hold an ever-decreasing significance in my life … I don't know how hundreds of us managed to climb into our aeroplanes time after time to fly straight into the face of the enemy, never knowing if it was to be our last day on earth. We just did. I do believe that a few people were exceptionally brave and took the war to the enemy. But for most of us, the truth was we were prepared to do a job, but we were not as bold as those few. That said, we certainly weren't cowards either … So what got me through? I don't know. In the final analysis I think it was just luck.

Certainly, William Walker, who flew Spitfires with 616 Squadron and survived being shot down on 26 August 1940, would have agreed: 'They were the most exhilarating days, but one lost so many friends, who were all so young. It is said that the best pilots seemed to get killed whilst the "hams" like me survived.'

Whilst pilots' memoirs served to boost morale and recruitment, after the war the public's demand for such stories appeared insatiable – and one writer cashed in on this like no other: Paul Brickhill.

An Australian, born in Melbourne in 1916, Brickhill's father and grandfather were both journalists, which he too became before the war. In 1939, however, he joined the RAAF and after training flew Spitfires in England before being shot down over the Mareth Line and captured in March 1943. Whilst a prisoner in the notorious Stalag Luft III, Brickhill began collecting the stories of his fellow 'Kriegies', with future books in mind. Upon repatriation, Brickhill resumed his journalist career, covering the Nuremburg trials for *The Sun* (Sydney), later working in America for two years before returning to Australia in 1948. In 1946, his first book was published *Escape to Danger*, comprising a selection of the many stories he collated whilst a prisoner. The book was so successful that Brickhill was convinced that the mass breakout from Stalag Luft III, which made a chapter in the book, would make a full-length book in its own right – so gave up his job, returned to London, wrote *The Great Escape*, which was published in 1951. The same year also saw publication of Brickhill's *The Dam Busters*, telling the epic story of 617 Squadron's famous raid on the German dams. Both books were enormously successful – and then Brickhill's attention turned to the most famous RAF pilot of all time: the legless Group Captain Douglas Bader. With some reservation, Bader agreed to work with Brickhill to produce the story of his extraordinary life, the somewhat romanticised version of events becoming another global Brickhill best-seller in *Reach for the Sky*, published by Collins in 1954. This made Bader a worldwide household name, the book selling millions worldwide. Then, in 1955, the film based upon Brickhill's *The Dambusters*, starring Richard Todd as Guy Gibson VC, was released, again to global acclaim, and *Reach for the Sky*, starring Kenneth More as Bader, hit the silver screen a year later – another massive box office success. Unsurprisingly, Brickhill's commercial success prompted many a war hero to show an interest in publishing their memoirs.

In 1956, the RAF's officially top-scoring fighter pilot, Group Captain (later Air-Vice Marshal) Johnnie Johnson, published his memoir, *Wing Leader*, with a foreword by Douglas Bader. Johnson qualified for the Battle of Britain Clasp having made an operational patrol with 616 Squadron, but missed the Battle of Britain proper on account of being hospitalised with a shoulder injury. Nonetheless, this is an important account, Johnson being a gifted writer, tracking his whole wartime career from joining the RAFVR to the 'Great Adventure', the 'Long Trek' from Normandy into Germany. Then, in 1958, the Scottish film and television episode writer Larry Forrester, published his, also romanticised, biography of fighter ace and Battle of Britain squadron commander Wing Commander Robert Stanford Tuck, *Fly For Your Life*. Written in a similar style to Brickhill, although successful Tuck's story was never translated to screen, and it is fair to say that Brickhill remains unsurpassed as a writer of popular war stories. Such accounts, however, were no longer subject to the wartime censor and approval by Ministry of Information and the Air Ministry, although there was now, in the post-war world, a degree of sensitive self-censorship, as Forrester explained,

> There are no fictitious characters in this book, but there are a few fictitious names. It seems to me that so long after the war it would be needlessly cruel to reawaken anguished memories

A first edition copy of *Reach for the Sky*.

> for the families of those RAF men who did not die quickly or cleanly, or who died stupidly; those who contracted unpleasant disease or suffered extreme hardship in Nazi prison camps or 'on the run'; the one or two who weakened and failed their comrades …

Another author around at the time was Robert Wright, who had been a navigator on night fighters during the war and throughout the Battle of Britain he was on the staff at Fighter Command HQ, for some of that period as Dowding's personal assistant. Working with Squadron Leader C.F. 'Jimmy' Rawnsley, Wright co-authored *Night Fighter*, published in 1957, providing a contrast to the tales of daylight battles. Rawnsley had flown as Group Captain John 'Catseyes' Cunningham's radar operator, that great ace and test pilot contributing the foreword.

Two years later, another important text was published, *Nine Lives*, being the memoir of Air Commodore Al Deere, the great ace from New Zealand, who had flown Spitfires with 54 Squadron throughout the Dunkirk and Battle of Britain period, surviving nine brushes with certain death and was another hero straight from the pages of the *Boys' Own Paper*, or so it seemed. Indeed, in his foreword, Lord Dowding wrote that 'Alan Deere must have had an exceptionally efficient guardian angel who, even so, must have been hard put to it to extricate his charge from the apparently hopeless predicaments in which he was constantly finding himself.' In Deere's introduction, he explains that 'In 1939, as a headstrong young man of twenty-one, I welcomed war as a glorious adventure. In 1945, war-weary and wiser, I greeted peace with a fervent, "Thank God".' *Nine Lives* describes the author's experiences throughout those tempestuous years, not just the Battle of Britain, and being by a pilot from New Zealand, and by such a successful and highly respected fighter pilot and leader, makes an important contribution to the air war's bibliography.

In 1969, a crucially important account was published by Robert Wright: *Dowding and the Battle of Britain*. This, of course, was the year the epic film *Battle of Britain* was released, the subject therefore being topical. Lord Dowding, of course, had published his official despatch on the Battle of Britain in 1941, but had never produced an autobiography – which is both a pity and perhaps surprising. One of the reasons, of course, was the manner of his treatment and retirement after the Battle of Britain, which remained a sensitive subject.

By 1969, Lord Dowding was 87, and had decided,

> [It was] necessary to find some way in which I could say what I wanted to say, and for that to be placed on record by someone who I felt understood and shared, with discretion, my views on my career in the RAF. The one man whom I knew that I could reply upon in this somewhat delicate situation was Robert Wright, an old and trusted friend.

Dowding placed in Wright's hands all of his personal papers, and the resulting, hard-hitting but entirely factual book, laid bare, for the first time, the truth of the 'Big Wing Controversy' and the appalling treatment of both Dowding and Park once the battle had been won. Dowding considered that Wright's research had been 'painstaking', that the story was now 'complete', revealing 'points never been made known to the public. I have agreed to that being done with the hope that it will put an end to all further speculation.' Wright had been 'fair and faithful' in his recording of the sorry tale, and Dowding considered the book arising 'a full account from both the personal and the historical point of view, of all that I should like to have placed on record'. That being so, Wright's book can only be considered an extremely important text, extensively quoting Dowding himself. Similarly, and for the same reasons as Dowding, Air Chief Marshal Keith Park, victor of the battles of Britain and Malta, never wrote an autobiography, but after the great man's death in 1979, the historian Vincent Orange, also a New Zealander, worked with the Park family, with access to Keith Park's papers, to produce a detailed biography, *Sir Keith Park*, which is as honest and accurate an account as Wright's Dowding book. Air Chief Marshal Trafford Leigh-Mallory, however, who had caused much of the trouble over the 'Big Wing' and tactics, was killed in a flying accident in 1944, so never wrote a memoir; the other protagonist, MRAF Sholto Douglas, 1st Baron Douglas of Kirtleside, did do so – working with Robert Wright, in fact – in which he distanced himself from the controversy. And so he might.

Lord Dowding was not alone after the war in wanting to set the record straight regarding certain matters. Wing Commander Hubert Allen, who had co-edited *Ten Fighter Boys*, remained in the RAF until 1965, after which he continued writing. In 1979, he published *Who Won the Battle of Britain?*, which was promoted as 'A startling, controversial appraisal by one of The Few'. Allen began by acknowledging that 'The Battle of Britain is etched deeper in British minds than any other military campaign' – but then charged that 'Yet there never was a Battle of Britain', arguing that such a battle would only have been fought had Operation Seelöwe gone ahead. Allen made clear that his aim was 'merely to assemble and then face the historical facts'. According to the *Evening News*, the end result was a 'scathing indictment', whilst the *Daily Express* considered the book 'extraordinary', Times Literary Supplement adding that Allen's attempt to demythologise one of the most famous conflicts of the Second World War was 'skilfully advocated'. The work was ahead of its time. Allen based his appraisal on facts – facts highlighting Fighter Command's deficiencies and challenging, for the first time, the accepted narrative born of wartime propaganda. The book won him few friends amongst his peers – but it was the first effort to present a factual analysis and as such is an important landmark in Battle of Britain historiography. The same year, 1979, also saw Allen publish *Spitfire Squadron*, under the pseudonym 'David Guthrie', which was really a revisit of *Ten Fighter Boys* with a little more controversy thrown in, and his personal memoir *Fighter Squadron: 1940–1942*. A controversial character, Allen certainly contributed to the Battle of Britain's written record; he died in 1987.

As 'The Few' reached retirement age, for some the time now on their hands was spent recording their memoirs. In 1988, for example, Group Captain Sir Hugh Dundas, an auxiliary, published his, *Flying Start*, covering the immediate pre-war period, when he joined 616 'South Yorkshire' Squadron of the AAF, Dunkirk, the Battle of Britain, the offensive operations of 1941, and leading his Spitfire wing in North Africa, Italy and Sicily. Capturing so well the atmosphere of the AAF, it is another important first-hand account, and movingly recounts the sense of desolation following the loss of the author's fighter ace brother, Flying Officer John Dundas DFC of 609 Squadron, who, on 28 November 1940, shot down the German ace Major Helmut Wick before being shot down himself, seconds later, crashing into the Solent. Other pilot's stories made for chapters in books of such stories, such as my own *Last of The Few* (2010) and *The Final Few* (2015). Many accounts, therefore, and one way or another, have been recorded and shared – the most successful memoir in recent times being Squadron Leader Geoffrey Harry Augustus 'Boy' Wellum DFC's *First Light* (2002). During the Battle of Britain, Wellum was an 18-year-old Spitfire pilot on 92 Squadron at Biggin Hill, becoming an ace decorated with the DFC – but, exhausted, later suffered a breakdown in Malta. Returning to England, he then became a test pilot at Gloster Aircraft, testing the Hawker Typhoon, and ended the war a gunnery instructor. Having left the RAF in

1960, Wellum eventually retired to Mullion, in Cornwall, where he became deputy harbourmaster. He wrote *First Light* thirty-five-years after the war, from notes made in Malta, as a means of exorcising the past. 'The words', he told me, 'just poured out, and I didn't stop until I finished'. *First Light*, published twenty years after it was written, became a best-selling Penguin book, later made into a BBC docudrama by Matthew Whiteman in 2010 (see Chapter Five); in that film, the once teenage Spitfire pilot said,

> People say to me 'How do you remember these things?' How do you expect me to forget? You can't. I can remember it vividly, see things, see people, see aeroplanes. The experiences of being a Spitfire fighter pilot in the Battle of Britain stay with you forever. You can't do anything about it.
>
> I asked myself 'Was it worth it?' All those young men I fought and flew with, all those chaps no longer with us. I asked myself that question and I can't answer it. I suppose it must have been. I am still struggling.

Squadron Leader Geoffrey Harry Augustus Wellum, a great ambassador for 'The Few', died on 18 July 2018, aged 96.

Whilst English-speaking pilots produced countless memoirs, very little has been translated from Polish into English, although notably *On Wings of War: My Life as a Pilot Adventurer* (1975) by the Polish-Swiss ace Wing Commander Jan Zumbach, who had flown Hurricanes during the Battle of Britain with Northolt's famous 303 Squadron, was published by Corgi. Two years later, the Canadian Group Captain Johnny Kent, who had commanded a flight in 303 Squadron published his memoir, *One of The Few*, which told us more about the Poles, but nothing appears to have been published in English by Czech Battle of Britain pilots. Significantly, however, the diaries of Free French pilot Commandant René Mouchotte DFC, who was killed in action during 1943, were translated into English and published in London in 1956, seven years after the diaries were released in France. This is another important text, describing how Mouchotte and friends answered Charles de Gaulle's clarion call and made their way to continue the fight in England. Many years later, in 2007, the former BBC television newsreader and celebrity Jan Leeming sponsored Mouchotte's name on the Christopher Foxley-Norris Memorial Wall – thereby embarking upon a personal journey, a 'search for René' culminating in meeting the pilot's 101-year-old sister, Jacqueline, who was, at last, able to receive her brother's medals, which had gone unissued. Leeming, keen to share Mouchotte's story, made a short BBC documentary, 'Searching for René Mouchotte DFC – Free French WW2 Pilot' (see Bibliography), in 2020, and more recently, in 2022, we have published a new edition of the diaries, *Free French Spitfire Hero*, with extra appendices, including Leeming's account of her project, and many previously unpublished photographs. This, therefore, has updated and given currency to what is a rare English language account by a foreign pilot.

Similarly, comparatively little has been published in English from German survivors. There are, however, some notable titles.

Having commanded *Luftflotte* 2 throughout the Battle of Britain, *Generalfeldmarschall* Albert Kesselring commanded Luftwaffe forces in the invasion of Russia, and later, as *Wehrmacht* commander-in-chief south, was in command of all German forces in the Mediterranean theatre; his final command would be German forces on the Western Front. At Nuremburg, Kesselring was convicted of war crimes and sentenced to death, which was later commuted to life imprisonment. Whilst incarcerated, Kesselring wrote his memoir before campaigners secured his early release in 1952. A year later, *The Memoirs of Field-Marshal Kesselring* were published in English – and the only *Luftflotte* commander in the Battle of Britain to so share his story. Consequently, they are of great historical significance.

A year later, *General* Adolf Galland published his memoir, which appeared in English, courtesy of Corgi, in 1957. Galland, of course, was one of Germany's greatest aces, the *Kommodore* of JG 26 during the Battle of Britain who ended the war as General of Day Fighters, flying the new Me 262 jet. Like Kesselring's, this memoir, *The First and The Last*, is an important historical document, given that Galland had first fought in the Spanish Civil War, where the Luftwaffe tested their new weapons and tactics, and went on after the Battle of Britain, as a fighter general, to witness and experience the *Jagdwaffe*'s ultimate demise from a unique perspective.

In 1964, *The Luftwaffe War Diaries*, by Cajus Bekker, were published in Germany, providing a wider perspective of the Luftwaffe at war on all fronts, the narrative based upon the official war diaries, personal papers of leading officers, archives and material in private collections, in addition to interviewing hundreds of former German airmen. Although playing down the Luftwaffe's defeat in the Battle of Britain, when published in English during 1967, also by Corgi, Bekker's book became a big seller and remains a standard subject reference. Although not a memoir, because Bekker included many first-hand accounts, it is included here.

In 1989, British historian and publisher Peter Osborne published the first memoir of a trilogy by former *Oberleutnant* Ullrich Steinhilper, an ace who had flown Me 109s with 3/JG 52 during the Battle of Britain, until being shot down and captured on 27 October 1940. This first volume, *Spitfire on My Tail: A View from the Other Side*, is a superb account of growing up in Hitler's Germany, learning to fly and the early war period from the Luftwaffe perspective. In this account, German airmen become real people, human beings with their own stories, and not unlike our own airmen of the RAF. Steinhilper's account is a gripping and honest one, the other two volumes covering his time as a prisoner of war. It is perhaps fitting to conclude this chapter with Steinhilper's opinion of the Battle of Britain's outcome: 'There is no doubt in my mind that the RAF broke the back and the spirit of the Luftwaffe during the Battle of Britain. The losses of aircraft could be made up but the experienced men who had formed the cadre of the Luftwaffe could not be replaced.'

Chapter Five

The Battle of Britain in British Cinema

The art of cinematography was discovered in the nineteenth century as a by-product of scientific research, and is essentially the rapid projection of still photographs onto a screen, providing an illusion of reality and movement. Cinema soon became enormously popular as a means of mass entertainment, and by 1914, the film studios of Europe, Russia and Scandinavia led the way. This new means of storytelling was big business, given the vast audience, and those companies involved began investing greater sums in increasingly ambitious productions, which were initially silent, black and white, 'movies'. The First World War, however, disrupted the European film industry, cinemas in Britain being closed for the duration – suggesting that the authorities back then had yet to appreciate cinema's virtually unlimited potential for communicating news, information and propaganda to the public. And in war, propaganda is crucial to all sides, to promote their cause and rally the people. In simple terms, propaganda could be defined as a process of managing, aligning and widely sharing information to promote a specific goal and positively influence public opinion and morale – and because film reached all strata of society, it became pivotal to that process.

This had, in fact, already been recognised in Germany, where cinema functioned throughout the First World War and utilised for propaganda purposes; with the ban on importing and screening foreign-made films, the German film industry burgeoned. How highly this medium was rated by the government as a propaganda tool became evident in 1917, when the German film industry was partially nationalised by the creation of *Universum* Film AG (UFA) – in part a response to the success of American cinema in the propaganda war. By this time, it was clear that war inexorably linked film with propaganda as a potent means of influencing public opinion and morale – and demonising the enemy. Indeed, N.J. O'Shaughnessy, a leading historian of propaganda, considers that 'in history the function of propaganda has often ultimately been the creation of a mind-set that facilitates the act of killing' and that propaganda frequently reflects a 'voracious need … to demonise'. So crucial, in fact, did A.J. MacKenzie consider propaganda to be by 1938, that he considered it the fourth 'defence service', after land, sea and air.

After the First World War, American studios forged ahead and were dominating the industry by the 1930s, which became the 'Golden Age of Hollywood'. By now, films had synchronised sound and, by the mid-1930s, some were even in colour. Throughout that decade and the next, cinema would be the primary form of popular entertainment, with people often attending cinemas twice weekly. The extent of the cinema's popularity, in fact, is evidenced by the fact that 'picture palaces', essentially super cinemas, could accommodate up to 3,000 people in a single sitting. This was, of course, the pre-home television age, radio and newspapers providing news and entertainment – and these mediums were no match or substitute for the escapism Hollywood delivered.

In Germany, Adolf Hitler was in no doubt as to the power of propaganda, and praised the British effort during the First World War in his autobiographical manifesto *Mein Kampf*, published in 1926 and which outlined his political manifesto and vision for Germany. Hitler became chancellor of Germany in January 1933, two months later making Dr Josef Goebbels *Reich* minister for popular enlightenment and propaganda (*Reichsministerium für Volksaufklärung und Propaganda* – RMVP). Goebbels clearly understood the power of film, stating in 1934 that 'film is one of the most modern and far-reaching methods of influencing the masses. A regime must not allow film to go its own way.' That year, Goebbels legitimised complete state control of the German film industry through the *Reich* Cinema Law (*Reichlichtspielgesetz*), which permitted 'positive' censorship by the state. With any kind of criticism of the state now impossible, the German film industry was now an arm of the totalitarian Nazi state – which Hitler fully intended to maximise. Shortly after coming to power, Hitler approached Leni Riefenstahl, a popular German actress who had directed her first film in 1932, with a view to producing a documentary featuring the 1934 Nazi Nuremburg Rally, which would 'appeal to, impress, an audience which was not necessarily interested in politics'. The resulting film – *Triumph des Willens* (Triumph of the Will) – was an orgy of Nazi pageantry – and an unprecedented success. There was absolutely no question by now of the infinite potential of the propaganda-based film – or, given this early exploitation of the medium by the Nazis, what Britain was up against in the propaganda stakes.

When the Second World War broke out, as we have explored, the British public's greatest fear was of bombing. Clearly, inspiring public confidence that Britain's aerial defences were sound would be a high priority for British propagandists. Due to certain doom-laden and influential films made during the 1930s, however, this was not necessarily straightforward.

Given the international fear of bombing between the wars, it was no surprise that this terrifying subject attracted the attention of popular literature and film. The novelist H.G. Wells, for example, wrote a script for London Films called *Things to Come*, which was brought to the cinema screen by Alexander Korda, a Jewish immigrant from Hungary, in 1936. This foreboding and sinister film provided a futuristic look at a war beginning in December 1940 – in which 'Everytown' was flattened by hordes of enemy bombers. Unnervingly, 'Everytown' was deliberately made to look very much like central London. The film, however, was considered too frightening, too realistic, to be popular, and public attendance was comparatively low. The following year, the prophecy of *Things to Come* appeared fulfilled, in fact, when newsreels were broadcast showing the suffering of Guernica. Appearing that same year, 1937, *The Gap* (written by E.V.H. Emmett, more of whom shortly) was hardly optimistic. An Air Ministry-backed film aimed at encouraging volunteers for Territorial Army anti-aircraft units, the film showed an enemy raid succeeding because of a deficiency of manpower in those units. Again, like *Things to Come* and especially so soon after the real, dreadful, spectacle of Guernica, the public's reaction was that the film only emphasised that the 'bomber would always get through'. Similarly, on 6 June 1939, *The Warning* was released in the hope of recruiting volunteers to the ARP network, showing the development of a raid and the defenders' response. The new Spitfires and Hurricanes were filmed scrambling, described as 'incredibly fast', but, again, the imagined enemy raid, this time on Nottingham, was successful. RAF pilots were seen being shot down in obsolete Gladiator biplane fighters – which hardly inspired confidence and only reinforced the bomber's perceived invincibility. What was required now was an antidote to this doom and gloom – which would ironically be provided by Korda – previously responsible for the dark and worrying *Things to Come*.

After *Things to Come*, Korda had negotiated with the Air Ministry to make an officially sanctioned film emphasising that from 1936 onwards the RAF had expanded and had the weapons and defence system to deal with any aerial threat. Perhaps significantly, the deal was agreed on 1 September 1939 – the day Hitler invaded Poland. Two days later, Britain and France declared war on Nazi Germany – and the government ordered the closure of all places of entertainment, including cinemas, so as to avoid concentrations of people who would be vulnerable in the event of air attack. This was not good news for Korda, who had decided that the best means of delivering the Air Ministry's message was via a feature film. Following complaints to the press, fortunately, two weeks later the ban was lifted. Given that 1940 would record over a billion cinemas admissions in Britain, a figure which increased as the war progressed, it was a wise decision. Consequently, Korda, who enjoyed a personal friendship with and had the support of Sir Winston Churchill (then the newly appointed First Sea Lord), successfully garnered support for the project from both the Air Ministry and Ministry of Information, the latter having been formed on 4 September 1939 and responsible for promoting the 'national case to the public at home and abroad in time of war' through producing 'national propaganda and controlling news and information'. The resulting film was *The Lion Has Wings* – the first British film of the Second World War.

Produced in haste during the autumn of 1939, owing to the urgent need to bolster public morale, Korda recruited three directors, Brian Desmond Hurst (whose later work included the 1945 Battle of Arnhem classic *Theirs is the Glory*), Michael Powell and Adrian Brunel, and set-to making the film at Denham Studios. The actor Ralph Richardson, himself in the process of becoming a FAA pilot and who had appeared as Mussolini in Korda's *Things to Come*, was recruited to play 'Wing Commander Richardson', and Korda's own wife, the beautiful Merle Oberon, became Richardson's on-screen spouse. Interestingly, Ronald Adam was chosen to play the German bomber chief, the actor himself having been a fighter pilot in the First World War, during which he was shot down and wounded, possibly by the Red Baron, Manfred Albrecht *Freiherr* von Richthofen, who sent compliments to the vanquished Camel pilot in hospital. In 1939, Adam returned to active duty in the RAF as a wing commander, serving as a sector controller at Hornchurch during the forthcoming Battle of Britain.

Narration (for the British release) was provided by E.V.H. Emmett, a veteran newsreader whose voice was well-known and reassuringly familiar to the public. The film's musical score was composed by Richard Addinsell (who later found fame for his *Warsaw Concerto* in Hurst's 1941 film *Dangerous Moonlight*). Screenplay was written by Ian Dalrymple, previously an experienced editor-in-chief with Gainsborough Pictures and Gaumont-British, whose contribution to the writing of the 1938 film *Pygmalion* had earned him an Oscar nomination. Dalrymple, who in 1940 would head-up the new Crown Film Unit and produce official propaganda films, was conscious that he had a delicate balancing act: on one hand, too much detail regarding Britain's air defences could not be revealed, but, on the other, he felt passionately, and arguably quite rightly, that the public deserved to know 'everything that does not (a) inform the enemy, or (b) provoke untimely debate'. Korda was given the use of Hatfield aerodrome, with Hurst directing both the aerial scenes and those involving Richardson and Oberon. According to another of the directors, Michael Powell, Korda had promised Churchill personally that he would make this important film – which would be ready in just one month.

On the afternoon of that fateful day 3 September 1939, off Inishtrahull a German U-boat inadvertently sank the SS *Athenia*, a passenger liner out of Glasgow, bound for Montreal. Over 100 passengers and crew lost their lives, including twenty-eight citizens of neutral America. Condemned as a war crime, the RAF was ordered to retaliate. The following day, Powell was tipped off by Squadron Leader H.M.S. Wright, the film's RAF liaison officer, that 149 Squadron's Mildenhall-based Wellingtons were poised to attack German shipping in the Kiel Canal, along with the Blenheims of 9, 107, 110 and 139 Squadrons. Powell dashed off to Mildenhall with camera crew and filmed 149 Squadron's take-off and triumphal return. This was important. In addition to showcasing Britain's aerial defences, it was equally necessary to reassure the public that the RAF also possessed sufficient offensive capacity to hit back at Germany. Whilst this made for impressive film footage, the actual truth of the matter was that 149 Squadron was poorly prepared for war. Astonishingly, Flying Officer Bill McRae only noticed at the last minute before take-off that his aircraft's bomb bay was empty, and when, on route to the target, Squadron Leader Paul Harris ordered his gunners to test their weapons, all failed to fire. Nonetheless, what was lacking in preparedness was compensated by the aircrew's spirit: although defenceless, Harris had pressed on.

Naturally, however, the Spitfire, which had already captivated imaginations and won hearts and minds, was destined to be the star of *The Lion Has Wings*. On the afternoon of 6 September 1939, and all the following day, Hurst's crew filmed Flight Lieutenant 'Treacle' Tracey's 'B' Flight of 74 'Tiger' Squadron at RAF Hornchurch, an important sector station north of the Thames in Essex. Given that on the morning of 6 September two pilots of 74 Squadron's 'A' Flight were responsible for destroying two 56 Squadron Hurricanes in the so-called 'Battle of Barking Creek' friendly fire tragedy, it was perhaps a quirk of fate that the 'Tigers' were chosen for this starring role. Nonetheless, it was a welcome distraction for 'B' Flight, the pilots of which entered into the spirit of the thing, socialising and happily cooperating with the 'luvvies'. Hurst was impressed, especially when the Spitfires mischievously beat up the film crew at low-level, and later cooperated at close quarters, enabling air-to-air footage to be filmed from an Avro Anson piloted by a female ferry pilot. Once cut and edited, these scenes certainly helped promote the message that the RAF, according to Powell, was perfectly equipped, able and ready to 'blow the *Luftwaffe* out of the sky'.

The Lion Has Wings was made with a budget of £30,000 – equivalent today, given inflation, to a still comparatively modest £181,737. The three directors successfully interwove actors with real newsreel footage and Emmett's commentary to produce a documentary style propaganda and morale-boosting film – the first of its kind made during Second World War. What audiences wanted from cinema was entertainment – and Korda's film demonstrated to the government how the extraordinary reach and popularity of the cinema could be harnessed and manipulated to communicate messages and themes via an engaging storyline. It was, however, as Michael Powell later admitted, 'an outrageous piece of propaganda'. Indeed, at least one audience treated with contempt the claim by 'Wing Commander Richardson' that 'We have never been so prepared'. Nonetheless, overall the film was well-received by critics and the public, being shown at over 200 cinemas in November 1939, finding favour with 73 per cent of viewers – and became that month's top cinema attraction, the second most profitable film of 1939.

Clearly, the film was a blatant and overt attempt to reassure the public that Britain's aerial defences were cutting-edge and perfectly capable of seeing off any aerial threat, in addition to striking back at Germany. If the intention was to reduce the public's fear and anxiety of bombing, it certainly helped – one young lady commenting to mass observation that having seen the film, she felt 'much safer'. The other thing, much more significantly, that had increased public confidence, however, was that by the time *The Lion Has Wings* was released, over two months after war broke out, the imminently expected and dreaded 'knockout blow' had failed to materialise. Indeed, there had been an urgent flurry of activity when general mobilisation was ordered, the size and composition of the RAF, for example, literally changing overnight as ranks were swelled by countless auxiliaries and reservists, and the BEF and Advanced Air Striking Force had dashed over to France – but nothing had yet happened. On the Continent, British troops had dug in for the winter on the Franco-Belgian border, awaiting events. The initial surge of activity and anxiety had subsided, the so-called 'Phoney War' now in full-swing, and many evacuees had returned home;

Cambridge, for example, accommodated 6,700 children in September 1939, but by November only half remained. Indeed, as Flight Lieutenant Brian John Edward Lane wrote, it was 'a queer war'.

The Lion Has Wings was authorised to be surprisingly open regarding the system of air defence – except in two crucial respects. Firstly, understandably, no mention is made of radar, the true significance of which the Germans had even failed to appreciate by the Battle of Britain, the film implying that the tracking of enemy aircraft was entirely reliant upon the eyes and ears of the Observer Corps and sound locating devices. Perhaps even more secret was the fact that in 1932, the Polish Cipher Bureau had cracked the German Enigma code, a machine used to send encrypted messages, although by 1939 the German system's complexity outstripped the Poles' capacity to keep up with it. Before war broke out, Poland provided Britain and France reconstructed Enigma machines and their knowledge of decryption, enabling British mathematicians and codebreakers to advance this work from the now famous Bletchley Park. At the time Korda's film was made, the Germans were still able to make much use of landline communications, but by the Battle of Britain signals traffic was constant. The Poles' pioneering work accelerated the Allies ability to eavesdrop on German messages, informing strategy and tactics. Exactly to what extent, owing to documents still being secret, we may never know, but nonetheless this, and radar, was something that the public could not be made aware of in 1939, for obvious reasons.

Whilst, unlike the other films in this book, *The Lion Has Wings* does not show an interpretation of the actual Battle of Britain, which had yet to occur, it certainly predicted such an aerial assault – and was the first Second World War film to heroicise the fighter pilot. For those reasons, and because investigating this film requires an examination of the broader context of air power and propaganda, it remains an important work.

In 1939, *The Lion Had Wings* had conveyed its message through a 'docudrama' style, which had proved immensely popular, featuring determined and daring Spitfire pilots beating back an enemy raid; during summer 1940 there was no need for fictional interpretations – the battle in the air was happening for real, and with it came an insatiable thirst for news. Naturally, at the time, the 'fighter boys' were upheld as the modern equivalent of heroic, chivalrous, knights, the glamorous duellists of the skies – and cinema was now well accepted as a powerful means of communicating news and propaganda. The Ministry of Information capitalised on this through the production not of feature films but on 'shorts', providing the public information, some featuring fighter pilots. More popular were newsreels, made by such companies as Pathé Gazette and British Movietone News. One newsreel made by the latter, appearing in 1940, was entitled *Well Done! The Fighter Command.* Today, this, and other newsreels like it, provide us unique glimpses of the past. This particular newsreel (available on YouTube) comprises a number of separately entitled sequences, one, for example, being *RAF Fighters Ever on the Alert*, featuring Hurricanes landing and the pilots of 56 Squadron awaiting the call to scramble at North Weald. Amongst the pilots featured lounging around at dispersal, awaiting the call to scramble, are Squadron Leader G.A.L. 'Minnie' Manton, Flight Lieutenant 'Jumbo' Gracie and Flight Lieutenant Percy 'Squeak' Weaver, dating this footage as before 31 August 1940 – the date Weaver was reported missing over the Essex coast. Later, another sequence, using graphics, show tactics used when a Spitfire intercepts a He 111 bomber, and real camera-gun footage of a *Stuka* under attack. Newsreels such as this were well-received by and highly popular with the public, showing as they did, albeit censored, authentic images of the war in progress. During the Battle of Britain, of 250 newsreels, eighty-three featured the RAF. Although there was no shortage of cinematic exposure for Fighter Command, the Battle of Britain would have to wait until 1942 for its first British feature film proper.

Nonetheless, the director Brian Desmond Hurst worked the Battle of Britain into his film *Dangerous Moonlight*, released on 26 June 1941. During 1940, the RAF's ranks had been gratefully increased by volunteers, many being trained pilots and airmen, from the occupied lands – men who had been evacuated or escaped, via various routes and means, to continue the fight. The largest national group amongst these freedom fighters desperate to liberate their oppressed homelands was the Poles, who fought with distinction during the Battle of Britain and beyond. In this love story, Hurst focuses on the fictional tale of 'Stefan "Steve" Radecki' (Anton Walbrook), a Polish fighter pilot and gifted concert pianist who meets an American reporter, 'Carole Peters' (Sally Gray) in Warsaw. After the German invasion, 'Radecki' volunteers, but is not chosen, to fly a 'suicide mission' (hence why the film's American release became *Suicide Squadron*). Nonetheless, he is amongst the last to leave Warsaw, ending up in New York, where he meets up with and marries 'Carole'. The couple travel to England, for 'Radecki' to continue the fight to free his homeland, where he gives a concert – the scene famous for the *Warsaw Concerto*, written by Richard Addinsell. Later, Radecki is shown as a pilot in a British Spitfire squadron, newsreel footage of 222 Squadron being amongst those clips used, and in action, for a full-on fourteen minutes, when he ultimately only narrowly survives ramming a He 111. Baling out, wounded and 'shell-shocked', 'Radecki' suffers memory loss. Recovering in hospital, our hero recalls the *Warsaw Concerto* and meeting his wife, whom he recognises and repeats the words spoken when they first met: 'Carole, it's not safe to go out with you when the moon is so bright' – and lived happily ever after. Whilst *Dangerous Moonlight* became a box office hit in Britain, it was less well-received in America, and Walbrook was unhappy with his own performance. Again, this film was, though, important propaganda.

Released a few days after Hitler's invasion of Russia, *Dangerous Moonlight* was a timely reminder of Britain's achievement less than a year previous, when Fighter Command successfully defied the mighty *Luftwaffe*. The film was also an acknowledgement of the contribution made by foreign nationals, in this case the more numerous Poles. It is no surprise, however, that the Spitfire, yet again, was the featured fighter.

On 26 September 1941, an American-made film, *A Yank in the RAF* was released by 20th Century Fox. Although not a British film, like certain other productions mentioned in this text, this cinematic story, based upon a story by Darryl F. Zanuck (under the pseudonym 'Melville Crossman'), is relevant to the development of cinema-goers' experience during wartime. When the film was made and released, America remained neutral, the Neutrality Acts preventing American citizens joining the armed forces of belligerent powers. Consequently, those so-called 'Gun Jumpers' who were unable to wait for America to enter the war before playing their part, first had to travel to Canada and enlist in the RCAF. In the film, 'Tim Baker' (Tyrone Power) is a self-focused but intrepid adventurer clandestinely ferrying American-built aircraft across the border to Canada, before similarly flying a Hudson to England, and rekindling acquaintance with his periodic girlfriend 'Carol Brown' (Betty Grable) who has joined the WAAF. Not to be outdone, 'Baker' joins the RAF but is disappointed at his posting to a bomber unit, and less impressed further still when his first operation involves not dropping bombs but leaflets. Cutting a long story short, 'Baker' answers Fighter Command's call for volunteers and finds himself operational on a Spitfire squadron in time for Dunkirk. After shooting down two enemy fighters, 'Baker' is himself shot down but manages to return to England – and, as inevitably as he ends up flying a Spitfire, gets the girl. Although ostensibly not an overt propaganda film, *A Yank in the RAF*, nonetheless drew attention to those American volunteers already fighting the Axis, and through a comparatively light-hearted look at the war and clever pairing of two of Hollywood's most popular stars, the film became the studio's second most successful film of the war (after *How Green Was My Valley*, about a Welsh mining community). Again, the storyline of the central character's desire to become a fighter pilot, and evocation of the dark days of Dunkirk, all helped to romanticise the Spitfire.

The wider RAF, however, was not being ignored by either newsreels, shorts, or film. Bomber Command had come into sharp focus when *Target for Tonight* was released on 18 August 1941. Produced by the Crown Film Unit, the popular film featured the story of a raid on Germany, from start to finish, showing the RAF at work. *One of Our Aircraft is Missing*, released on 27 June 1942, told the story of a Wellington crew forced to bale out over the Netherlands and whose successful evasion was greatly assisted by brave Dutch civilians. Directed by Michael Powell (previously one of *The Lion Has Wings*' three directors) and Emerich Pressburger, the film received two Oscar nominations and remains one of Britain's best-loved films of the Second World War. Nonetheless, it was behind two films in the box office ratings, namely *Mrs Miniver* and *The First of The Few* – both of which returned to Fighter Command and, of course, the Spitfire.

Mrs Miniver was not a British-made film but a Hollywood production, providing Americans a utopian view of an upper-class British family's part in the 'People's War'. By the time Metro-Goldwyn-Mayer released the film on 4 June 1942, the United States had been in the war for over six months, following the surprise Japanese attack on Pearl Harbor on 7 December 1941 – and it was now equally crucial to maintain morale and public confidence in America. To that end, the US Department of War had already commissioned Frank Capra to direct a series of seven factual documentaries explaining why America was in the war, and why it had to be fought and won. The first of these, *Prelude to War*, was released on 27 May 1942, explaining the causes of the Second World War and placing blame firmly at the Axis Powers' door. *Mrs Miniver* took this theme further through a storyline revolving around a peace-loving, functional and thoroughly decent British family.

'Kay Miniver' (Greer Garson) is the family's unassuming but wise and stoic matriarch, whose son, 'Vin' (Richard Ney, who in real life was to marry Garson) returns from university, meets, falls in love with and marries 'Carol' (Teresa Wright), the daughter of 'Lady Beldon' (Dame May Whitty). Determined to do his 'bit', 'Vin' joins the RAF, becoming, inevitably, a Spitfire pilot. 'Mr Clem Miniver' (Walter Pidgeon) takes his boat off to join the heroic 'Little Ships' assisting the Dunkirk evacuation, and upon return the 'Minivers' take in their stride being nearly killed when a bomb hits their home, and 'Mrs Miniver' capturing a fugitive Nazi airman (Helmut Dantine). After 'Vin' and 'Carole' are married and return from their Scottish honeymoon, the now two 'Mrs Minivers' accompany 'Vin' in his sports car to his nearby aerodrome, watching with concern his Spitfire squadron scramble. Eventually, the ladies, with 'Mrs Miniver' senior driving, leave the airfield – comprising most unlikely timber-built buildings – and head home, through the black-out. On the way, they are forced to stop when the 'village' is heavily bombed (clear message there: not a legitimate military target, and throughout the film the viewer has come to know some of the villagers and their peaceful, simple, way of life). A German *Stuka* machine-guns the car – killing Carole. 'Vin' returns from duty and surviving aerial combat to the devastating news that his wife of only a few days has been tragically killed by enemy action. The film's subsequent finale is sheer genius. The 'Minivers' and villagers are seen attending a service in the bombed-out local church, complete with Medieval knight's effigy, where the 'Vicar' (Henry Wilcoxon) takes his central theme from Psalm 91:5: 'You will not fear the terror of the night, nor the arrow that flies by day, nor the pestilence that stalks in the darkness, nor the destruction that wastes noonday.' The 'Vicar' then delivers a powerful and deeply moving sermon affirming their cause's moral right and emphasising that this, above all others, was the 'People's War'. The roar (actually more of a wine, definitely not the Merlins supposed) of aero-engines then interrupts proceedings as through a gaping hole in the church roof we see an endless stream, or so it seems, of Spitfires heading out, presumably, to once more engage the Luftwaffe – to the rousing hymn *Onward Christian Soldiers*, and finally *Land of Hope and Glory*. The Battle of Britain is not specifically mentioned, but clearly this is an allusion to it, and so influential did America's President Franklin D. Roosevelt consider the final sermon that he ordered it produced as leaflets in various languages for dropping over enemy occupied territory, and had it published in the magazines *Time* and *Look*.

Mrs Miniver became the top box office attraction of 1942, making an initial profit of $4,831 and becoming the studio's most profitable film of the year. It was particularly well-received in America, which Churchill considered vitally important, and was named by 555 of 592 American film critics as the year's best film – doing great service in rallying support in America for Britain and the war. In Germany, the film even won the admiration of Goebbels, who acknowledged that the propaganda power of *Mrs Miniver* was of a level only previously 'dreamed of', and that the anti-German sentiment was subtly achieved without one hostile word spoken against Germany. Although popular in Britain, the cinema-going public's reaction was mixed – but the film remains the benchmark for the nation's perceived popular memory of and identity during the Second World War.

More important than *Mrs Miniver* to British audiences in 1942, however, was *The First of The Few*.

Given the enormity of the achievements of 'The Few' and the unprecedented place this unique victory had in the contemporary national consciousness, it is perhaps surprising that it would be two years before the event was celebrated and featured in a British feature film. Several ideas were considered but rejected until the Australian writer Henry C. James hit the right note with a story that had everything: the life, premature death and inspirational achievement of the genius Reginald Joseph Mitchell, tragic designer of the iconic Spitfire, who had died of cancer on 11 June 1937 – without ever knowing the immense contribution his Spitfire made during the Second World War.

Film producer George King and his partner John Stafford bought the option to James's idea, and set up a company, 'British Aviation Pictures', covering the rights. Metro-Goldwyn-Mayer expressed interest but only if they controlled all rights, which was unacceptable to king. The British actor Leslie Howard was approached with a view to him playing the lead role of R.J. Mitchell, but Howard had no interest in working on another Hollywood-backed project. After Metro-Goldwyn-Mayer left the arena, however, Howard agreed to the starring role – and also became both director and producer, buying the film's rights – which was then financed by Rank. When war broke out, Howard had returned to Britain from America, to assist the war effort by making morale-boosting films – and was now embarking upon what would prove to be his greatest contribution in that endeavour.

King and Stafford had already identified the genius of Churchill's use of language by eulogising Fighter Command's aircrew as 'The Few', and received the prime minister's consent to use his words on-screen. Knowing that this stirring film about the Spitfire needed Air Ministry and other official support to ensure the best possible result, Howard also enlisted Churchill's help, who endorsed the project in writing and even personally called Air Chief Marshal Sholto Douglas, air officer commanding RAF Fighter Command, to impress upon him that all necessary cooperation must be provided British Aviation Pictures. With Churchill aboard, anything was possible: a Supermarine S6 Schneider Trophy seaplane was produced for studio scenes, along with a Spitfire fuselage, and access for Howard to experience the atmosphere and rituals of the RAF fighter station at Biggin Hill. Best of all, the film makers were given permission to film at the 10 Group Sector Station airfield of Ibsley, near Ringwood in Hampshire – home to Squadron Leader Christopher 'Bunny' Currant's Spitfire-equipped 501 Squadron, and Squadron Leader Frank Howell's 118 Squadron; both pilots were decorated Battle of Britain aces, and their men included more of 'The Few'. Filming was also to go ahead at RAF Warmwell, on the coast near Weymouth in Dorset. Unlike Ibsley, Warmwell, the satellite and forward airfield of the Middle Wallop Sector Station, had played an active part in the Battle of Britain. Howard now had Spitfires, pilots, a Blenheim for use as a camera-ship – and even use of an airworthy He 111 bomber! This aircraft had been shot-up by Spitfires on 9 February 1940 and made a forced-landing at North Berwick Law, East Lothian. Having suffered only minor damage, the German bomber was repaired and subsequently operated by the AFDU based at Duxford, and 1426 (Enemy Aircraft) Flight. Howard could not have asked for more, and was positioned, therefore, to make a spectacular British aviation film.

Another advantage Churchill's involvement secured was the temporary release from war service of the British actor David Niven – chosen to play 'Geoffrey Crisp', a composite character based upon various test pilots, in what would be his first major British film. Rosamund John became 'Diana Mitchell', 'R.J.'s' wife (although in real-life Mrs Mitchell's name was actually Florence). The Russian-born Anton de Grunwald, who had worked with Howard on *Pygmalion* in 1938 and wrote the screenplay for his *Pimpernel Smith* of 1941, collaborated with the prolific screenwriter Sir Miles Malleson, producing a workable film script from the original story written by King and Stafford. Many years later, Dr Gordon Mitchell, son of 'R.J.' and Florence Mitchell, considered that the eventual script pursued two key themes: firstly 'the widely-held public image of the high-powered, highly intelligent "boffin"' and secondly 'the idea of someone literally killing himself by grossly overworking to produce something of vital importance, in this case, of course, the Spitfire.' How accurate these themes were in relation to Mitchell's story, however, was a quite different matter.

Considering what a huge box-office success *The First of The Few* was in 1942, it is perhaps surprising that the British film industry did not rush to make more films featuring Fighter Command – although in terms of newsreels, shorts and general press coverage the 'Fighter Boys' were hardly in danger of under exposure. An interesting – and now virtually forgotten – film for our purposes, however, is *The Flemish Farm*, made in 1943.

Whereas *Dangerous Moonlight* had focused on the Poles, Jeffrey Dell's *The Flemish Farm* was a nod towards free Belgians. The story concerns a Belgian fighter squadron forced to flee their homeland, who first continue the fight in France before arriving in England and fighting in the Battle of Britain. Before escaping from the continent, however, the hero, 'Jean Duclos' (Clifford Evans) buries the squadron's colours on a Flemish farm – and resolves to return and retrieve the flag. Having parachuted into enemy occupied Belgium, 'Duclos' recovers the banner and returns to England, with help from the resistance. Upon return, the precious flag is formally presented to the Belgian Air Force in exile. The interesting thing about *The Flemish Farm* is that although there is footage of a Spitfire landing, the film revolves around Hurricanes. Whilst no aerial combat is recreated, there is some good footage of Hurricane Mk IIs – a departure from the 'Spit-centric' films to date.

The year 1943 also saw the release of a particular American information film: *The Battle of Britain*, the fourth in a series explaining to American servicemen and women, and the public, why their country was at war. The director was Frank Capra, an Italian-born American citizen, who, although established in Hollywood, volunteered to serve after the Japanese attack on Pearl Harbor. Capra was tasked with making the series of *Why We Fight* films by the chief of staff, George C. Marshall. Capra had watched, and been intimidated by, *Triumph of the Will*, which, he considered, even 'Satan couldn't have devised a more blood-chilling super spectacle' upholding Germans as the invincible master race. Capra decided to counterattack using a simple strategy: using original footage to let America's enemy demonise themselves through actual hostile events. *The Battle of Britain* used existing archival material, much of it German and very rare, cut together to tell the story together with a powerful voiceover by well-known Canadian actor and entertainer Walter Huston. The film projected what is now the traditional narrative of the Battle of Britain: 'Showing the gallant and victorious defence of Britain by the Royal Air Force, at a time when shattered but unbeaten, the British were the only people fighting the Nazis.' Like *The Lion Has Wings*, Capra's film explains how Britain aerial defences worked, and predominantly, but not exclusively, featured many clips of Spitfires. These include a few seconds showing Johnnie Johnson, at the time of filming a flight lieutenant on 616 Squadron, exiting his Spitfire and telling the waiting intelligence officer that he got 'a 109 destroyed'. Some superb footage shows German aircraft from the early war period in action – and somehow disturbing cine-gun camera film showing Spitfires under fire – and being fatally hit – by an Me 109. On 15 September 1940, the viewer is told that Fighter Command met the Luftwaffe's 'challenge by throwing in everything they had' – which, of course, is simply untrue. Certainly, Air Vice-Marshal Keith Park committed 11 Group to battle, with reinforcements from 10 and 12 Groups, but plenty of resources remained in the latter two and 13 groups. This is, however, an underpinning pillar of the 'David and Goliath' popular narrative. Capra's film, however, does not ignore Bomber Command's early efforts, or the stoic response of British civilians to the night blitz. Cleverly, the final scene is borrowed from *Mrs Miniver*, showing the mass formation of Spitfires seen through the bombed church's holed roof. Finally, the chief of staff's words appear, leaving viewers in no doubt as to why the war was being fought, and to what end: 'victory of the democracies can only be complete with the utter defeat of the war machines of Germany and Japan'. It was powerful stuff – but this was a narrated documentary, not even a docudrama like *The Lion Has Wings* – and it was also another American production.

The next major British-made film featuring the RAF, *The Way to the Stars*, was released a month after the cessation of hostilities in Europe, in June 1945. This was the first retrospective film about the Second World War, in which we witness life and death on a Blenheim bomber squadron through the eyes of 'Flying Officer Penrose' (John Mills). Joining his unit during the Battle of Britain, fresh from training, shortly after 'Penrose' arrives the airfield is attacked – and Hurricane Mk IIs scramble to defend it. After the raid, a Hurricane beats up the airfield at low-level before performing a victory roll – prompting an acerbic remark from 'Squadron Leader Carter' (Trevor Howard): 'Line shoot. These fighter types, you know, top button undone, victory rolls, bad show, I think.' Unlike that epic, however, not one Spitfire appears in *The Way to the Stars* – which remains in the opinion of many the best film about the wartime RAF. Be that as it may, this was still no attempt to tell the Battle of Britain story.

In America, the air war featured in cinema four years later, in 1949, when 20th Century Fox released Henry King's *Twelve O'Clock High*. Starring Gregory Peck as 'Brigadier Frank Savage', the film re-visited the United States Eighth Air Force's early missions, flying from bases in England. Owing to the lack of a long-range offensive escort fighter, losses amongst the American bomber crews were high, leading to division in public opinion at home regarding the wisdom of the daylight bomber offensive. The Americans literally stuck to their guns, however, and this film paid tribute to the bravery and sacrifices of the aircrews involved. According to *The New York Times*, *Twelve O'Clock High*, which won 2 Academy Awards, was in the year's top 10 films, and even in 2009 was considered amongst the best 1,000 films ever made. Clearly, air war films generated more than sufficient commercial interest in the new post-war world to attract investors, which Hollywood had certainly proved and cashed in on with *Twelve O'Clock High*, which firmly focused on America's pivotal contribution to the strategic bombing offensive. Conversely, although Fighter Command's victory in the Battle of Britain was infinitely more significant strategically, and universally upheld as the nation's 'Finest Hour', it was not until 1952 that a film, British or otherwise, featured the epic aerial conflict as its central theme.

That film was *Angels One Five*.

It was actually the English film producer and actors' talent agent Cecil Gordon Tenant who floated the idea of a Battle of Britain related film, with a view to finding a suitably commercial project for two of his clients, namely John Gossage and Derek Twist. Gossage's film credits, as producer, associate producer and production manager dated back to 1936, and included *Hamlet* (1948), in which Laurence Olivier's genius was demonstrated as both actor and director. Twist was an even more experienced industry professional, whose work as an editor included *The 39 Steps* (1935) and *The Lion Has Wings* (1939), and as a writer eight previous films including the comedy *Green Grow the Rushes* (1951), on which he had worked with Gossage and also directed. Both Gossage and Twist had served in the wartime RAF – and Tenant's suggestion piqued their interest. The pair set up Templar Productions to front the project, receiving the backing of the Scottish film executive Robert Clark, head of production at the Elstree-based Associated British Picture Corporation, for a project entitled *Battle of Britain*.

With the summer of 1940 only eleven years distant at the time preparations for this film were being made, the often-traumatic events involved remained crystal clear in the memories of many, including both survivors and those who had lost loved ones. The 'Finest Hour' also enjoyed a unique status in the British popular memory of the Second World War and national identity, so the subject had to be treated both sensitively and, indeed, reverentially. For this reason, Gossage and Twist resolved that the only way forward was to produce as authentic a film as possible – and to do that, they needed as many people who had actually served in the RAF both behind and in front of the cameras. The chosen director, for example, George More O'Ferrall, had been an army liaison officer at Fighter Command HQ. A former

Portuguese air force Hurricane pilots during the making of *Angels One Five*. *(Historic Military Press)*

Shakespearean and West End theatre actor, O'Ferrall had also directed plays and in 1936 became the BBC's first drama producer, directing the 1948 television adaptation of *Wuthering Heights* and receiving a Royal Television Society award for his two-part *Hamlet* production. This new project, however, was his first film as director.

Battle of Britain also needed an informed screenplay, which would be written by Twist, who chose as the basis for this the book *What Are Your Angels Now?* By Wing Commander A.J.C. Pelham-Groom – a retired Fighter Command staff officer and Biggin Hill sector controller, since turned actor and writer. Typically, Pelham-Groom's novels, including *David Farlow Takes the Air*, *The Little Hanging Men* and *The 'Black Eagle'*, were tales of aerial high adventure and mystery, aimed at boys, so unsurprisingly Twist had to re-work Pelham-Groom's Battle of Britain book to produce a more serious script suitable for an adult audience. Nonetheless, it was a break for Pelham-Groom, who also acted as the film's technical advisor, and, by all accounts, was quite a character. Other former RAF officers involved included Ronald Adam, who played the 'Group Controller' – and had served as Hornchurch sector controller during the Battle of Britain – as Cyril Raymond, who would play 'Squadron Leader Barry Clinton', apparently had at Kenley. Humphrey Lestocq, who had become famous as a radio comedian for his 'Flying Officer Kite' character on the *Merry Go Round* series, was chosen as 'Flight Lieutenant "Batchy" Salter', a Hurricane pilot – the aircraft being a type Lestocq himself had actually flown during the war (he also flew Typhoons operationally with 609 Squadron). Indeed, so soon after the war, finding actors with service backgrounds was straightforward – but the producers would find sourcing aircraft somewhat more difficult.

The Air Ministry was supportive on the grounds that such a film could encourage recruitment during what was now the so-called 'Cold War', and provided the film-makers access to RAF Kenley, a crucial 11 Group Sector Station defending London in 1940, which remained operational, and Air Vice-Marshal Keith Park's underground operations room at Uxbridge, in addition to seconding a number of personnel to the project. What the Air Ministry was unable to conjure, however, was numbers of period aircraft – a somewhat essential ingredient to a film telling the Battle of Britain story. Few Hurricanes were available: Mk Is L1591, used for in-studio cockpit shots and dressed in 56 Squadron codes as US-N – but criminally broken up after filming; L1592, dressed as US-D and used as a static aircraft, whilst P2617 taxied as US-B. Hawker Siddeley Aircraft Ltd provided the airworthy Mk IIC PZ865 (under civilian registration G-AMAU), masquerading as US-P, and apparently the RAF LF363, although no evidence of the latter has been identified on-screen. At the time, authentic Spitfires were similarly scarce, but salvation was at hand from an unanticipated source: the Portuguese air force still operated Hurricanes and provided five Mk IICs for the film. So it was that the Hurricane – not Spitfire – for once became star of the proposed film.

By now, Twist had substantially worked the screenplay, the film's title morphing from *Battle of Britain* to *Hawks in the Sun, Angels Fifteen,* and finally settling on *Angels One Five*, a derivative of Pelham-Groom's book title upon which the production was loosely based. The producers also emphasised that the film's focus was on people, not aeroplanes, and the title changes may have been because the lack of available aircraft prevented the making of an aviation-based extravaganza. The screenplay sought to tell the story of one fighter station's experience under attack during the summer of 1940, and that of a new pilot in particular, rather than a blow-by-blow account of the Battle of Britain as a whole. This change of tack may well have been influenced by the shortage of authentic aircraft, although the film's budget was comparatively small anyway and incapable of funding extensive flying scenes. The final title was one heard many times in pilots' headphones as they scrambled and were directed by the controller towards the enemy – 'Angels', in the radio jargon of the day being height measured in thousands of feet.

With screenplay, actors, aircraft, and locations all good to go, *Angels One Five* was filmed in July 1951 – later than anticipated owing to a poor spring, postponing the anticipated release from 4 August 1951 to 19 March 1952.

Angels One Five was intended as a tribute to 'The Few', and upon release was appraised by Group Captain Douglas Bader, who attended the premiere: 'I can't fault it in any detail … depicts life on any fighter station in the South of England during the Battle.' Whilst the gutter press shared this positive view, the more upmarket newspapers and magazines were less enthusiastic, however, feeling that the film lacked real drama, excitement and tension. Rightly, Thomas Spencer, of the albeit communist newspaper the *Daily Worker*, complained at how the working-classes were portrayed in the film. Indeed, the whole production was arguably a romp for public school boys and girls rallying round and seeing off the jolly old Hun, backed up by some pretty dim and uncultured lower ranks. The only glimmer of hope, in fact, is at 0.30.52, when 'Batchy' assures 'Baird' that 'Pete', the only sergeant-pilot seen throughout the entire film, and for a second at that, is a 'good type'. A tribute to 'The Few' *Angels One Five* may have been intended – but the end result was a very selective one, there being no foreign pilots at all, and just that one fleeting glimpse of the lone sergeant-pilot.

Whilst the film is undoubtedly of its time, and not dissimilar in approach to other British war films of the period, it fails to actually tell the Battle of Britain story in any detail, and would have benefited from a narration, providing context. Admittedly, the Battle of Britain is a very difficult and expensive story to translate to cinema, not least because accuracy involves using large numbers of aircraft, and these were simply unavailable. Nonetheless, the Hurricanes and Spitfires assembled provided for some excellent ground and aerial footage – but *First of The Few* proved that a realistic impression of combat could be achieved through splicing newsreel and cine-gun footage. Surprisingly, *Angels One Five* made no attempt to do this, relying instead on graphics primitive even by 1951's standards.

So far, films either revolving around the Battle of Britain, or at least referring to it, had focused upon the story of an individual, *The First of The Few* being a distinct case in point, whilst *Angels One Five* had majored on the importance of team-work, not individualism, through the story of '"Sceptic" Baird' and 'Pimpernel Squadron'. The next relevant film, Daniel Angel's 1956 biopic *Reach for the Sky*, focused on that one, larger than life, personality: Douglas Bader – whose life, of course, defied fiction. Bader had become a household name during the Second World War, the legless Battle of Britain fighter ace who ended up an unappeasable prisoner in the notorious Colditz Castle. Beyond doubt, even today, Bader remains the most famous of 'The Few', and in conquering his double-amputation, personified determination and courage at a superhuman level – which is what was required in wartime and, moreover, something post-war Britain needed reminding of.

Times were changing. The Conservative dominated Britain of the 1930s, for example, was disappearing. In 1945, in spite of Churchill's enormous popularity as Britain's war leader, Clement Attlee's Labour Party won the general election. The socialists immediately set about creating the welfare state, providing more educational equality and nationalising key industries, public transport and the Bank of England. The truth was that although Britain had emerged victorious from those long years of struggle, it was financially exhausted. The immediate post war period saw a shortage of food and clothing, meaning that rationing and 'austerity' continued into the 1950s. Nonetheless, that decade saw virtually full employment and the majority of Britons had never been so well off. On the wider stage, though, whilst Britain remained a leading European power, America had emerged leader of the Free World, and the Soviets had retired behind the 'Iron Curtain' – heralding the Cold War between democracy and communism.

Moreover, Britain's Empire was now rapidly waning: in 1947, India won independence, and British influence in Africa was in decline; large-scale immigration transformed post-war Britain into an ethnically diverse and multi-cultural society. It was in many ways a difficult time for Britain. The British contribution to victory in the Second World War, however, was – and is – the supreme moment in the modern national story and identity, providing a declining post war Britain with a mythic reminder of the country's great past. Against this backdrop, Douglas Bader's story was screaming out to be told. It had all the ingredients for a book and film to 'stir a glow in English hearts', as the *Daily Mail* later wrote of the story – which was very much needed in austerity Britain at the time. So far as Group Captain Douglas Bader was concerned, however, there was only one man to write his story: Paul Brickhill.

Noting the plethora of wartime memoirs being published, Douglas Bader had started writing his own, working with an unnamed author whose idea of a film was rejected by Rank, after which the project foundered. After his collaborator walked away, Bader, kept the 100,000 words manuscript and pondered how to progress getting it into print. After reading *The Dam Busters*, both Douglas and Thelma Bader were convinced that Brickhill was the man to tell their story. The Baders reached out, inviting the best-selling author to dinner in London and putting the prospect to him. Brickhill, however, was aware that whilst everyone had nothing but respect and admiration for how he conquered his disability, inspiring in the process people the world over, Bader was in other respects very much a 'marmite' character. Whilst his inner sanctum of close friends and cronies worshipped the man, others found him arrogant, rude, opinionated, unreasonable and imperious. Over dinner, Brickhill decided that Bader's huge personality 'hits you like a bolting steamroller' – and, with full access to the original manuscript and Bader's personal records and papers, he agreed to take the job on. Soon, Brickhill's agent, David Higham, lined up Collins to publish the Douglas Bader story: *Reach for the Sky*. Published in 1954 – the year Britain's austerity measures ended – the book was an overnight success.

In the same year that saw *Reach for the Sky* become an international publishing phenomenon, Brickhill's *The Dam Busters* was made into a film, which became a box office hit in 1955. The film rights to *Reach for the Sky* were actually purchased by independent film-maker Daniel Angel for £15,000 – even before he had read Brickhill's book. Angel, a former army major, was a producer, the director he worked with being Lewis Gilbert. The pair had previously collaborated to make two films concerning the

The actor Kenneth More, who portrayed Douglas Bader, on set with Johnnie Johnson, the official top-scoring RAF fighter pilot of the war, during the making of *Reach for the Sky*.

wartime the RN, *Albert RN* (1953), a story about naval officers in a German prison camp, and *The Sea Shall Not Have Them*, telling the story of an RAF High Speed Launch's daring rescue of a downed RAF bomber crew from beneath the Germans noses. With *Reach for the Sky*, Angel was to produce the film whilst Gilbert both directed and wrote a screenplay based upon Brickhill's book. Clearly, the story's key points were the devastating crash in Woodley followed by Douglas Bader's astonishing survival and relentless determination to walk – and fly – again, his war service confirming his incomparable courage and personal victory over the loss of both legs. There was never any question that a film based upon Bader's incredible life story and Brickhill's latest best-seller could be anything other than a massive success.

Richard Burton was preferred to play Bader in the film but turned the role down. Instead, Kenneth More was chosen, who desperately wanted the part:

> I admired Douglas Bader. He was to me a Rudyard Kipling figure; you don't find them anymore. I understood him. He was a harder man than I am. To me he represented everything that every Englishman wants to be: courageous, honest, determined – but knows he hasn't the nerve or capacity to be. He has got his faults – who hasn't? He was difficult, impulsive, strong-headed; he was all these things. But I felt that someone had to give him to the world.

That More certainly did. During his research for the part, More met Bader twice: firstly over lunch before golfing at Gleneagles. The pair got on – and most importantly Bader trusted the actor. Naturally, Bader wanted the film of his life to be as accurate as possible, so some of his friends became involved, advising the film-makers. Group Captain Harry Day, for example, became official technical advisor. It was a good job, as Air Marshal Sir Denis Crowley-Milling remembered:

> When Angel discovered that I had been shot down and was hiding in St Omer at the same time Douglas [Bader] was in hospital there, he immediately came up with the ridiculous idea that the story should be changed to show me leading an attempt with the French Resistance to break Douglas out. We swiftly put a stop to that nonsense!

Bader was adamant that everyone who had played a part in his life story should be faithfully represented – which was impossible in a film of 136 minutes, dictating the need for composite characters and the 'telescoping' of certain events. For example, Cambridge graduate Lyndon Brook, who had already starred alongside Gregory Peck in *The Purple Plain* (1954), became 'Johnny Sanderson' – a composite character based upon Geoffrey Stephenson; 'Sanderson' was also used as the narrator. After the Woodley crash, in the film it was not the Australian Jack Cruttenden portrayed lifting Douglas from the wreckage, as in fact had happened and which would have dictated introducing and explaining another character, but 'Sanderson'. This was a great worry to Douglas. Some of his RAF friends were included by name, however: Harry Day was represented by Michael Warre, Stan Turner by Lee Patterson, 'Woody' Woodhall by Howard Marion Crawford, and Crowley-Milling by Basil Appleby. No. 242 Squadron's engineering officer, Warrant Officer West (Michael Ripper) also appeared, as did Air

Chief Marshal Hugh Dowding (Charles Carson) and, of course, Air Vice-Marshal Trafford Leigh-Mallory (ironically' given the 'Big Wing' dispute between 11 and 12 Groups, played by former 11 Group Battle of Britain controller Ronald Adam). Certain medical staff were also included: Nurse Brace (Dorothy Alison), the surgeon Mr Joyce (Alexander Knox), and consultant Robert Desoutter (Sydney Tafler). Naturally, a crucial character was Thelma Bader – played by former Royal Shakespeare Company and ENSA actress Muriel Pavlow (who in 1953 had starred alongside Alec Guinness in *Malta Story*).

The film was shot at Pinewood Studios, Denham Aerodrome (which became Woodley), and RAF Kenley, the latter providing a setting for multiple locations, including pre-war Cranwell and Kenley itself, Duxford, North Weald and Tangmere. As always, finding authentic aircraft was an issue. Permission was granted by the Science Museum for use of the sole surviving Bristol Bulldog (the type Bader was flying when he crashed at Woodley), whilst the Shuttleworth Collection of historic aircraft provided a Bristol Fighter, Avro 504 and Hucks Starter. Only one airworthy Hurricane, the RAF's LF363, was available, along with two static aircraft and the replica built by the film's art department. More Spitfires were available, but these Mk XVIs were visibly very different to the Mk Is, IIs and Vs Bader had flown in wartime, with a pointed rudder, cannons, tear-drop canopy, razor-back fuselage and a four-bladed propeller. The American-engined Mk XVI's nose, like the IX, was also 18in longer than the earlier Spitfires, to accommodate its more powerful engine's two-stage supercharger, which also required twin under-wing radiators. Nonetheless, they *were* Spitfires – and airworthy – eight Mk XVIs and a Griffon-engined F.22. Unsurprisingly, no airworthy German wartime aircraft were available, and so Gilbert would rely upon newsreel footage, gun camera film, studio close-ups and models to recreate combat scenes. As usual, flying kit was also improvised, using whatever surplus was readily available – none of it authentic.

Reach for the Sky was released in July 1956, the film's premier attended by the Duke of Edinburgh – but not Group Captain Douglas Bader, who, in fact, only watched the film on television some years later and declared it 'Rather good'. It was certainly an entirely sympathetic depiction – which became the biggest box office success of 1956. Indeed, the *Daily Mirror* considered Gilbert and Angel's work to be 'one of the greatest British films ever made and one of the most inspiring'. Like the fateful crash in 1931, the film was also a defining moment in Douglas's life. Millions of people watched the film worldwide in 1956 and when re-released in 1959, and have since done so on television and at their leisure since videos, DVDs and online streaming became available. The book and film super-charged the Bader story and presented it to countless people globally, making Bader a household name the world over – enabling him to do great work, it must be said, for the disabled community, to whom he was an obvious source of inspiration. Whilst, according to film industry chronicler Josh Billings, the film was a 'colossal money maker', it was not for Bader himself. Having agreed to a one-off payment, the Baders received no royalties.

A massive success though *Reach for the Sky* was, it had focused upon one hero, providing a somewhat inaccurate view of the 'Big Wing', making no mention of the controversy and row surrounding it, and made no attempt to tell the Battle of Britain's overall story. Whilst *Reach for the Sky* was another film focused on an individual's story framed by wider events, it was evident from its success that aviation related war films were lucrative business. Surprisingly, it was still some time before the overall Battle of Britain story would be told.

One notable thing about 1950s British war films, and *Angels One Five* and *Reach for the Sky* are no exceptions, is that it remained unthinkable to show the Germans in any kind of positive or sympathetic light. Bravely, Roy Ward Baker had directed *The One That Got Away*, released in 1957, based on the book of that name by James Leasor and Kendal Burt, telling the story of *Oberleutnant* Franz von Werra – an enemy fighter pilot shot down and captured during the Battle of Britain and who infamously became the only German prisoner of war to escape from Allied custody and return home. Baker was heavily criticised for heroicising a German airman (nonetheless his film was popular in both Britain and West Germany, making a profit of £3 million). Moreover, in 1956, a former Luftwaffe fighter ace currently serving in an RAF squadron on an exchange visit through NATO, was not allowed to take part in that year's annual Battle of Britain flypast over London. That same year, the Foreign Office had expressed concerns that the German war trophies displayed annually at Horse Guards could offend the democratic West Germans, who were a valued Cold War ally. Four years later, this commemoration was discontinued, and in 1961, the annual RAF flypast was scaled right back. Clearly, things were changing, the old 'triumphal mood', as the *Daily Express* put it, evaporating – and with it, potentially, the opportunity to translate the Battle of Britain's big story to the silver screen.

By the 1960s, times had very much changed in post-war Britain. The domestic television was making a significant impact, a negative one so far as British cinemas were concerned, the population increasingly watching the 'box' at home, rather than go to the 'flicks'. With reduced cinema attendance, the British film industry suffered financially. Indeed, from now on, the world of film would be dominated by America, and in Hollywood there was little or no interest in Britain's Finest Hour. Moreover, by 1960, twenty years after the event and fifteen after the Second World War ended, there were generations of young people with no personal experience of what was seen as their parents' war, with which most modern teenagers had little or no affinity. Indeed, they actively sought to distance themselves from their parents' world and values, and, owing to the fear of nuclear weapons and America's controversial war in Vietnam, the decade saw a growing and vocal peace movement. The world and internal order had also changed – and many did not now see the Battle of Britain as a big story to trumpet, but one best buried and forgotten. Fortunately, the former RAF pilot and successful Polish film producer Ben Fisz was not amongst them. Fisz, together with his director, Guy Hamilton, was determined to 'tell it how it was' and produce 'a tribute to The Few'. Both were aware of their self-set task's enormity – an even greater undertaking than most realise, perhaps, against the backdrop of the 'Swinging Sixties'.

In more recent times, however, various academic historians, not least amongst them Clive Ponting (*The Myth of 1940*) and Angus Calder (*The Myth of the Blitz*), have argued that the 'Finest Hour' was nothing of the sort and little more than a manufactured myth, something explored in detail by Malcolm Smith in his excellent study *Britain and 1940: History, Myth and Popular Memory*, and who wrote that 1940 and the Battle of Britain seems 'to have been the one genuinely heroic moment in twentieth-century British history. Britain was fighting alone against something which simply had to be stopped if any kind of acceptable values were to survive in Europe.' Guy Hamilton certainly acknowledged that 1940 was undoubtedly heavily myth-laden – but took a very different tack, one with which this author wholeheartedly supports – proclaiming that his intention was 'to destroy the myth, only to create a greater myth, because it's a fantastic story'.

Although upon release in 1969, the American financed and British made *Battle of Britain* failed to excite the critics or aspire to investors' box-office expectations, there is no doubt that Fisz and Hamilton tried their best, under often difficult wider circumstances, to tell this 'fantastic story', and, for the first – and probably last – time, succeeded in telling the big story that the Battle of Britain most certainly is. Unlike previous films lauding individuals, Fisz and Hamilton showed the disparity between the politicians' agendas and Fighter Command's requirements, and touched upon the internal argument over strategy and tactics (more of which later). The contribution of foreign aircrew was not ignored, and neither was the WAAF. The suffering of civilians, work of the emergency services and Observer Corps, along with the contribution made by radar, is all included. Bravely, the Germans, twelve years after Baker was criticised for *The One That Got Away*, were shown as a brave and skilled adversary, although the portly and flamboyant Luftwaffe chief and Hitler's deputy, Hermann Göring, rightly, was not portrayed so sympathetically. To aviation enthusiasts the world over, though, what made – and still makes – the film unique was the extensive use of actual aircraft, and brilliantly filmed and edited aerial sequences, married to a superb soundtrack by Sir William Walton and Ron Goodwin. Unlike *Angels One Five* and *Reach for the Sky*, it was also in full technicolour, making it more contemporary to modern audiences.

Just how historically accurate the film is, however, is not an easy question to answer, for it is a complex one. At the film's press conference, Battle of Britain ace Squadron Leader James 'Ginger' Lacey, who had worked as a technical advisor on the project, claimed that *Battle of Britain* was a catalogue of no less than 193 errors. Some were unavoidable and dictated

A recreated RAF fighter squadron dispersal in the 1969 *Battle of Britain* film. *(Historic Military Press)*

The hangar actually being blown up during filming at Duxford! *(Historic Military Press)*

'Messerschmitts!' *(Historic Military Press)*

by the availability of aircraft types and flying kit, for example, but clearly an effort was made to align these things as closely as practically possible with the real deal. These are, in any case, arguably micro details unaffecting the overall storytelling and end result, and noticed only by we enthusiasts. On the macro stage there are certain things not quite right, or correctly interpreted and presented. Without question, though, the producers of *Battle of Britain* have left behind a rich legacy – and have done this big and '*fantastic* story' a great and lasting service.

Battle of Britain, without doubt, succeeded in telling the big story, whilst taking some liberties, by necessity with micro detail and concluding with the false impression of an abrupt and final defeat. The aerial scenes remain second to none and out takes are film makers' standard go-to source for such footage even today. The film was made over fifty years ago now, long before the digital age, and those aerial scenes, using largely real aircraft, are its strength. Today, flying Spitfires and Hurricanes are aplenty, and we still have a number of airworthy Buchon 'Me 109s' in addition to actual Me 109Es – but we have no airworthy *Stuka* or any of the twin-engined German bombers or fighters. The other problem is that the numbers of aircraft required would be financially prohibitive. Computer Generated Images (CGI) provide a cost-effective alternative and compromise – but this technology is not yet sufficiently advanced, in my personal view, to be entirely convincing, and seems to be more a matter of providing a shock and awe viewer experience. So, the issues around using real vintage aircraft are a significant factor in why there has been no other film like *Battle of Britain* – and Guy Hamilton did such a good job in 1969 that another film is probably unnecessary anyway. Furthermore, whether there would be sufficient interest in today's world to make such a project commercially viable is a moot point, and, of course, the British film industry is not what once it was.

Although the Battle of Britain has not featured in British cinema since 1969, the subject has been visited by eastern and central European cinema. In 2001, the Czech director Jan Sverák gave us *Dark Blue World*, a film about free Czech pilots fighting with the RAF. In the film, a Spitfire attacks a train – that scene alone costing more to film than the entire budget for the director's previous movie, the Oscar-winning *Koyla*. The reception to *Dark Blue World* was mixed, but nonetheless it grossed $2,300,000 worldwide and won several international awards. In 2018, Polish director David Blair made *303 Squadron* (also released under the titles *Hurricane* and *Mission of Honour*), telling the story of the famous Polish squadron during the Battle

Left: The iconic poster and logo: *Battle of Britain*.

Below: The invitation and passes for the film's premier sent to Battle of Britain Spitfire pilot Wing Commander Roger Boulding.

of Britain, recreating combat scenes using CGI – the result being more spectacular than convincing. Blair's film only made $7,694,425, less than the reported $8,000,000 budget, and there, for now, the Battle of Britain story in cinema ends.

But what about television? The advent of domestic television saw a burgeoning interest in producing programmes for broadcasting on the 'telly', whist concurrently the British film industry declined. In 1988, Derek Robinson's irreverent novel *Piece of Cake*, following the fortunes of 'Hornet Squadron' during the early war period, including the Battle of Britain, appeared on our television screens as a six-part London Weekend Television series. Like the book itself, reaction to the series was mixed, the highlight for aviation enthusiasts being some thrilling low-level flying by the late, great, Ray Hanna in Spitfire MH434, and the series failed to live up to expectations. There were 12.1 million viewers who watched episode one, but only 9.2 million saw the series out. In 1991, the popular British actor Nigel Havers appeared as 'Hugh Fleming', a Battle of Britain Spitfire pilot recovering from horrific burns, in *A Perfect Hero*, loosely based upon a novel, *The Long-Haired Boy* by Christopher Matthew, which had been inspired and informed by Richard Hope Hillary's classic memoir *The Last*

Squadron Leader Geoffrey Harry Augustus Wellum at RAF Coningsby with Squadron Leader Anthony Parkinson and Spitfire P7350 in 2012. *(Jarrod Cotter)*

Enemy. Unfortunately the series was bland at best and poorly received. Nearly twenty years would pass before the Battle of Britain again appeared dramatised on our home televisions.

During the Battle of Britain, one Geoffrey Harry Augustus Wellum was an 18-year-old Spitfire pilot serving at Biggin Hill with 92 Squadron. Known as 'Boy', Wellum survived intensive action, earning the DFC, became an ace and later fought in the defence of Malta before suffering a breakdown. Although Wellum did not keep a diary, he did make some notes on his experiences whilst en route to Malta, and retained his personal pilot's flying log book. Thirty-five years after the war, partially as a means of exorcising the violent and traumatic past, he sat down with these aged references and started writing – and didn't stop until his story was committed to paper. The book, though, would not be published for over twenty years, until produced and distributed by Viking Books, under the evocative title *First Light*, in 2002. The following year, Penguin distributed the title – which leaped onto the best-seller list and catapulted its very modest author into the public eye. The book was lauded as amongst the most honest, accurate and gripping memoirs to have emerged from the air war, with which assessment I would entirely agree. As the seventieth anniversary of the Battle of Britain approached, Wellum's best-seller also inspired film producer and director Matthew Whiteman:

> In a way, this was a dream come true – getting the chance to dramatise *First Light* for BBC Two to mark the 70th anniversary. The book is Geoffrey Wellum's memoir of what it was like to be an eighteen-year old Spitfire pilot, thrust into the gut-wrenching, life and death struggle of the most violent aerial combat ever. And it also deals with his mental disintegration in eighteen relentless months on the frontline.
>
> This was one film where we had to get not just the emotional thrust right, but also the historical detail. There are a lot of people out there for whom this really matters – and I am one of them. It's not a question of being 'nerdy' – I believe we all know when something feels right; whether it is in the tone of a performance, costume, props, or whatever else clouds the mind of a director trying to truly evoke the time and place of a story.
>
> The conversations started early about getting Spitfires airborne. But what is it they say? Never work with animals, children … or, in my case, vintage aircraft! We were discussing

a scene in which [Geoffrey Harry Augustus] 'Boy' Wellum, the hero of our story, makes his first flight in a Spitfire, and our actor, Sam Heughan, couldn't wait to get into the air. The problem was how to convince the audience that he was actually at the controls of a Spitfire for the first time, rocketing through the clouds. The big snag was that there was no way we could get Sam airborne in a real Spitfire. This scene was crucial to the story, appearing little more than ten minutes after the opening of the film. We had to produce a sequence breath-taking enough to make the audience believe that flying the Spitfire was love at first sight for 'Boy'. We had access to a real Spitfire – and the budget for maybe forty-five minutes flying time – but the Spit is a single-seater and there was no question of anybody but a very experienced pilot taking the controls of several million pounds' worth of vintage aeroplane. And we also had access to a replica Spitfire, which could be shoved about on the ground, but had no proper cockpit interior. We soon decided that rather than shooting costly air to air footage, we would use outtakes from the Battle of Britain movie – and enhance it with CGI.

This was a huge task in itself; viewing around fifty hours-worth of unused and unseen material, but it was great that we could give some of this footage the light of day at last! The old movie footage was lovely stuff, but the code letters and numbers on the side of Spits in the movie footage didn't begin to match our real or replica planes. One plane was brown and green, the other brown and grey. And the real one was based at Wycombe Air Park, whilst our replica was eighty miles away on the drama set outside Dunstable. Bringing the replica down would nuke what little was left of the budget, but if we didn't, Sam could be walking in the rain to the replica on one location, and then climbing into the cockpit (to shoot an authentic start-up sequence) in bright sunshine on the other. It was quite a headache! Somehow, we wangled it in the end. New codes and numbers were put on the replica – and the owner was persuaded to bring his baby to stand side-by-side with the real McCoy.

Then we found a friendly pilot, prepared to have the back cockpit of his two-seater Russian YAK trainer converted to look like a Spitfire cockpit interior. Sam leapt in, surrounded by high definition (HD) mini-cams, and took to the sky with his script taped to the instrument panel. Meantime, our real Spit took off with the pilot delivering [Geoffrey Harry Augustus] 'Boy' Wellum's point of view (by way of a specially designed camera mounting on his flying helmet). When we got into the edit, the whole story came together. By combining Sam walking to the replica Spitfire, the real thing taxiing, Sam in close-up in the back seat of the YAK – and then cutting to his point of view, shot in the real Spit, we got the hair-raising images of 'his' first take-off. Once airborne, we started to inter-cut Sam in the cockpit with flying footage from the Battle of Britain movie.

… And that was the easiest of the flying sequences in the film!

Then we had to work out how to create a full-blooded dogfight, and a nightmare flight in torrential rain over the channel – during which 'Boy' shoots down a German bomber. Looking back on it all now, I can't believe that we shot the whole drama, including the flying, in just nine days. We couldn't have done it without the orchestration of the first assistant director Chris Carreras, whose experience spans the *Bourne* movies, *United 93*, *Harry Potter* and many other big films. And Chris was dead right when he took one last long look at the schedule just before we began the shoot, and, having considered the weather and all the other infinitely frightening variables, commented dryly: 'We're going to have to be 100% lucky on this one!'

Geoffrey Wellum didn't have time to visit us on set – but before the shoot, as I was scripting, we spent a huge amount of time together. And afterwards, during post-production, Geoff worked very closely with the CGI artists to make sure we got the tracer fire absolutely correct in the air battles. Geoff explained to the CGI folks that real tracer doesn't fly in straight lines – like *Star Wars*; it curves and snakes across the sky, governed by the motion of the aircraft and the air.

Working so closely with Geoffrey has made *First Light* a unique experience both for me as a director and I think, for the audience. The combination of Geoff's expert eye-witness

> guidance, and actually getting Sam up in the air – instead of in some faked-up studio cockpit – has made the film an incredibly rich experience for everybody. And, I guess, is just about as close as any of us would want to get to the nerve-jangling terrors of air combat, Battle of Britain style.
>
> Creating the tension on the ground, however, was just as important as in the air. I love the waiting scene in dispersal before Geoff's first combat – the tinkling of teaspoons in cups, the rustle of a magazine and flight leader, Brian Kingcome, chewing on his match … And then the sudden shrill ringing of the phone – scramble! Geoff watched these scenes with great interest and said that he felt the film perfectly caught the mood and emotions he felt at the time, both on the ground and in the air. The war literally tore Geoff's emotions apart. If he had not been rested from flying before going back for a second tour of combat, I think he would be the first to say he would no longer be with us now. But at that time – as he reflects in the film – he was desperate to fight on until the bitter end. Geoff still carries a sense of guilt that he survived when so many he knew died. This was the truth for many soldiers – the feeling that they had been taken off the line before the 'job was done', and now were left to watch others die whom they could no longer help or protect.
>
> Geoffrey hates to be called a hero, but his efforts, and that of all those around him seventy years ago, saved us from the terrors of Nazi occupation. I believe that his war – the Battle of Britain, was the key turning point of World War Two. If England had fallen to Germany, the Britain could not have been used as the launching point for the D-Day landings and the liberation of Europe. I salute you, Geoff – however reluctant you are to be called a hero. I salute you and all those that fought alongside you. And I'm sure the audience will, too.

Sam Heughan, who more recently found fame in the excellent historical *Outlander* drama series, played Geoffrey Harry Augustus Wellum in Whiteman's docudrama:

> I have always been particularly interested in World War Two and the Battle of Britain. I guess my first contact was through

Ben Aldridge (left) portraying Brian Kingcome, and Sam Heughan depicting Geoffrey Harry Augustus 'Boy' Wellum in Matthew Whiteman's BBC 2 docudrama *First Light*. *(Etienne Bol)*

Sam Heughan's '"Boy" Wellum' was convincing. *(Etienne Bol)*

my grandfather; he took me to the Imperial War Museum etc at an early age, and had himself been called up to fight. I think this influenced my career. I have always been cast in many period productions. My first job leaving drama school was *Island at War*, a big budget ITV drama focusing on the Channel Islands and the German occupation. I did a lot of research; there are a few documentaries and books on the subject. We filmed on the Isle of Man, which in its own way lent itself to feeling like a small community removed from the mainland. I have also filmed several period documentaries and worked on many stage productions set in that period. I guess what fascinates me is the 'spirit' of the time. It seems to me that the British Isles were isolated and the war brought out the 'British' spirit, one where the people were industrious and collaborative, and learnt to survive. Also, the great tragedy, the bigger cause and the personal struggle. I guess everything seems more poignant at wartime, time and life is precious, and should not be wasted. It lends itself to a great setting for drama – I guess that's why there are so many fantastic TV and film productions about the war. I also grew up watching the old 1940s movies, which all had a slight glamour, the uniforms and hairstyles. Only in more recent years, though, has the true grim reality of war been more accurately portrayed. To me, productions based on reality or history are a real gift to an actor, as you have so much research and source material.

When I was asked to audition for *First Light*, I read the script and instantly loved it. I did some research, saw that it was a book and read it. I think I finished it in one day; it was SO good, readable and touching. It became the whole casts' handbook. An insight into the world of 92 Squadron and the characters who fought, lived and died alongside each other. The pictures were evocative and the honesty in which Geoffrey revealed his inner most thoughts were a gift. I had to do it!

I met with Matthew Whiteman, the Director (also a pilot), and instantly felt that we got on. He has a great wealth of knowledge of the period, and, more than that, it's his passion. Matthew had also already done some great docudramas on the period (*Double X* is fascinating, I'd love to make it into a film), so had written and produced similar projects. In preparation, we talked, and had rehearsals. I re-read Geoffrey's book (the true inspiration and actually all we needed, it's all in there!), plus I wanted to understand more about Spitfires and what it meant to be a pilot. I found a reproduction of the Spitfire Pilot's Notes, an amazing pilot's aid. It was not a dissimilar way to how pilots learnt in those days. I studied the book and learnt all the controls for the cockpit and the start-up sequence. In the scene where I have my eyes closed and am being tested by the aircrew, I actually found I knew exactly where to find the 'Trim, brake, fuel select' etc. I also visited the Imperial War museum and RAF Museum site at Hendon.

However, again, on set it was Matthew who had the eye for everything. Much of the memorabilia in 'Boy Geoffrey's' home were Matthew's personal toys. I think in many ways, the film married Geoffrey's and Matthew's absolute love of flying. I felt that was the strong message in his book. Geoffrey's joy of flight, the freedom of the air. That's why the first flight in a Spitfire is such a large section of film. The ability to escape the dark goings-on of wartime and be free to glide anywhere, must have been amazing. These beautiful machines, being used for foul purposes. I was fortunate that we had a Spitfire to film in. I spent a large amount of time in the cockpit. It was a magical experience. I am six feet and three inches tall, not the perfect height for a pilot! However, once inside it felt very familiar. You can see what a great design it was, the mechanics beautifully engineered. The smell of grease, the ticking of the engine; I fell in love with the aircraft too. And when it fires up!

We also did some flying, an air sequence where I went up and did barrel-rolls, loop the loops etc. What a thrill! Terrifying also, to know these young men were put in charge of these powerful machines – fitted with guns – given comparatively little training, and then left to see if they'd survive ... I remember my first day, watching a Tiger-moth performing some aerial acrobatics and thinking how graceful and brave it was of the pilot. A young man's game, easier if one were less aware of the consequences. How those boys grew up quickly, we wanted the characters to age through the film. Experiencing the terrors and mundane side of the War, fraying our nerves and hopefully doing a little justice to what the real pilots went through. We can only imagine ...

The filming schedule was intense, maybe two-three weeks. I remember it was full on. We banded together as a team of young pilots. We drank beer in the evening, smoked cigarettes. The boredom of a filmset, waiting around, maybe not too dissimilar to the wait before being scrambled? (Without the threat!) The heavier themes of being at war were maybe found through our own personal experiences. We would discuss the book, the war, and I think everyone involved had some connection through relatives involved. As filming came to a close, we all felt deeply upset. We had all invested in it and knew how much we wanted to do Geoffrey a service.

Matthew had been working with Geoffrey for some time but thought it best I didn't meet him until after filming, so as not to try and mimic him, but find my own way into the part. Though Matthew knew him very well, and would answer questions or give me occasional insights into his character, I was desperate to meet Geoffrey and a few weeks after filming completed I did. We met at the RAF Club at Green Park. Geoffrey walked in, full of energy and humour. An amazing character, charming all around him, but yet clearly still living with the effects of living through World War Two. It's still with him and he'll never lose that, I also don't think he wants to. We must not forget.

The reason his book works, is his personal account of a tenacious young man surviving on his natural abilities during a time of great hardship. It doesn't feel dated, as it could apply to any period of history, however it was indeed a time of great change and high deeds. These days, challenges are different. I wouldn't say younger generations are forgetting, but I guess it's getting more distant, and more recent happenings (Afghanistan) are focused on.

I feel deeply honoured to have met Geoffrey Wellum. I'm lucky to have been able to work on this project and hopefully make sure people don't forget what these people did for us. Geoffrey wouldn't say he's a hero, he'd say that he and comrades did what they did just to survive. Yet we should be grateful – and celebrate their deeds.

The Lion Television docudrama *First Light* was broadcast on BBC 2, 14 September 2010.

In this chapter, we have seen how the Battle of Britain has been represented over the years, through wartime newsreels, official 'shorts' and feature films, and beyond into post-war Britain. In this investigation we have considered the factors influencing production and representation, including propaganda, the state of society at a given time, financial constraints, and how the film industry became dominated not by Pinewood or Denham, but Hollywood. We have seen how it took a long time for anyone to attempt telling the overall story, and, indeed, to date that has still only ever been done once, through Guy Hamilton's 1969 epic *Battle of Britain* – which has stood the test of time. Although Matthew Whiteman's BBC 2 docudrama *First Light*, based upon Geoffrey Harry Augustus Wellum's best-selling memoir, was made for television and not cinema, which is really the focus of this book, it has been included here because, so far as this historian is concerned, whereas *Battle of Britain* remains the highpoint of the subject in cinema, *First Light* occupies that position so far as British television is concerned.

Today, though, the broadcasting landscape has very much changed since 2010; back then, it was a limited number of television channels that monopolised viewing – but the internet has changed all that. Today, we have a plethora of broadcasting channels, unconnected the television broadcasting and accessed online – even the 2024 Spielberg and Hanks mini-series *Masters of the Air*, for example, concerning the American Eighth Air Force, was not broadcast on mainstream television but via Apple TV. YouTube is also an incredible sharing platform for would-be film-makers, amateurs and professionals, and these days the equipment and technology to make a simple film is relatively inexpensive. Indeed, we can all make a film today on our mobile phones. What all of this means is that there is much more chance of so-called specialist films being made and shared, via an increasing number of viewing portals. A great example of this is the recently produced *Forgotten*. A short, simple, effective film about a missing RAF pilot, *Forgotten* was initiated and written by Philip Harvey, a long-time researcher of 'The Missing Few' and deeply moved himself by this lack of closure. Deservedly, in 2024, *Forgotten* has rampaged through various film festivals, sweeping the board with, at the time of writing, twenty-seven domestic and international awards, eight of them winners, and numerous finalist awards. With, at the time of writing, nine more festivals to go, it is likely that *Forgotten* will enjoy further success – and once the BAFTA

Promotional graphic for the successful short film *Forgotten. (Philip Harvey)*

nominations are released in October 2024, the film will go on public release. So, in the recent past, times have changed, technology and communications have moved forward to unanticipated heights – making anything possible, or so it seems – as Philip Harvey and friends have proved with *Forgotten.*

So far as the Battle of Britain on screen goes, therefore, it is very much a case of 'watch this space'…

Chapter Six

Aviation Archaeology and the Battle of Britain – 'The Missing Few'

The epic *Battle of Britain* film, which premiered in 1969, inspired a whole new wave of interest in the near thirty-year old air battle. Thanks to the film, the vintage warbird movement, for example, began, as aged airframes were returned to the air for the flying sequences, and what became known as 'aviation archaeology', with its own peculiar cult following. Over time, however, an emotive and controversial matter developed, which would set the authorities and enthusiasts at odds: 'The Missing Few'. Aviation archaeology, though, is far from just about the recovery of missing aircrew, and, for sure, there have been countless legitimate recoveries contributing greatly to our understanding of this epic conflict. The saga of 'The Missing Few', however, is of primary importance when considering the impact of aviation archaeology on remembering the Battle of Britain – and hence why it is the focus of this chapter.

Essentially, aviation archaeology involves the discovery of aircraft crash sites and the recovery of remaining artefacts for conservation, sometimes by independent individuals, or, more often, back in the day, by one of the many amateur enthusiast groups or countless museums which sprang up, nationwide, to pursue the activity. The Battle of Britain, of course, held a particular fascination, and there was no shortage of crash sites, RAF and Luftwaffe, to investigate in southern England. These Battle of Britain sites were eagerly and impatiently sought in what could be described as a scramble as groups competed to dig the most sites and recover the most sought-after aircraft parts, control columns, engines, and armament being high on the list. Depending upon the nature of the crash and site, sometimes a dig would be by hand, perhaps only recovering small fragments; other times, in soft ground, a machine would be used to dig deep and lift out heavy items, such as propellers and engines. There was fierce rivalry, and given the speed at which Battle of Britain crash sites were picked over, digs were sometimes less than thorough.

The majority of the local aviation museums involved were small and self-funded, and over time various of these have disappeared, their collections sold off and absorbed by larger concerns.

Although crash sites and eyewitnesses were abundant, many official records remained secret and unavailable to the public, meaning that no list existed in the public domain of aircraft casualties. Appeals were made in southern newspapers for contact with eyewitnesses to crashes, who would show the enthusiasts the sites concerned. Sometimes the witnesses knew the type of aircraft concerned, often not. This meant, therefore, that digs sometimes began with no knowledge of which aircraft was concerned, the type and specific machine only being identified through items recovered. Back in 1969, there was no law or formal rules regulating this new activity, which was unprecedented, the only permission required to recover and crashed aircraft being that of the relevant landowner. That, however, would soon change.

Given how intense the fighting had been, the number of crashed aircraft involved, which often came down in remote rural areas, sometimes unseen by anyone, the RAF maintenance units and civilian sub-contractors were overwhelmed by the amount of recovery work involved. Frequently, pilots were killed or too badly wounded to abandon their aircraft, and so went in with their machines. Some were recovered, others not; at least two were only recovered at the time owing to investigative work by their own families, namely Flight Lieutenant William Rhodes-Moorhouse DFC of 601 Squadron, and Sergeant Peter McIntosh of 605 Squadron. Many casualties remained missing, it being assumed that they had crashed into the Thames Estuary or the sea; aviation archaeologists would soon discover that certain of the missing were still to be found in south-east England.

One very active early group was the former Ashford and Tenterden Recovery Group (A&TRG), founded in 1970 and chaired by the now late David Buchanan. By 1972, the Group had recovered nine aircraft and possessed sufficient wreckage to open a museum at Brenzett, on Kent's Romney Marsh. Having obtained vague information of a 'Spitfire' crash site near Goudhurst in Kent, Buchanan's team interviewed eyewitnesses who described having seen the pilot bale out and land safely in a hop field. The crash site was duly located at Bockingfold Farm and permission obtained for a recovery, which went ahead on 21 May 1972.

David Buchanan:

> We nearly didn't find the wreck at all. We were searching a wood about half a mile away until a local woman said she

> thought we were in the wrong place. We checked the new site that she showed us with metal detectors, and there it was. Once the impact spot had been located we brought in a mechanical shovel. Each load dug out was piled next to the hole and later sifted through a metal screen for bits and pieces of wreckage. At the bottom of the hole we found the engine and bits of armour plate from behind the pilot's seat. The plane had crashed into a stream when it was shot down and we could not have reached it had the farmer not diverted the watercourse four or five years before. Even so, we were digging in mud and slurry, and it was hard to find anything.

Amongst the wreckage found were certain items indicating that the fighter was actually a Hurricane, not a Spitfire, as claimed by eyewitnesses. On a piece of plywood airframe was found serial number 'P2728'. When the mechanical digger exposed a parachute pack, its contents spilling out, it was obvious that the unfortunate pilot remained buried at the site. Buchanan immediately halted the recovery and contacted the local police. Whilst awaiting the arrival of Kent Police, the 'spoil heap' was picked over, revealing certain of the pilot's personal effects: a nail file and a silver cigarette case. Upon attendance, the constable, having no experience of such an occurrence, sought advice from the Ashford coroner and CWGC. In due course, instructions were received for the recovery to proceed – and soon the pilot's remains were recovered from his shattered cockpit. The total depth reached during the excavation was 4.5m.

David Buchanan:

> This was the first time we had found human remains during an excavation. Normally if we heard of a wreck that may be that of a missing pilot, we did not dig. This time we did not know about the pilot, and in fact were searching for a Spitfire, the pilot of which we were told had baled out. After the pilot's remains were recovered they were treated with the utmost respect and handed over to the Police.

Having received the pilot's remains, Chief Inspector Walter Smith issued a statement on behalf of Cranbrook Police: 'The MOD is virtually certain that they have identified the plane and pilot, but no names will be issued until they are absolutely sure and have had a chance to contact any relatives who may still be living.'

The serial number, P2728, confirmed that this was a Hawker Hurricane of 607 'County of Durham' Squadron – and that the pilot was Pilot Officer George Drake, a South African, reported missing on 9 September 1940.

No. 607 Squadron, in fact, had only arrived at Tangmere from Usworth the previous day – as Squadron Leader Harry Welford, then a pilot officer, later recalled,

> We arrived at a completely blitzed aerodrome where we were greeted by the remnants of 43 Squadron: some on crutches, others with an arm in a sling, and yet another, who had had his face torn apart by an exploding cannon shell, with a head swathed in bandages. Though they had suffered so many casualties it was quite amazing to see them walking about. Needless to say they were very pleased to see us, having just been up on the third sortie that day and were still waiting for news of the latest casualties.
>
> We only had time to re-fuel when we were called out on an operational trip that evening. There was no interception, however, and no casualties. The next morning, to my great disappointment, I was not called upon to fly and later the Squadron went off. In the event I was the more fortunate, as of twelve Hurricanes *six* were shot down. Three officers were killed and three sergeants wounded. Amongst the casualties were Stuart Parnall, my best friend, Scotty Lenahan and the young South African George Drake.
>
> Somehow we could not believe it. No one talked about it and we all hoped for news to

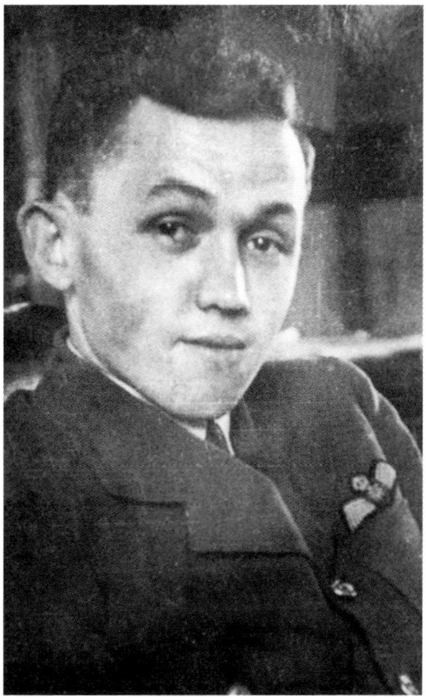

South African Pilot Officer George Drake – the first of 'The Missing Few' to be recovered.

> filter through from some remote pub or perhaps a hospital. No news came, so we hardened ourselves to the worst: 'Killed in Action'. We bit back our tears and our sorrow. It was 'You heard about Stuart and Scotty? Rotten luck, wasn't it?' Someone would add 'And young George, bloody good blokes all of them'. After that epitaph, the mater would be dismissed with the ordering of another round of drinks to avoid any trace of further sentiment.
>
> I had known George Drake for only a very short time. He came as a replacement to 607 at Usworth during the reformation after the losses in France. George Drake always seemed to me very young, with a boyish open face but beneath the surface was latent belligerence. He had a constant inquiring mind and seemed much interested in how the other half, we 'Brits', lived. No bad thing as he would expect to be amongst us for some time. I don't remember any particular incident but a feeling was that he was too young to be thrown into battle. I think he was barely out of his teens, but then so were others. It still hurts to talk about it.

New to the increased tempo of fighting over south-east England, 607 Squadron had arrived at one of the 'hottest' sector stations at an extremely busy time. Without time to adjust to these new operational conditions, it was inevitable that the lethal Me 109s would harshly treat the 'County of Durham' Hurricanes. New to the fray over 11 Group, 607 Squadron went on patrol flying the useless vic formation – and paid the price.

Pilot Officer George Drake's family were traced by the authorities in Boksburg, near Johannesburg. Although both parents had died, they had continued questioning the MOD regarding their son's fate right up to the 1960s. It was believed that Drake had crashed into the sea; although on 10 September 1940, Squadron Leader Goodman of 49 MU reported that a Hurricane had crashed at Goudhurst, the aircraft was not salvaged and nothing existed to connect the crash with 607 Squadron's missing man.

Naturally, the discovery of Drake's remains had by law to be reported to Her Majesty's Coroner, a judicial office independent of local and central government, whose duty is to ascertain the cause of any sudden or unexplained death, investigating any unusual circumstances and hopefully identifying the cause. The coroner's inquest into the death of Pilot Officer George Drake was held at Ashford on 7 November 1972, the verdict 'Killed by an Act of War' returned. Thereafter a military funeral was arranged at Brookwood Military Cemetery for 14.30 hrs, 22 November 1972, which was attended by the pilot's brothers, Eric and Arthur Drake. The coffin was borne by serving airmen from RAF Odiham, and riflemen of the RAF Regiment fired a six-gun salute as the coffin was lowered into the grave. An RAF chaplain, the Reverend David Barnes officiated, and said,

> This young man came from a part of the [British] Empire, like so many others only to die fighting for the sacred cause of human freedom. When he laid down his life pursuing what is the basic right of every man, he was a long way from his South African home and family.

Arthur Drake:

> Joining the RAF to fight for Britain was George's only ambition. He had to work his passage across here and then he went out to fight knowing that the odds were against him and his friends. He was very proud of what he was doing and we have always been proud of him, down the years.

The military funeral of Pilot Officer George Drake at Brookwood.

Left: Pilot Officer Drake's brothers, Eric and Arthur, at their long-lost elder sibling's military funeral in 1972.

Below: Eric (fifth from left) and Arthur Drake (fourth from right) with the now late David Buchanan and his recovery team with the shattered Merlin of Pilot Officer George Drake's Hurricane, P2728.

So it was that Pilot Officer George Drake was finally brought in from the cold and appropriately laid to rest – and made history as the first of 'The Missing Few' to be recovered long after the Battle of Britain.

The following year, David Buchanan's team were back in the news, having discovered a missing German airman in similar circumstances to the recovery of Pilot Officer George Drake. In September 1973, the A&TRG excavated a crash site at Burmarsh, also on Romney Marsh, confirming it to be a Me 109 – and discovering the pilot's remains at a depth of 24ft. Having notified the authorities, the pilot's remains were taken to Folkestone's Royal Victoria Hospital, the South Kent coroner, John Clarke, telling the press that 'We believe we can identify the pilot, but an inquest is necessary so that proper documents can be issued if, as we expect, the Germans wish to take him back home.' According the *Daily Mail*, 'Berlin has been asked for a formal declaration of the mission', and that the new Luftwaffe had been asked to check its records to confirm the pilot's identity. The *Folkestone Herald* quoted one of the diggers: 'Don't make us out to be grave-diggers. It was a shock for us to find the pilot still in the plane.'

Just forty-eight-hours after British newspapers broke the story that a Me 109 pilot had been recovered, the German authorities, having identified the casualty as *Leutnant* Werner Knittel, traced the pilot's widow, Dr Inge Knittel, her missing husband having been conclusively identified via his identity disc. A famous pre-war sports pilot, Spanish Civil War veteran and *Adjutant* of III/JG 51, Knittel was reported missing after a high-altitude fighter sweep over Kent on 28 October 1940; he was not returned to Germany, as the coroner had anticipated, but interred with full military honours at the *Soldatenfriedhoff* (German War Cemetery) on Cannock Chase in Staffordshire. So it was that from beyond the grave *Leutnant* Werner Knittel made the news once more – this time as the first Luftwaffe Battle of Britain airman to be recovered by aviation archaeologists.

By 1974, Buchanan had presented the authorities with the remains of two pilots reported missing in the Battle of Britain and another, German pilot, *Gefreiter* Richard Riedel of 2/JG 3, recovered that November; shot down just after the Battle of Britain officially ended, on 17 November 1940. Understandably, with missing pilots being recovered with such apparent frequency, the general public, unaware of the background context to these crashes, were confused and concerned as to why this was happening. Why had the authorities not recovered these fallen warriors either at the time or afterwards, and given them the decent and respectful burial they deserved, giving their families peace? It was an emotive issue – one which

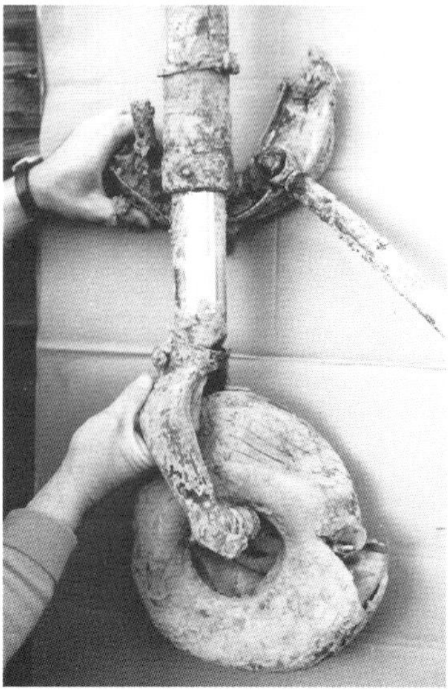

Above: *Leutnant* Werner Knittel, the first German Battle of Britain airman to be recovered post-war.

Left: The tail wheel of *Leutnant* Werner Knittel's Me 109.

embarrassed and became a public relations disaster for the MOD. The 'justified public disquiet' was alarming for the MOD, and at that time the exact number of missing airman still buried with the aircraft in south-east England remained unknown. Media coverage of aircraft recoveries led an increase in the number of groups and individuals pursuing the aviation archaeology interest, meaning that the recovery of more airman, further embarrassing the MOD, was a distinct possibility. Consequently, in March 1975, the MOD issued a set of guidelines in an attempt to regulate the activity.

These first 'Guidelines for Recovery Groups' required that in the event of human remains being discovered, they must be treated with respect, the recovery must cease and the authorities informed immediately. Also, the MOD demanded that under no circumstances should the pilot's identity, confirmed or speculative, be released until the casualty section had traced and informed surviving family. These rules were sensible but carried no weight in law, relying entirely upon the cooperation and goodwill of those concerned. Any contravention carried no fine or other formal punishment, only the withdrawal of MOD cooperation. Things would get much worse.

Another most active recovery group was the late Mike Llewellyn MBE's Kent Battle of Britain Museum (KBoBM), which was initially based at Chilham Castle and now located on the former forward airfield at Hawkinge (see Chapter Seven). Llewellyn had spoken to a Michael Wigmore, who, an 11-year-old schoolboy, had excitedly watched the air battle overhead; on one occasion, he recalled that 'A Spitfire's engine was screaming as the plane came down, very close to me. It crashed with a loud thud at a 45° angle and immediately burst into flame. It was completely out of control and the pilot made no attempt to pull out of the dive.'

The aircraft had crashed into the remote Grove Marshes at Wickhambreux, near Canterbury. At this time, official RAF records remained closed, until 1975, so when Mike and friends gathered at the crash site on 28 March 1971, all the recovery team had to go on was Michael Wigmore's recollection that the aircraft was a Spitfire. The site was owned by the Nature Conservancy, which preserved the site as a bird sanctuary, which gave conditional permission for a dig: as no eyewitness evidence suggested a parachute, as a precautionary measure, in case human remains were disturbed, the police must be present. This was duly arranged and on the day in question Llewellyn's team were met on site by a police superintendent and the Coroner's Officer (a constable), two sergeants and a scenes of crime photographer; a range warden was also present.

The late Mike Llewellyn and the Kent Battle of Britain Museum team with police officers during the recovery of the Grove Marsh Spitfire in 1971. *(KBoBM)*

A machine was brought in but conditions were extremely difficult in the marshy ground. At a depth of 8ft, a Merlin engine was found, confirming that this was a British fighter – but then another bucketful revealed an unopened parachute pack and what appeared to be human teeth and uniform fabric. This grim discovery was brought to the attention of the policemen present, and, having already recovered the Merlin, Llewellyn discontinued the recovery. This was, remember, a year before the discovery of Pilot Officer George Drake, by David Buchanan and friends, so there was absolutely no precedent. Given that human remains were obviously present, however, Llewellyn felt that it was inappropriate for KBoBM, an amateur civilian organisation, to proceed, and naturally assumed that the police officers would do the necessary with the coroner and military authorities. This, however, for whatever reason, did not happen.

The Merlin and parachute recovered from Grove Marsh was displayed at Chilham Castle, research indicating that the Spitfire was R6713 of 65 Squadron, in which a Polish pilot, Flying Officer Franciszek Gruszka, was reported missing on 18 August 1940. This reached the ear of Squadron Leader David Glaser DFC, a test pilot who had flown with Gruszka during the Battle of Britain, and he informed the Polish Squadron Leader Boleslaw Drobinski, who had escaped from Poland with Gruszka and was posted to 65 Squadron as a replacement after his friend was reported missing. The pair brought the matter to the MOD's attention, insisting that the RAF should mount an official recovery operation. Consequently, on 15 April 1974, an RAF team recovered R6713 and the remains of 30-year-old Gruszka, who was identified from an inscription on his gold-coloured propelling pencil, found with him.

Polish Flying Officer Franciszek Gruszka of 65 Squadron.

The coroner's inquest took place at Canterbury on 1 May 1975, at which the police officers attending the KBoBM dig in 1971 denied having been shown the teeth fragments at that time. As Mike Llewellyn's solicitor, John Tickner, argued, having arranged the police presence there was absolutely no reason for them not to have been informed of this gruesome discovery, not least because the officers were actually present at the time for that specific purpose.

Years later, Mike Llewellyn commented,

> I left the matter firmly with the authorities, the onus lay with them, not with us to recover the pilot … Hindsight is a wonderful thing … In those days we trusted the authorities, and having informed those present at the dig of the circumstances, we assumed that they would take over – that is, of course, why they were there. We wondered what was going to happen, and local rumour suggested that the location would be turned into a war grave. Another rumour was that due to the ongoing Cold War, and with Poland behind the 'Iron Curtain', no action

> would be taken and the status quo maintained. Whatever, so far as we were concerned the authorities were aware.

Ultimately, Mr Mowll's verdict was that Flying Officer Franciszek Gruszka had died of 'injuries sustained on war service'.

On 17 July 1975, Gruszka was buried with full military honours at Northwood Cemetery, joining there many other Polish comrades who had made the ultimate sacrifice. Because Poland was still behind the 'Iron Curtain', the first his family knew of the recovery and funeral was when a shocked Piotr Gruszka, the pilot's brother, heard the news on the BBC World Service. Present at the funeral, were three former 65 Squadron pilots who had fought shoulder-to-shoulder with Flying Officer Franciszek Gruszka: Commander Jeffrey Quill OBE, and Squadron Leader Boleslaw Drobinski and Squadron Leader David Glaser DFC. As Jeffrey Quill said, 'There were at least two coachloads of Poles present from the London community. I had no idea there were so many Poles still over here! They were so proud, and shared the moment with David, "Gandy" and I, when our missing man was at last laid to rest.'

Flying Officer Franciszek Gruszka's military funeral at Northwood Cemetery, near Northolt, in 1975.

Flying Officer Franciszek Gruszka's grave today – the original CWGC and not Polish style headstone remains at the behest of the Gruszka family, given that the pilot is acknowledged as being Polish and was served in an RAF fighter squadron. In 2020, the CWGC was asked to ensure that this always remains the case.

Flying Officer Franciszek Gruszka was one of 145 Polish pilots who fought with the RAF during the Battle of Britain, seventy-nine of them, like him, in British squadrons, whilst sixty-four flew with the Polish 302 and 303 Squadrons. With them, these men brought experience, an offensive spirit, and a burning desire to one day liberate their homeland. Twenty-nine Polish pilots lost their lives during the Battle of Britain – Gruszka was the eighth of them to die, and the first Polish Spitfire pilot lost in the Battle of Britain. Today, the wreckage of his aircraft can still be seen at the Kent Battle of Britain Museum, and is a memorial in itself to those sacrifices.

After the highly publicised Gruszka recovery, and issue of the 1975 guidelines, aircraft recoveries continued unabated, some groups even visiting several crash sites in a day. With this level of activity it was just a question of time before more missing airmen were found.

On 7 October 1940, Me 110s of ZG 26 escorted the Ju 88s of II/KG 51 on what was the last major daylight raid of the Battle of Britain, an attack on Westland Aircraft at Yeovil. At 16.00 hrs, 10 miles north-west of Portland, Squadron Leader Michael Robinson of 609 Squadron engaged a circle of Me 110s, shooting one down which dived vertically and crashed 5 miles north of the Dorset coast. This machine went in near Kingston Russell House, Long Bredy, near Poole, and so violent was the crash that what little could be found of the two crewmen were buried on site as unknown German soldiers, later being interred at Cannock Chase.

In August 1976, the WAAG excavated the Long Bredy site, recovering the substantial remains of both crewmen, along with various personal effects naming them as Herzog and Schilling. Surprisingly, however, the Central Dorset coroner, Mr Morris Bailey, refused to accept that these were the remains of 6/ZG 26's missing crew from 7 October 1940, *Oberfeldwebel* Karl Herzog and *Gefreiter* Herbert Schilling, when the aircraft was known to have crashed. Indeed, a destruction order was placed on the remains, and understandably the WAAG were dissatisfied, to say the least, with the coroner's actions. The Group alerted the German War Graves organisation, which did accept the identification and arranged for the remains to be buried at Cannock Chase, named as the airmen they were.

It was just a month before 'The Missing Few' hit the headlines again.

At 15.03 hrs on 11 September 1940, Squadron Leader Harry Hogan led eight 501 Squadron Hurricanes off from Kenley to patrol with 253 Squadron, and at 15.30 hrs were engaged by over Ashford. The Hurricanes were attacked from above by twenty Me 109s, Squadron Leader Hogan hitting one, which was 'seen to turn inland'. Sergeant James 'Ginger' Lacey DFM, however, was shot down and baled out, unhurt – but Sergeant Eddie Egan was missing.

Sergeant Tony Pickering:

> I was flying with Sergeant Eddie Egan when he was killed. I didn't know Eddie terribly well, but I suppose I could count him as a friend. We were flying along, just the two of us,

Above left: The tattered uniform of *Obergefreiter* Herbert Schilling. *(Andy Saunders)*

Above right: Sergeant Eddie Egan of 501 Squadron, recovered in 1976, identified in 1977, and given a military funeral at Brookwood.

looking out all the time for trouble, and I saw four Spitfires, or what we thought were Spitfires, behind us. We were talking to each other on the R/T, monitoring the movements of these fighters. Suddenly one of them zoomed forward, just left the others standing, shooting Eddie down. I turned towards Eddie's assailant but the old Hurricane was just too slow. The Hun just shot Eddie down and flew off with the others, they just climbed high and left us. I looked over the side and saw Eddie going down, the aircraft in flames. Eddie crashed in a wood outside Ashford in Kent. After landing I filed a report on the location, and six months later had to see the Air Ministry and pin-point the site as Eddie had not been found.

Brookwood Military Cemetery in Surrey – wherein now lie a number of 'The Missing Few'.

On 11 September 1976, the London Air Museum (LAM) investigated a crash site at Daniels Wood, Tuesnoad, near Bethersden, recovering the remains of a Hurricane – and its pilot. Although nothing was found amongst the wreckage to identify the aircraft or pilot, it was known that the crash occurred on 11 September 1940 – and Fighter Command's only missing pilot from the fighting that day was Sergeant Eddie Egan. Despite that irrefutable fact, the MOD refused to accept the identification.

John Tickner was present at the recovery:

> In those early days we just used to drive to a village, seek out elderly residents and ask whether they could recall any aircraft crashes in the vicinity. We would then locate these with a view to a recovery, but frequently until that went ahead we were actually unaware of even what type of aircraft was involved, much less its identity. This was so in the case of Sergeant [Eddie] Egan's aircraft, as prior to the excavation we had no idea that a missing airman was concerned. It is difficult to understand, however, why the authorities were unable to locate the wreck in 1940, as it was, in fact, easily accessible.

Squadron Leader (as he became) Tony Pickering:

> The next I ever heard of Eddie Egan was when I happened to read a newspaper article about his bones being found by an aviation archaeology group – at the very spot I had told the authorities about in 1940. I got in touch but was not called as a witness by the resulting inquest, which was rather surprising given that I had actually seen Eddie go in.

The MOD having refused to accept the LAM's identification, the Daniels Wood pilot was buried by the CWGC as 'Known Unto God' at Brookwood; relatives of Sergeant Eddie Egan, however, attended the military funeral, including the pilot's sister, Mrs Jane Somerville, who fully accepted that her brother had been found.

On 1 October 1977, the next recovery took place – not by a civilian group but as a training exercise for No. 590 Explosive Ordnance Disposal Unit, a Territorial Army formation. The site chosen was that of a Me 109 located behind Mountain Street in Chilham, from which the EOD team recovered much of the aircraft and its pilot. This was found to be *Oberleutnant* Ekkehard Schelcher, the III/JG 54 Staff Officer, shot down on 2 September 1940. The pilot was buried at Cannock Chase with full military honours, in the presence of his brother and sister-in-law. Mike Llewellyn, in fact, had been called in to assist with the identification, and, in his words, 'was praised by the Coroner, in direct contrast to the Gruszka fiasco'.

Oberleutnant Ekkehard Schelcher of Stab III/JG 54, recovered in 1977 and buried at the German War Cemetery on Cannock Chase. *(KBoBM)*

The following year, in November 1978, a conglomeration of recovery groups cooperated to re-dig the Daniels Wood site, determined to discover evidence irrefutably confirming the aircraft's identity.

This was successful: the manufacturer's plate was recovered, bearing the serial number of Sergeant Eddie Egan's Hurricane: P3820. The MOD consequently accepted that Egan had been found – and the Brookwood grave was named accordingly.

All of this activity, however, continued to concern the MOD, the Air Force Board Secretariat issuing updated 'Notes of Guidance to Recovery Groups' active in the recovery of 'Crashed Military Aircraft of Historical Interest'. The guidance involved covered various subjects, most of which were common sense, and included a section on 'Human Remains', essentially demanding that in the event of human remains being found the recovery must be suspended, the MOD informed, and, significantly, that recovery groups were not to make any effort to trace next-of-kin, which would be handled by the MOD. The main difference between this and the previous guidance was that recovery groups were required to submit a report detailing what, if anything, had been found. Still, though, the guidance was unsupported by legislation, and so in terms of regulating the activities of those enthusiasts actively seeking to recover the missing, was just yet another paper tiger. Consequently, this latest guidance had little or no effect.

September 1979 saw the LAM and WAAG cooperate to excavate the crash site of a Hurricane at the rear of the Post Office at North Fambridge. Research at Essex County Records Office had revealed a report from the Eastern Report Centre confirming that at 15.30 hrs on 5 September 1940, a Hurricane had crashed at the location concerned and burnt out, there being 'no trace of the pilot'. According to a report from Billericay Region ARP warden's log there was 'no trace' of any 'occupants', the 'plane' having 'buried itself 10–15 feet in the ground. Pilot believed to be in the wreckage'. An eyewitness, Jack Friedlein, remembered 'a mighty explosion and a huge ball of flame … no trace of the pilot was ever recovered, so I presumed he had been blown to pieces.' By this time, RAF records were available for public inspection at the Public Records Office (now The National Archives) at Kew, and at the MOD AHB. It was therefore learned that on the day in question, 73 Squadron had been sent south, from Church Fenton to Castle Camps, in the Debden Sector of 11 Group – and, like 607 Squadron, was roughly handled in its first encounter with Me 109s: five Hurricanes were shot down, and one pilot, Sergeant Alexander Logan McNay, was missing – the only Hurricane pilot still outstanding from this particular day's fighting. It was therefore clear that the Fambridge Hurricane could only be McNay's.

During the recovery, the Merlin was recovered, along with various cockpit items, including the pilot's head armour, pieces of his Sutton

The crash site of Sergeant Alexander Logan McNay's Hurricane in 1940. *(Philip Harvey)*

The 1979 dig in progress at North Fambridge. *(Steve Vizard)*

harness and even a map named 'McNay'. Unfortunately, as John Tickner, who was also present at this dig, recalled, 'only a few pieces of life jacket were discovered, nothing else connected with the pilot' – so Sergeant Alecander Logan McNay remains missing to this day, no doubt owing to the violence of the explosion.

Later that month, the WAAG undertook a recovery for the television cameras, a BBC 2 'Forty Minute' documentary, *Missing: No Known Grave.*

On 7 September 1940, the Luftwaffe began its round-the-clock attack on London, and amongst the squadrons in action that day was 257 – which lost both flight commanders fighting over the Thames Estuary, Flight Lieutenant Hugh Beresford and Flying Officer Lancelot Mitchell both being reported missing. On 4 October 1940, 49 MU was informed that a Hurricane had crashed on the Isle of Sheppey and suggested than a Bren-gun carrier from nearby RAF Eastchurch could be used to drag the wreckage from the marsh in which the aircraft had crashed. For some reason, however, the RAF undertook no work at this site.

In 1971, the KBoBM partially excavated the site concerned, at Elmley, Spithead Point, Sheppey, during which the serial P3049 was discovered. When the RAF's 1940 records were placed in the public domain, it was ascertained that this was the Hurricane of a missing pilot: Flight Lieutenant Hugh Beresford. No human remains had been found in 1971, so it was likely that the cameras would not be disappointed – and nor were they. On 29 September 1979 the recovery went ahead, the cameras rolling, and Beresford was recovered. Sheppey Police took possession of the human remains, and the MOD were informed. Either in compliance with the new MOD guidelines, or more likely to keep the dig quiet until it could go ahead and be filmed, WAAG made no attempt to trace and contact the Beresford family. A married man, his widow, Cherry, had re-married to Australian VC winner Wing Commander Hughie Edwards, but had died prematurely in 1966. The MOD ascertained that Flight Lieutenant Hugh Beresford's sole surviving relative was his spinster sister, Pamela, who was traced and later admitted having previously always clung to the hope that somehow, somewhere, her brother was still

The recovery of Flight Lieutenant Hugh Beresford in progress at Spithead Point in 1979. *(Andy Saunders)*

alive. Sadly, that was now confirmed not to be the case, and Beresford was given a full military funeral at Brookwood.

Soon after the Beresford dig, on 6 October 1979, the WAAG recovered the remains of another missing Hurricane pilot: Sergeant Hubert 'Padding' Hastings Adair, of 213 Squadron. Although one of 'The Few', like *Gefreiter* Richard Riedel, Adair was killed just after the Battle of Britain ended, on 6 November 1940, but his story is relevant to the ongoing saga concerning MOD policy.

Sergeant Hubert Hastings Adair of 213 Squadron, recovered in 1979. *(Andy Saunders)*

Geoffrey Stevens was also a sergeant-pilot during the Battle of Britain, and remembered,

> Having joined 151 Squadron in early August 1940, I became very friendly with a fellow NCO pilot called 'Paddy' Adair, who was posted to us in early September. He had been with a Fairey Battle squadron attacking bridges in the Low Countries and France, and was lucky to have survived. When I volunteered to go to a squadron in the South, Paddy, who by then was my best friend, somehow managed to follow me to 213 Squadron. We were therefore able to continue our friendship. He was a volatile Irish redhead, who could fly off the handle only to return to earth just as quickly. We had many violent arguments but these never affected our close friendship.
>
> On 6 November 1940, I did not have a serviceable aircraft and was therefore left on the ground. I watched the battle in the air, over the Portsmouth area, from the Tangmere tarmac, and saw a lone fighter plunge almost vertically from 15[,000]–20,000 feet. I remember thinking 'Poor devil, whoever you are'. Of course I had no way of knowing if it was one of ours or theirs. I had even less idea that it was Paddy, who was sadly killed.
>
> As his best friend, I was sent by transport to identify Paddy Adair, but there wasn't very much to see. It was most unpleasant and very depressing.

Adair, in Hurricane V7602, had been shot down by the German ace and *Kommodore* of JG 2, *Major* Helmut Wick – and was reported missing.

By August 1979, an aircraft crash site art Pigeon House Farm, Cosham, had attracted the interest of the WAAG, it being confirmed that the incident occurred on 6 November 1940 – and in which action two RAF fighter pilots were killed: 238 Squadron's Flying Officer James Tillett, who was buried at nearby Gosport, and Sergeant Hubert Hastings Adair – who was commemorated on Runnymede. Nonetheless and somewhat surprisingly, permission for an excavation was forthcoming from the MOD. On the day, Mr Robert Ware, the tenant farmer on whose land the aircraft crashed was present and who was an eyewitness, was present and remembered that at the time, 'air force people came to the scene and stood guard for several days. After that a long trailer came and removed the parts of the plane above ground. To my knowledge there was no attempt made to remove the pilot's body.'

The first items of wreckage were found at a depth of 3ft, and further down all eight Browning machine-guns were recovered, together with human remains and a flying boot – but nothing, however, which identified the pilot or aircraft. The police duly attended and removed the Browning's and human remains to Cosham Police Station, and the coroner informed.

On 22 October 1979, the Coroner's Officer reported having had several discussions with Whitehall following the aircraft's recovery, the upshot of which was that the MOD had been 'unable to trace any next-of-kin in this case and in any event cannot positively identify the plane or pilot'. Adastral House's attitude 'was that this matter is best dealt with by NOT holding an inquest, by calling the pilot an unknown aviator and by disposing of the remains locally.' The MOD, however, acquiesced that the decision was that of the coroner's to make, and if he decided to hold an inquest, the ministry would cooperate.

Two days later, the MOD wrote formally to the coroner, confirming the detail of the conversations reported, acknowledging that the aircraft was 'a Hurricane fighter' and that 'the location of the human remains indicate that they are those of a pilot'. 'Identification', however, had 'not been possible'. There was no inquest, which was doubtless a relief to the MOD, which thereby averted further adverse publicity.

There being no unknown burial corresponding with a loss on 6 November 1940, the question is, though, what became of the remains viewed by Sergeant Stevens?

The human remains recovered by the WAAG were cremated and scattered in the Garden of Remembrance at Portchester Cemetery on 29 October 1979.

The recovery of Sergeant Hubert Hastings Adair in progress – all eight Brownings in the foreground. *(Steve Vizard)*

Sergeant Hubert Hastings Adair, therefore, remains missing. The MOD, however, had not disputed the date of the crash, and as Adair was the only pilot still missing from that day, and known to have been lost in the area concerned, refusing to accept that he had been found was pedantry in *extremis*. It is clear to anyone that WAAG had found Adair; as Steve Vizard said, 'Given the evidence, how can the MOD justify both not accepting the pilot's identity and destroying his remains?' It is a fair question.

Following a protracted search, in 1980 the LAM found and excavated a crash site at Theydon Bois, Essex, recovering the substantial remains of a Hurricane – and its pilot – known to have crashed on 7 September 1940. Nothing, however, was found to identify either aircraft or pilot, and with Flight Lieutenant Beresford having been recovered the previous year, there were still two Hurricane pilots missing from the day in question: 257 Squadron's Flying Officer Lancelot Mitchell, and 242 Squadron's Pilot Officer John Benzie, a Canadian. Although the enthusiasts' erred on the side of having most likely found Benzie, the MOD, understandably, would not be moved, and so the remains were buried at Brookwood as an unknown airman.

Canadian Pilot Officer John Benzie of 242 Squadron. *(Andy Saunders)*

Could the remains buried here at Brookwood be those of Pilot Officer John Benzie? *(Andy Long)*

In May 1940, Steve Vizard's Tonbridge Aircraft Museum (TAM) obtained permission from the MOD to recover Hurricane L2118, safely abandoned by 73 Squadron's Sergeant John Griffin, on 14 September 1940. The excavation, at Park House Farm, Chart Sutton, Kent, however, found a completely different aircraft: P2542, another 73 Squadron Hurricane – and its pilot: Sergeant John Brimble. To say that this recovery was untimely, considering that the BBC 2 documentary *Missing* had been broadcast only the week before, would be an understatement. A veritable media storm broke over the recovery, one headline reading 'Death Plane Runs into Flak', the RAF claiming to be 'upset and angry' because the licence application concerned a completely different machine and pilot. The inference, of course, was that TAM knew full-well that it was not Griffin's Hurricane at Chart House, but knew that an application to excavate the crash site of a missing pilot would be refused. Steve Vizard, however, maintained that his actions were perfectly justified because Sergeant Brimble would now receive a decent burial – which he did, at Brookwood, on 16 October 1980.

The MOD, however, was mighty upset and revoked permission for all aircraft recoveries. On 7 January 1981, there followed a meeting between senior RAF officers and MOD officials and the major recovery groups, and various other stakeholders, the purpose of the meeting being to discuss the MOD's current policy towards aircraft recovery and, in particular, the

The recovery of Sergeant John Brimble in progress. *(Steve Vizard)*

problems arising when human remains were found. The MOD explained that its policy was to permit recoveries at sites where there was no likelihood of human remains being find or risk from explosives. Clearly, the MOD policy towards ‘ The Missing Few’ was very much one of ‘letting sleeping dogs lie’, for a variety of reasons and not least a lack of resources and finance. Representatives of various ex-servicemen’s organisations and the War Widows’ Association were in support of the MOD and were strongly opposed to the disturbance of wreckage containing human remains, which, the MOD press release arising, stated was ‘very upsetting for the next-of-kin, many of whom are now of advanced age’. It was an emotive issue, for sure, and a highly charged meeting at which certain aviation archaeologists argued their equally strongly held view that all wrecks thought to contain human remains should be recovered with the consent of next of kin, for decent burial. Others felt equally strongly that such sites were in themselves a last resting place. As the chairman, summing up, said, ‘there were no easy answers’, there being ‘a wide range of strongly held views’, asking ‘all aviation archaeologists to have respect for the Ministry policy based on the very sincerely held views of a great many people.’ Although the meeting was a valuable public relations exercise, there was never any chance of the MOD changing its policy. Surely, though, instead of a blanket refusal, matters should be considered on a case by case basis?

Undeterred, on 23 August 1981, TAM was back in the news. Having located a crash site in a field north of Wrotham, Kent, TAM applied for a licence to recover a Spitfire in which a pilot had been killed, but had been recovered and buried. Permission was granted and the dig went ahead: a Hurricane, not a Spitfire, was found, and from records available those involved knew that this aircraft was L1965, flown by Pilot Officer Colin Dunstan Francis of 253 Squadron on 30 August 1940. On that day, the Squadron, freshly arrived at Kenley, fought its first combat and was typically hammered by the Me 109s, losing four Hurricanes: two pilots were killed, and a third, Pilot Officer Colin Dunstan Francis, reported missing. The discovery of shredded uniform fabric made it obvious that the pilot remained in the wreckage, and so the recovery was suspended and the MOD informed. This time the MOD agreed that the recovery could in due course resume, under the supervision of RAF personnel from Biggin Hill. This was duly carried out, the pilot being recovered and removed by the RAF to the local police station. Before the subsequent inquest was held at Tonbridge on 8 September 1981, recording the verdict of ‘Death on active service’, the MOD traced the pilot’s next of kin, a cousin, who attended the

Above left: Sergeant John Brimble pictured off-duty during flying training. *(Andy Saunders)*

Above right: Pilot Officer Colin Dunstan Francis. *(Andy Saunders)*

Below: The battered plate identifying Hurricane L1965. *(Steve Vizard)*

Pilot Officer Colin Dunstan Francis's grave at Brookwood. *(Andy Long)*

military funeral of Pilot Officer Colin Dunstan Francis at Brookwood on 29 September 1981.

Two years later, Steve Vizard found another of 'The Missing Few': 'We were searching for a Spitfire at Holliwell Point, near Burnham-on-Crouch in Essex, but found the modification plate confirming it to be a Hurricane.'

Further research indicated that the aircraft concerned was most likely flown by Pilot Officer John Basil Ramsay, of North Weald's 151 Squadron, reported missing on 18 August 1940.

Steve Vizard:

> By coincidence, around this time Pilot Officer [John Basil] Ramsay's mother's death notice appeared in the *Daily Telegraph*, placed by his cousin, Miss Joan Worth. Andy Saunders contacted her, and discovered that Miss Worth worked for the MOD and had actually grown up with Pilot Officer Ramsay. It was explained to her that we had found a crash-site which we believed to be his Hurricane, and Miss Worth concluded that her cousin must be recovered as her aunt had always agonised over her son's fate.

Instead of going straight ahead with a recovery, it was agreed that Miss Worth, as a family member of the missing pilot, would formally request that the authorities undertook an official recovery – which was refused on the grounds that another pilot, Squadron Leader R.H.A. 'Dickie' Lee DFC of 85 Squadron had also been reported missing on the day in question: a lame excuse indeed, considering contemporary accounts confirming Lee's loss 30 miles out to sea. Naturally, Miss Worth and the WAAG were disappointed with the MOD's decision, and a visit to the crash site strengthened the lady's resolve to see her cousin recovered. Consequently, at Miss Worth's request, the WAAG carried out a major recovery on 11 August 1983. The mortal remains of Pilot Officer John Basil Ramsay were duly recovered and identified, and buried with full military honours at Brookwood.

Steve Vizard:

> This time we had the backing of a pilot's relative, by the MOD still refused to cooperate. Our unauthorised recovery was only undertaken as a last resort, therefore. At the funeral, the MOD tried to prevent us from communicating with the relatives – not for the first time – but Miss Worth kindly took us back to

The recovery of Pilot Officer John Basil Ramsay in 1983. *(Steve Vizard)*

> her hotel where a buffet had been arranged for us. That, I think, indicates her level of support and appreciation for our efforts.

It would be three years before another of 'The Missing Few' was brought in from the cold.

On 13 August 1978, the Essex Aircraft Historical Society (EAHS) excavated a Hurricane crash site south of Wennington Church, near

Pilot Officer John Basil Ramsay's grave at Brookwood. *(Andy Long)*

The MARG recovery underway at Wennington. *(David Smith)*

Romford. Although nothing was found to identify the machine, but the EAHS believed they had found P3159, which crashed on 31 August 1940 – the pilot of which, 310 (Czech) Squadron's Pilot Officer Jaroslav Sterbacek, remained missing. Given that no human remains were reported, however, it is difficult to understand how such a firm conclusion could be reached. Sterbacek was, in fact, the first Czech fighter pilot to be killed in action during the Battle of Britain, and, according to the 310 Squadron ORB, it was 'presumed that he went into the Thames'. Some years later, the Medway Aviation Research Group (MARG) suggested that the Wennington Hurricane was more likely that of Pilot Officer Miroslav Kredba, who was also shot down on 31 August 1940, in what was 310 Squadron's first combat, and safely baled out. An eyewitness, John Burton, remembered the crash, and saw a parachute descending, which, it was assumed, was the pilot of this Hurricane; he also recalled the RAF recovery team telling inquisitive locals that the pilot had abandoned his machine. On that basis, the MOD gave permission for a recovery, although, according to MARG member David Smith, the group was aware that the Sterbacek family were 'very keen that Jaroslav [Sterbacek] should be found and buried'.

On 27 April 1984, the MARG found dry conditions at the site, unlike the wet weather which had hampered the EAHS recovery. The site was still marshy, however, and the Hurricane had buried itself deep below the surface. A mechanical digger was brought in, but having reached a depth of 15ft its tracks became stuck in the thick clay.

David Smith:

> By that time very little of the aircraft had been found, and as it was mid-afternoon time was moving quickly on. At a depth of

> about twenty feet, the digger lifted out the tail wheel, complete with inflated tyre, but five feet further down lifted something which shed a completely different light on the operation: a complete and unopened parachute pack. We knew then that the aircraft concerned was not [Miroslav] Kredba's … The pilot was still in the wreckage, and as we knew that both [Jaroslav] Sterbacek and 601 Squadron's Flying Officer Michael Duke Doulton, of the famous bone China and porcelain family, were both missing from action on 31 August 1940, the question now was which pilot had we found?

It was decided to continue with the excavation, and at a depth of over 25ft the remaining wreckage and pilot's remains were recovered. A panel from the aircraft's tail section was found with the serial number R4215: the Hurricane of Flying Officer Michael Duke Doulton. The local police subsequently attended and the identification as Doulton was officially accepted by the South Essex coroner. The pilot was buried at Salehurst, Sussex, at a private service, surrounded by his family and friends … Tragically, the only thing Michael Doulton's son, born in April 1941, was ever able to do for his father was 'arrange that funeral'.

The brother of Pilot Officer Jaroslav Sterbacek, who was aware of the 1978 investigation, travelled to England upon hearing of the 1984 recovery, before the coroner announced the identity of the pilot involved as Doulton; the man was devastated when told by the MOD that it was not his long-lost brother who had been found. This was significant. The MOD had long argued that without positive identification from a crash site of aircraft and/or pilot, those identities, despite strong circumstantial and eyewitness evidence could not be assumed. The danger was that a family's hopes and expectations could be unnecessarily raised, and distress caused, as had happened to the Sterbacek's in this case. The Doulton recovery, therefore, provided concrete evidence with which the MOD could vindicate its stance and justify its inflexible policy.

The year 1984 also saw the first missing Luftwaffe airman recovered since 1977.

In 1975, the BAM excavated a crash site at Shuart Farm, St Nicholas-at-Wade, on the Isle of Thanet, but abandoned the operation owing to the depth at which wreckage lay and limitations of the digging machine available at the time. Nonetheless, a plate was discovered identifying the aircraft as a Me 109, and specifically WN 3874, a 109E-1 of 6/JG 3 shot down on 26 August 1940 by 56 Squadron's Flying Officer Ken Marston; the enemy pilot, *Unteroffizier* Fritz Buchner, remained missing. There the matter lay until 21 September 1984, when a team led by Steve Vizard and Andy Saunders dug the site. Using a tracked machine with a long-reaching arm, the engine and cockpit section were recovered from a depth of 40ft, together with the pilot's remains. *Unteroffizier* rank badges, a handkerchief with the embroidered initials 'FB', and given that BAM had previously identified the aircraft, left no doubt as to the irrefutable fact that Buchner was no longer missing. Bizarrely, however, the German authorities refused to accept the identification and ordered the remains to be buried as unknown at Cannock Chase. The enthusiasts involved, however, traced Fritz Buchner's sister, *Frau* Emma Heumos, which the authorities had failed to do, and made the family aware of the facts.

Similarly confusing is that the coroner's inquest in Broadstairs was not held until nearly two years after the recovery, on 1 July 1986. Proceedings lasted three hours, the coroner, Rebecca Cobb, concluding that *Unteroffizier* Fritz Buchner had been found and, indeed, shot down by Flying Officer Marston. Buchner's grave at Cannock Chase, therefore, was named to him and, thanks to the tenacity of the recovery team, another missing airman was found, his family given closure.

Between 1972 and 1984, the MOD had been presented with the remains of sixteen Battle of Britain and other airmen. Public opinion had weighed down heavily on the side of the enthusiasts prepared to go head to head with the authorities and contravene the MOD's guidelines, and the MOD policy of non-disturbance was seen as inhumane. The MOD, however, had been powerless to impose any sanction or punishment upon those flouting the rules, which were not backed by legislation. That, however, was about to change.

Unteroffizier Fritz Buchner. *(Andy Saunders)*

Michael Mates MP, a former army officer, was working on a private member's bill with the intention of legally protecting certain military sites awarded the status of war graves. This would mean an end to, for example, recreational diving and souvenir hunting on shipwrecks from the two world wars – and rein in certain aviation archaeologists. A formal aircraft recovery licence, it was proposed, would be necessary from the secretary of state for defence, rather than just written consent from the MOD, and the crash sites of missing airmen would become protected sites, the interference of which was prohibited. Most importantly, contravention was punishable. On 30 January 1986, the Protection of Military Remains Act received its second and third reading in the House of Commons – so the cat was out of the bag, so to speak, and only approval from the House of Lords was now required for the Act to become part of the law of the land. Needless to say, feelings were running high – and before the Act was ratified more problems lay ahead for the authorities.

On 1 September 1986, a photographic reconnaissance Spitfire pilot, Pilot Officer Charles Barber, who had crashed near Winchelsea on 24 April 1942, was recovered by Andy Saunders's team, and four days later the same independent group found *Leutnant* Helmut Strobl, of 5/JG 27, shot down by Sergeant Charles Hurry of 43 Squadron on 5 September 1940 – and therein lies a sorry tale indeed.

Leutnant Helmut Strobl of 5/JG 27, reported missing on his twenty-fifth birthday, 5 September 1940, and recovered on the forty-sixth anniversary. *(Andy Saunders)*

In 1971, the A&TRG (later the BAM) excavated a Me 109 crash site close to Appledore railway station, recovering some highly prized artefacts, including the aircraft's Revi gunsight, the pilot's parachute harness release buckle, and his Iron Cross. Moreover, the aircraft was identified as WN3627 – Strobl's Me 109E-1. No human remains, however, were reported. The site was re-dug on the forty-sixth anniversary of the crash, 5 September 1986 –Strobl's remains being discovered, along with his identity discs, in a plastic carrier bag. Further comment on that fact would be superfluous. Suffice it to say, with identity established beyond doubt, after the coroner's inquest in March 1987, at his family's request, *Leutnant* Helmut Strobl were interred at the family plot in Kolbnitz, near Badgastein, Germany.

Five days after Strobl was recovered, on 9 September 1986, the Protection of Military Remains Act (PMA) was passed by the House of Lords, the preamble stating the new statute's purpose: 'An Act to secure the protection from unauthorised interference of the remains of military aircraft and vessels that have crashed, sunk or been stranded and of associated human remains; and for connected purpose.' Sub-section 7 made clear the penalties for contravening the Act: on summary conviction, a fine, not exceeding the statutory maximum, and conviction on indictment, also a fine. Sub-section 5 made it an offence for any person to 'make a statement, or furnish a document or information, which he knows to be false in material particular', or be 'reckless' in making 'a statement or representation'. Subsequently, the MOD made a booklet of 'Notes for Guidance' available to the aviation archaeology movement, emphasising the Act's key points and reiterating MOD policy. This included reference to 'Adverse Publicity': 'The Ministry of Defence is concerned that neither the Services or Department should become involved in any adverse publicity as the result of any recovery activities. Groups are requested to take all possible steps to prevent such an occurrence.' The PMA, the MOD, considered had brought aviation archaeology under control – but had it?

In the run up to the PMA, there was another site under investigation by Andy Saunders and friends, at Rookelands Farm, Newchurch, on Romney Marsh – which was known to be the Hurricane of 504 Squadron's Pilot Officer Arthur 'Bill' Clarke, reported missing on 11 September 1940. This had been confirmed, in fact, back in 1971, when the KBoBM excavated the water-logged site, recovering substantial wreckage before abandoning the exercise. Amongst the items recovered were the engine, a pair of pilot's silk inner gloves, and a handkerchief bearing the embroidered name 'CLARKE'. No human remains, however, were reported, and nor were they by various other groups which picked over the site subsequently. Contacted in 1986, however, the pilot's sister, Mrs K.L. Freeman, confirmed in writing on 30 July 1986 that the family 'proposed to leave Bill's remains where they lie and hold a memorial service close to the spot'. This wish was respected, and that service, and the unveiling of a roadside memorial arranged by Andy Saunders, was held on the forty-sixth anniversary of the crash, 11 September 1986 – two days after the PMA became enforceable.

Pilot Officer Arthur Clarke of 504 Squadron – who remains buried at his crash site in respect of his sister's wishes.

The PMA, however, did not bring an end to the matter of ' The Missing Few', as the MOD intended. In 1977, Steve Vizard had located a Spitfire crash site at Greenway Court, near Hollingbourne in Kent, which RAF personnel of 49 MU had confirmed in 1940 as being P9364 – the pilot of which, Sergeant Ernest Scott of 222 Squadron, shot down by *Major* Werner Mölders on 27 September 1940, remained missing. Many years later, in 1990, enthusiasts showed the pilot's brother the crash site, after which Scott's sister, Mrs Irene Hukin, wrote to the (then) Prince of Wales, His Royal Highness Prince Charles, asking for his support to see her brother recovered. On 30 September 1990 – the Battle of Britain's fiftieth anniversary year, Prince Charles asked the MOD to investigate. Research into 49 MU records confirmed that no wreckage had been recovered from the Hollingbourne site – and to quantify the Unit's workload at the time, 618 RAF aircraft crash sites were attended between 1 September 1940 and 29 November 1940. Now, following intervention by Prince Charles, on 15 December 1990, an RAF Support Command team excavated the crash site, recovering the Spitfire and Sergeant Ernest Scott, whose identity was confirmed. On 1 February 1991, after a funeral service at RAF Manston, Scott was laid to rest at nearby Margate Cemetery. Naturally, the story aroused great media interest, Mrs Hukin being quoted, who summed the situation up: 'It now seems that they (the authorities) knew, very early on, where Ernest's plane could be located. It is sad that it has taken all this time but we are indebted to Prince Charles.'

Three years later, this emotive subject was back in the news yet again.

On 1 September 1940, a Hurricane crashed at Court Road Orchard, Highways, Chelsfield, which was investigated by on behalf of 49 MU by the civilian sub-contractor A.V. Nicholls on 22 September 1940. The CO of 472 Battery RA, located at a listening post in Highways, was interviewed, his men having guarded the site, who confirmed that RAF personnel from Uxbridge had attended and cleared surface wreckage from the site a fortnight previously, stating their intention to return later to recover the engine. Nicholls confirmed that 'the machine had gone five to six feet into the ground, a propeller blade was visible embedded in the bottom of the crater made by the machine; the engine was still in the ground; one or two pieces of fuselage remained.' A gang was instructed to clear the site of what was reportedly Hurricane L2062 – that of Pilot Officer Brian Noble of Biggin Hill's 79 Squadron, who baled out, wounded.

The Nicholls gang began digging at the site on 23 September 1940, Mr Nicholls reporting further to Squadron Leader Goodman of 49 MU:

> They came across a flying boot containing a foot; digging further they came across an unopened parachute, pulling on the parachute exposed the pilot's body. Police were called to the site by gang supervisor, digging operations continued under surveillance of the Police, came across money, opened pilot's pocket, found cigarette case also small wallet containing photographs of two ladies. All above articles handed over to Police ... The Police took charge of the Pilot's remains. We cleared the remaining fuselage, one propeller blade and engine parts; filled in crater and left tidy.

Clearly, this was not L2062, although the Nicholls gang found nothing to correctly identify the aircraft or pilot, the remains of whom appear to have been buried as unknown in plot 128, Star Lane Cemetery, St Mary Cray, near Orpington. The headstone, however, attributed to 'An Airman of the 1939–45 War, Royal Air Force', wrongly recorded the date of death as 12 October 1940. Later, travellers scouring the area for scrap metal found further body parts, which were handed to the police and subsequently buried in another 'unknown' grave at Star Lane, no connection having been made with the first burial. There the matter was left until the advent of aviation archaeology.

In the late 1970s or early 1980s, enthusiasts hurriedly dug the site whilst the field was being ploughed, recovering some easily found items, including the maker's plate identifying the aircraft as Hurricane P2673 – that of a missing pilot, namely Sergeant John Mortimer Ellis of 85 Squadron, shot down on 1 September 1940. Nothing further was done, however, until September 1992, when another enthusiast, Mark Kirby, re-located the site,

The grave of Sergeant John Mortimer Ellis at Brookwood. *(Andy Long)*

Andy Saunders tracing the pilot's family, which confirmed their desire to see any further remains recovered from the site. The landowner and the enthusiasts agreed that this being the case, regardless of the PMA and MOD policy, a dig would go ahead. So it was that in September 1993, the substantial remains of Sergeant John Mortimer Ellis were recovered and handed over to the police, with identification. On 1 October 1993, Sergeant Ellis was buried at Brookwood Military Cemetery with full military honours – so now has three graves. Surprisingly, the case attracted little publicity and the MOD took no action under the PMA against those responsible for the recovery.

On 20 April 1994, the same enthusiast team recovered Sergeant John 'Gilly' Gilders of 41 Squadron, one of 'The Few' who was reported missing after the Battle of Britain, on 21 February 1941, having inexplicably dropped out of formation whilst patrolling over Folkestone, presumably due to oxygen system failure. No. 49 MU attended the crash site of a Spitfire reported on that day, near Chilham, confirming the aircraft to be Sergeant [John] Gilders' P7816. On 24 March 1941, the Air Ministry wrote to the pilot's father with distressing news: the aircraft had buried itself 16ft deep, exploding on impact; although parts of the aircraft had been recovered, no trace had been found of the pilot, his parachute or clothing, convincing the officer in charge that 'the pilot concerned was not in the wreckage'. Mr Gilders was bitter and confused: had enough been done, he repeatedly inquired to find his son?

In 1970, the LAM investigated the site at Chilham Beeches, recovering sufficient parts, John Tickner recalled, to identify it as a Spitfire, but nothing to suggest that the pilot remained aboard. The group intended to return, but the landowner refused permission. The situation had changed by 1993, the land having changed hands, and having had no action taken against him following the Ellis recovery, Mark Kirby decided to petition the family and, if supportive, go ahead and recover Gilders, irrespective on the law. The family, however, was divided in opinion but the final decision was made by the pilot's sister, Mrs Margaret Lawson: go ahead. On 20 April 1994, Sergeant John Gilders was duly recovered, along with his identity card, it being apparent that 49 MU had actually made little effort to undertake a recovery. On this occasion, Kirby was arrested and charged with having contravened the PMA. At court on 1 December 1994, he pleaded guilty with mitigation, that the 1993 recovery discredited the 49 MU report, and the documented wishes of the pilot's late father, and family support. The guilty plea was accepted by the sympathetic justices – who discharged the

Sergeant John Gilders of 41 Squadron at Hornchurch in 1940.

matter by way on an absolute discharge – which is essentially a criminal conviction but without any actual punishment. Four days later, the inquest was held at Ashford, and on 11 May 1995, Sergeant John Gilders was buried with full military honours at Brookwood. As the presiding chaplain, David Osborne, said, 'What we owe John and the others like him we cannot repay'. Inevitably, the whole saga whipped up a veritable media storm, in which the RAF stated its view in *Kent Today*: 'The exhuming of bodies is not a hobby in this country. If it must be done, it should be done by professionals and within the strict constraints of the law.' That, nobody could deny – but clearly there has been little will by the 'professionals' to take positive action in these matters.

In 1996, another of 'The Few' was recovered within the law, but nonetheless sparking further controversy.

On 30 August 1940, Sergeant Dennis Noble of 43 Squadron was shot down and killed, his Hurricane crashing at the junction of Portland and Woodhouse Roads in Hove. A recovery team duly attended, recovered the pilot for burial, and tidied the site. Consequently, 20-year-old Sergeant Noble was buried back in his home town, at East Retford Cemetery in Nottinghamshire. Fast-forward to 1995, and the Southern Counties Aviation

The grave of Sergeant John Gilders at Brookwood. *(Andy Long)*

Club (SCAC) became aware that a major property development was starting the following year in the area of Noble's crash site, there being a suggestion that a block of flats would be named after the pilot. The development also provided an opportunity to recover any remaining wreckage of Hurricane P3179, and permission was duly obtained from Hove Council and all companies with services running through the site, and a recovery licence issued by the MOD. The dig went ahead on 8 November 1996, and being in an urban area attracted much public interest. Sightseers, however, got more than they bargained for when substantial human remains were discovered. Coinciding with Remembrance time, the recovery generated great media interest, and the obvious question was asked: as the pilot had been buried in 1940, how could this have happened?

At the original funeral, certain onlookers were suspicious that the coffin, which listed heavily to one side, contained only ballast, so may not have been surprised to learn that the greater part of Sergeant Noble remained buried at his crash site. The aircraft, however, had gone in 15ft deep, creating a water-filled crater and difficult digging conditions for an already overwhelmed recovery service using comparatively primitive equipment. The recovery of human remains is also an extremely unpleasant task, especially when such a violent death is involved, so it is understandable that in this case only partial remains were recovered. Nonetheless, it was another embarrassing

The crash site at Woodhouse Road, Hove, on 30 August 1940. *(KBoBM)*

Above left: Sergeant Dennis Noble, 43 Squadron, recovered in 1996. *(KBoBM)*

Above right: Flying Officer John Cutts of 222 Squadron.

scenario for the MOD, which ultimately saw Sergeant Dennis Noble given a second funeral, in early 1997, with full military honours, when finally laid to rest in the original East Retford grave. The case of Noble, however, is not unique.

Two particular graves at Bell Road Cemetery, Sittingbourne, both interred on 28 September 1940, have quite a story.

According to the Kent County Council War Diary, at 14.03 hrs on 4 September 1940, there was a 'Spitfire down at Chart Sutton. Pilot baled out'; this was the first in a catalogue of errors. On 7 September 1940, 49 MU recorded that Spitfire X4278 was the machine down at Chart Sutton, the recovery of which was 'in hand' – and presumably that of its missing pilot, Flying Officer John Cutts of 222 Squadron. No recovery was reported, however, but the unknown airman's remains buried in Plot W, grave 143, at Bell Road, were recorded in the burial register as having come from 'Amberley Farm, Loose', on 14 September 1940 – which was not necessarily, therefore, the date of death. There has never been an 'Amberley Farm' at Loose, a suburb of Maidstone, some 2 miles north-west of Chart

Sutton – but there is Amberfield Farm at Chart Sutton, which is where X4278 crashed on *4* September 1940. The only Spitfire pilot missing from that day's fighting was Cutts. In 1998, this author and friends presented the evidence to the MOD and it was accepted that the remains in W143 were indeed those of Flying Officer John Cutts – who, at last, was provided

The grave now named to Flying Officer John Cutts at Bell Road Cemetery, Sittingbourne.

a named headstone. So it was that one less of 'The Few' was missing, without a recovery being needed to take place. The same, in fact, was true of 501 Squadron's Sergeant Geoffrey Pearson, shot down on 6 September 1940; buried as unknown at St Stephen's, Lympne, whose identity was accepted in 1982 and headstone named accordingly following research undertaken by his brother-in-law, Richard Griffiths.

The second unknown airman at Bell Road was interred in plot W49, the burial register stating that the casualty 'Died at Park House Farm, Chart Sutton', again on 14 September 1940, these details being confirmed by the relevant death certificate. That is the site from which the TAM recovered Sergeant John Brimble in 1980, who was buried accordingly at Brookwood. At that time, what was overlooked was that the remains in W49 were also those of John Brimble. A complication was that another Hurricane had also crashed at Park House Farm, Chart Sutton, the pilot of which was known to have died in the crash. A.V. Nicholls attended the site and reported to 49 MU that this was P7382, the aircraft of 1 Squadron's Pilot Officer Richard Shaw, shot down on 3 September 1940. This, however, was a different site to that from which TAM had recovered Brimble's remains, and in 1998 the authorities accepted our evidence confirming that W49 were also his, and the Bell Road grave named accordingly. Brimble, therefore, now has not one but two graves.

Over time, the many Battle of Britain crash sites have been dug, some many times, and are now virtually exhausted. It is highly unlikely, therefore, that any further missing Battle of Britain pilots will be recovered – but at least three are known to remain buried with the wreckage of their aircraft. As we have seen, Pilot Officer Arthur Clarke's sister required him to stay with his Hurricane at Burmarsh; Pilot Officer Richard Shaw was never, for whatever reason, recovered from Park House Farm in 1940, a local couple erecting a modest memorial at the crash site to an 'RAF Pilot'. Having long since fallen into disrepair, in 1970, the Headcorn branch of the RAFA adopted the site, creating a memorial garden and holding a memorial service annually on the anniversary of the crash. In 1978, before the PMA 1986, it was confirmed via the police constable who attended the crash that the aircraft wreckage – and presumably, therefore, Pilot Officer Richard Shaw – was definitely never recovered by the A.V. Nicholls gang, so Andy Saunders made the Shaw family aware with a view to an excavation. In view of the memorial garden and annual service, however, the forthcoming decision was to maintain the *status quo*.

The case of 46 Squadron's Flight Sergeant Eric Williams, however, was rather more complex.

The grave at Bell Road now named to Sergeant John Brimble.

On 15 October 1940 the opposing fighters clashed over the Thames Estuary, after which combat Williams was reported missing. The Kent County Council War Diary recorded that at 14.25 hrs, a 'British plane down at Albion Parade … Pilot missing, plane burnt out, slight damage to wharf buildings.' The aircraft, in fact, had crashed through the roof of Barton's Timber Wharf, alongside the Thames Estuary at Gravesend,

Above left: Pilot Officer Richard Shaw of 1 Squadron. *(Andy Saunders)*

Above right: Flight Sergeant Eric Williams of 46 Squadron: still missing in action.

burying itself deep underground. A team of Royal Engineers attended the site and attempted to recover the wrecked machine, but the depth and waterlogged nature of the site prevented this. It was, however, identified as Flight Sergeant [Eric] Williams' Hurricane, V6550, and although no trace of the pilot was found, a flight sergeant's crown was recovered. There was no doubt, then, that Williams remained entombed with his machine.

In 1981, Steve Vizard identified the crash site, and in 1990 David Smith, who had recovered Flying Officer Michael Duke Doulton, arranged a memorial commemorating Flight Sergeant Eric Williams in Gordon Gardens, close to Albion Parade. The enthusiasts had traced the missing airman's widow, Mrs Joan Eddleston, now re-married and living in Canada, who made the journey to Gravesend and unveiled the tribute. Moved though the lady was, Mrs Eddlestone remarked that 'it would have been better if Eric had been buried'. In March 1995, Mrs Eddlestone was made aware by enthusiasts of a potential building development over the crash site, and sent her written approval for Mark Kirby to 'locate and recover the body' of her missing first husband. The site is a very difficult one, however, owing to its physical nature, and there was no recovery made.

Having achieved a level of cooperation from the MOD in relation to a missing non-Battle of Britain pilot, in 1998 I met with Peter Edwards, the head of the (then) RAF Personnel Management Agency at RAF Innsworth, during the course of research for my book *Missing in Action: Resting in Peace?* Amongst other things, the purpose of the meeting was to try and persuade the MOD, given the prospect of development, to make another attempt to recover Williams, which, given the more sophisticated digging machines available, could possibly be successful. In due course, the site was surveyed by the Royal Engineers and RAF personnel, who decided that a recovery attempt was impractical. Frustrated, on 8 February 1998, two enthusiasts made an illegal but unsuccessful recovery attempt – and there the matter lay for nearly ten years, during which time Mrs Eddlestone passed away.

On 6 October 2006, the Medway Aircraft Preservation Society (MAPS) wrote and advised the MOD Joint Casualty & Compassionate Centre (JCCC) that the site at Albion Quayside was the subject of a major development as part of the Thames Gateway Rejuvenation Project, due to begin in 2008. On 20 July 2007, JCCC issued POMRA Licence No 1562 to Mr Lewis Deal of the MAPS, who achieved support from the Royal School of Military Engineers (RSME), based at Chatham. The Joint Air Recovery and Transport Squadron from MOD St Athan also committed to the operation, an unsuccessful recovery attempt taking place between 25-27 July 2007.

Prior to this, a Defence Science & Technology Laboratory (DSTL) search team had recorded two significant readings at the site, their reference being a 1941 aerial photograph of Barton's Timber Wharf, showing a hole in the roof believed to have been caused by the crashing Hurricane. According to a subsequent official report, 'a huge excavation took place' but 'no trace of the aircraft was found. The two readings obtained by DSTL were, however, confirmed as being 1'the metal upper works of an old Thames barge and 1970s era rubbish'. The water table was at 2-metres, 'the rate of water ingress was very high', so much so that pumps on-site were 'barely able to keep pace'. Although the recovery attempt once more came to naught, a BBMF Hurricane flew over the site in tribute to the missing pilot, and an on-site memorial service for Flight Sergeant Williams was held on 29 July 2007.

As a result of the extensive media coverage, a British aviation archaeology enthusiast living in France contacted Wing Commander David Lainchbury, Commandant of the MOD Fire Services Central Training

Establishment at RAF Manston, and provided further information: two eyewitness accounts suggesting that the bulk of wreckage had impacted towards the rear of Barton's yard, and an account of an unofficial excavation pre-POMRA during which parts of the Hurricane's battery were recovered. On 5 September 2007, a POMRA recovery licence was issued to Wing Commander Lainchbury, and the Joint Air Reconnaissance Intelligence Centre then produced 'new mapping based on a modern satellite-based overlay of the contemporary imagery', this data then being 'fed directly into the DSTL search equipment'.

Nonetheless, the excavation subsequently undertaken between 21-23 September 2007 was also fruitless: 'A variety of metal rubbish was recovered but, with one possible exception, no tangible remains of aircraft were found. Moreover, just as before, once the metal contaminants were removed, the DTSL equipment could find no trace of a main body of wreckage… which would emit an enormous electronic signature'. Significantly, a 91-year-old eyewitness contacted the RAF team following further publicity, who claimed to have been first on the scene. According to this witness, the hole in the roof was unconnected with the crash, which actually occurred at the 'western-most building, not the eastern-most where we had been previously working' - this being consistent with a sketch map recorded by a policeman who guarded the site in 1940.

This new potential site, however, is beneath a warehouse erected in 1978, in good order and still in commercial use. In January 2008, with the consent of all stakeholders involved, DSTL carried out a further survey, recording two major readings in the new area. RSME then deployed a 'mobile drilling rig', removing 'core samples from the 5-7 metre band. These samples revealed various small fragments including bone, leather, laminated wood and some nits and bolts. Sadly, none of these fragments can be directly attributed to the aircraft, although the laminated wood is of a type consistent with 1930s aircraft construction. Both of the large electronic readings were further analysed by means of a magnetometer that was inserted into the drill holes; neither reading proved to be an aircraft, nor were any other significant readings located in the vicinity'.

In 2014, with building work yet to start, at Barton's Timber Wharf, another public campaign was launched to pressure the MOD into making another recovery attempt, but the response was that any further digs would be unlikely, and no further licences for the site issued, given that it had already proved impossible to locate and recover the wreckage and missing pilot on multiple occasions. That said, eleven years later there has still been no development at the site, and the current attitude of JCCC is that a new POMRA licence may be issued in the event of new evidence being presented likely to positively identify the crash-site and prior to any building work.

And so, despite multiple attempts, Flight Sergeant Williams remains missing, and Hurricane V6550 steadfastly defies discovery.

In 2025, there was a happier outcome in the case of Flying Officer Philip Anthony Neville Cox of 501 Squadron – although this did not involve a recovery.

On Saturday 27 July 1940, Dover harbour, was attacked by 3/Erprobungsgruppe 210, the destroyer HMS *Walpole* being damaged at 1430 hrs, before the Germans returned at teatime to sink another destroyer, HMS *Codrington*, and damage the depot ship HMS *Sandhurst* (these two ships being moored alongside each other in the Submarine Basin).

The previous day, 501 Squadron had moved from Middle Wallop in 10 Group to Gravesend in 11 Group, and at 1745 hrs on 27 July, 'B' Flight was on patrol one and a half miles north-east of Dover, as Pilot Officer Kenneth Lee (Blue 1) described:

> Sighted E/A diving onto Dover docks and immediately led the Squadron towards them when the Dover Defence Barrage opened up. I engaged one Me 109 pulling up from machine-gunning or bombing the docks, attacked with full deflection and then followed it round to take a further shot from full astern. My tracer ammunition passed through the E/A, which dived steeply towards the sea, followed by Blue 3, who himself could not get within effective range and quickly lost sight of it. There were our Spitfires and other Me 109s engaged in the vicinity.

Flying Officer Cox, however, failed to return from this action. At the time, it was believed that Cox, often referred to as P.A.N. Cox, had been hit by the Dover barrage, but more recently it has become clear that this popular flight commander was shot down by an Me 109 pilot , namely Leutnant Horst Marx, of 3/Erprobungsgruppe 210:

> After a bombing attack on a relief cruiser in Dover harbour, the Staffel was returning in the direction of Calais. The last machine was engaged in combat and the whole Staffel turned. The English machine veered away, but was caught up by us. After two other aircraft had already fired at it, I managed to get

> within 40m and my first burst, from behind and below, set it on fire. It immediately dived blazing into the Channel.

That day, Oberleutnant Otto Hintze, 3/Erprobungsgruppe 210's Staffelkapitän, was flying no less than his 100th combat mission, and confirmed Hintze's report:

> The English fighter, a Hurricane, attempted to escape in the direction of Dover. After a short burst I had to pull away to my left due to my greater speed. After completing the left turn, I saw that the Hurricane was hit by the third machine and shortly afterwards fell burning into the sea.

Feldwebel Büttner, flying No 2 to Hintze, added that:

> After being told over the W/T to turn back for combat, we saw an enemy aircraft (Hurricane) which, as we drew close, sought to escape in low flight. The Staffelkapitän, behind whom I flew closely, reached the enemy aircraft, which tried to avoid the bursts of fire by turning, whereupon I was able to give two short bursts at the enemy. With the enemy aircraft suddenly pulling upwards, No 1 and 2 passed by it, due to greater speed. I then saw one of the following machines fire a heavy burst into the opponent, which crashed into the water.

Cox was reported missing, but we now know, thanks largely to the efforts of Dutch researcher Philip Reinders, that his was the body washed ashore a month later at Westenschouwen on the Zeeland coast. This body was buried by the Germans as an unknown British RAF officer. How this happened is unclear, though, because burial records indicated the name Cox and the first two digits of his service number – 33184.

When reinterred at Bergen-Op-Zoom War Cemetery in 1946 those details were somehow lost, leading to the remains once more being 'Known unto God'. Those lost details, however, were rediscovered by Reinders, and CWGC and JCCC accepted that this particular unidentified burial was actually Flying Officer P.A.N. Cox. On 4 June 2025, Reverend (Squadron Leader) Jonathan Stewart RAF presided over a rededication service at Bergen-Op-Zoom, during which a new headstone named to Cox was unveiled.

Above left: Flying Officer PAN Cox, 501 Squadron.

Above right: The headstone of Flying Officer Philip Anthony Neville Cox in Bergen-Op-Zoom War Cemetery, photographed on the day of his rededication ceremony on 4 June 2025. (Courtesy of Martin Mace)

Going forward, whether any further recoveries of the 'Missing Few' will take place is doubtful, but thanks to the due diligence of mainly civilian researchers, it is quite possible that more 'unknown' graves could be identified. Time will tell.

Chapter Seven

A Selective Guide to Key Memorials Commemorating 'The Few', Battle of Britain Museums and Sites of Interest

There are, in fact, an astonishing number of memorials and monuments, official and unofficial, museums, both large and small, professional and amateur, and a host of associated sites of interest from former airfields to crumbling fortifications, and much more besides. To comprehensively list them all would be an impossible task, so the purpose of this guide is therefore to provide information on certain of these sites, sign-posting the way for the would-be Battle of Britain tourist to obtain more information, and hopefully find these interesting and, in some cases, essential locations to visit.

The websites, where relevant, of sites listed below can be found in the Bibliography.

The Battle of Britain Memorial

The National Memorial to 'The Few' has to be the primary site to visit, and is described in Chapter Two. High on the cliffs overlooking Folkestone, and on a good day France, this award-winning memorial and visitor centre is managed and maintained by the Battle of Britain Memorial Trust CIO, which we can all support by becoming a 'Friend of "The Few"' (see website).

This crucially important and dignified site of pilgrimage also includes the Christopher Foxley-Norris Memorial Wall, commemorating each of 'The Few' by name, and busts of Air Chief Marshal Hugh Dowding and Air Chief Marshal Keith Park.

The Battle of Britain Memorial and 'Wing' Visitor Centre, including the 'Cockpit' café and a well-stocked shop, can be found on New Dover

Detail of 'The airman' at the National Battle of Britain Memorial.

Road, between Dover and Folkestone, at Capel-le-Ferne, Kent CT18 7JJ. Admission is free but parking charges apply; please see website for opening times and further information.

RAF Chapel, Westminster Abbey

At the eastern end of King Henry VII's Lady Chapel, is the RAF Chapel, commemorating all RAF aircrew who perished in the Battle of Britain. Featuring the impressive Battle of Britain memorial window, two panels of which include Shakespeare's words from Henry V: 'We few, we happy few, we band of brothers'. The illuminated roll of honour commemorates the 1,497 pilots and aircrew killed or mortally wounded during the Battle, of which 449 were in Fighter Command (whom the window specially commemorates), 732 in Bomber Command, 268 in Coastal Command, 14 in other RAF commands and 34 in the FAA. The names include those of forty-seven Canadians, forty-seven New Zealanders, thirty-five Poles, twenty-four Australians, twenty Czechs, seventeen South Africans, six Belgians and one American, as well as those from the United Kingdom and Colonies.

The tablet beneath which lies Air Chief Marshal Lord Hugh Dowding's ashes in Westminster Abbey.

Air Chief Marshal Hugh Dowding is buried in the RAF chapel, a simple tablet in the floor reads 'He Led The Few in The Battle of Britain'. There could be no greater epitaph.

Also to be found in Westminster Abbey is the plaque commemorating the American volunteer, Pilot Officer Billy Fiske (whose grave is at Boxgrove Priory, in West Sussex).

Admissions times and charges apply.

The Battle of Britain London Monument

The Battle of Britain Monument, situated on Westminster's Victoria Embankment, commemorates everyone who experienced the Battle of Britain, from aircrew to civilians, and, being outdoors and in a public space, is free to view.

Detail of Westminster's Battle of Britain London Monument.

The RAF Memorial

Situated at Whitehall Stairs, Victoria Embankment, London SW1A 2HR, the RAF Memorial is topped by a great bronze eagle sculpted by Sir William Reid Dick and unveiled in 1923. A short distance from the Battle of Britain London Monument, again, being in an open space, admission to view is free.

The Air Forces Memorial at Runnymede

Commemorating by name over 20,000 men and women of the RAF, including foreign nationals, who failed to return from operations during the Second World War when flying from bases in the United Kingdom and

Entrance to the tower of the RAF Memorial.

The cloisters at Runnymede record the names of over 20,000 missing aircrew.

north-west Europe, this imposing memorial is situated on Cooper's Hill, Englefield Green, between Windsor and Egham on the A308, overlooking the Thames. The memorial is open every day except Christmas and New Year's Days, and admission is free. Maintained and managed by the CWGC, opening times vary with the season.

The Polish Air Force Memorial

Another suitably imposing memorial, commemorating the 2,408 Polish airman who lost their lives in the Second World War, 1,241 of these, being those lost on operational sorties, are commemorated by name; the Polish

The Polish Air Force Memorial.

Air Force Memorial can be found beside the A40/A4180 traffic island near RAF Northolt, between Ruislip and Northolt in Middlesex, west of London. Behind the memorial is a small park with commemorations concerning the famous Polish 303 Squadron, which flew from nearby Northolt during the Battle of Britain.

RAF Bomber Command Memorial

The late Queen Elizabeth II unveiled the Bomber Command Memorial, in Central London's Green Park, on 28 June 2012. Made of Portland stone and featuring larger-than-life-sized bronze statues of a bomber's crew, this impressive memorial commemorates the 55,573 Bomber Command aircrew

The Bomber Command Memorial in London's Green Park.

who made the ultimate sacrifice during the Second World War, including the Battle of Britain. Significantly, one wall is inscribed with these Churchillian words, spoken in September 1940: 'The Fighters are our salvation but the bombers alone provide the means of victory.'

Appropriately, the memorial is situated opposite the prestigious Royal Air Force Club in Piccadilly, and close to Hyde Park Corner tube station. There is no admission charge to the Bomber Command Memorial.

Perhaps surprisingly, although there is a comparatively modest Coastal Command memorial at Westminster Abbey, and one at North Berwick commemorating Coastal Command's crews lost flying from Scottish bases, there is no specific memorial to Fighter Command.

The Lee-on-the-Solent Memorial

Standing on the Hampshire coast looking out across the Solent towards the Isle of Wight, the Lee-on-the-Solent Memorial bears the names of over 1,900 servicemen and one woman of the RN's FAA who have no known grave. They died in operations across the globe, serving alongside the sailors of the RN and Merchant Navy in almost every theatre of the Second World War – including the Battle of Britain, in which fifty-six FAA pilots flew with Fighter Command units.

St Clement Danes, the Central Church of the RAF

Situated in Central London's Strand, St Clement Danes has been the scene of memorial services to countless RAF officers and personalities, outside which is the statue of Air Chief Marshal Hugh Dowding, made possible by the BoBFA. The statue is in a public space, but opening times apply to access the church itself.

The Dowding Memorial, Moffat

Born in Moffat in 1882, the town erected a memorial wall and plaques in Lord Dowding's honour at Station Park, on the right-hand side of the road when entering the town.

The Moffatt Memorial to Air Chief Marshal Lord Hugh Dowding. *(Tanja Anderson)*

Tributes to Sir Keith Park

Having first stood on the fourth plinth in Trafalgar Square, the huge statue of Keith Park, made possible through the Sir Keith Park Memorial Campaign, was re-located to Waterloo Place, London, and unveiled on 15 September 2010. Being in a public space, there is no admission charge.

The statue of Air Chief Marshal Keith Park at Auckland's MOTAT.

Copies of this impressive piece can also be seen at the Battle of Britain Bunker, Uxbridge (see separate entry) and The Museum of Transport and Technology (MOTAT) in Auckland, New Zealand. In fact, there are a number of tributes to Keith Park in New Zealand: at MOTAT is also the Memorial Garden of the Sir Keith Park Memorial Airfield, and a plaque erected by Sir Keith's fellow Auckland councillors to the memory of this 'distinguished citizen'; adjacent is a replica of Sir Keith's Hurricane, 'OK1' (albeit unauthentically painted); a (more accurate) replica is on the gate at the Sir Keith Park Memorial Airfield at Thames, and Sir Keith's uniform and medals can be seen at the Auckland War Memorial Museum.

In 2025, Keith Park's name will be added to the Christopher Foxley-Norris Memorial Wall at The National Battle of Britain Memorial, following this author having proved him to be a legitimate holder of the Battle of Britain Clasp and, therefore, both a leader and one of 'The Few' himself.

Memorials to the Battle of Britain VC

On 15 September 2016, headmaster Richard Hutchinson arranged the unveiling of a large plaque at Sholing Junior School, Southampton,

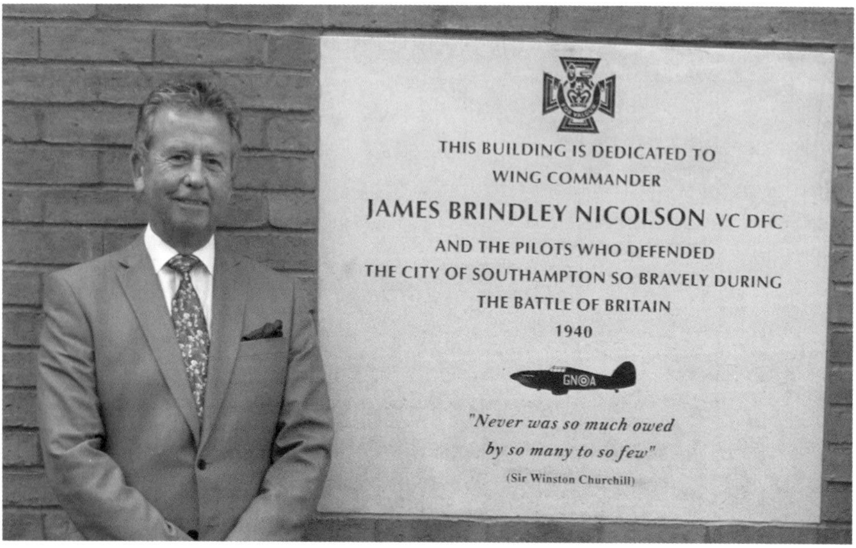

Jim Nicolson with the plaque commemorating his VC-winning uncle, Flight Lieutenant James Brindley Nicolson, at Sholing School, Southampton. *(Richard Hutchinson)*

Jim Nicolson with the plaque at Southampton Guildhall. *(Richard Hutchinson)*

dedicating a school building in memory of Wing Commander James Brindley Nicolson VC DFC 'and the pilots who defended Southampton so bravely during the Battle of Britain 1940'. The plaque was unveiled by the VC's nephew, Jim Nicolson.

The original memorial erected in 1970 near the spot where the VC landed by parachute at Millbrook, Southampton, having been dismantled during development work, on 19 October 2018, Jim Nicolson also opened 'Nicolson House' at the Leonardo's defence business premises now occupying the site. On 5 April 2019, Jim Nicolson also unveiled a similar plaque to that at Sholing School, also arranged by Richard Hutchinson, in Guildhall Square, Southampton.

Blue Plaque to Squadron Leader Brian Lane DFC

There are countless memorials to individual Battle of Britain airmen, at schools attended and elsewhere, including an unofficial blue plaque at the house where Squadron Leader Lane, CO of 19 Squadron, grew up, 17 Barrow Point Avenue, Pinner, Middlesex. Organised by local resident Paul Baderman, the plaque was unveiled on 25 September 2011, by

English Heritage having refused a blue plaque, Paul Baderman went ahead and organised his own to Squadron Leader Brian John Edward Lane.

19 Squadron's last surviving Battle of Britain pilot, Ken Wilkinson, and Squadron Leader Lane's one-time flight rigger, John Milne.

Roadside Memorial to Pilot Officer Arthur Clarke

This stone of remembrance, resembling a headstone, can be found on the west side of the road, by a coppice between two fields, 1km south of Newchurch, on Romney Marsh (post code TN29 0DJ). Pilot Officer Arthur Clarke remains buried at his crash site, in the field behind the memorial.

Brookwood Military Cemetery

Those of 'The Few' killed during the Battle of Britain and who have known graves can be found scattered throughout the land, in churchyards, both military and civilian cemeteries, and, if cremated, commemorated in various crematorium gardens of remembrance. Graves are a mixture of those for which the CWGC is responsible, and private family plots. Naturally

The fitting roadside memorial to Pilot Officer Arthur Clarke on Romney Marsh.

Brookwood Military Cemetery – immaculately maintained by the CWGC.

the larger plots and specific war cemeteries managed by the CWGC are immaculate, but sometimes those graves which are isolated in churchyards and cemeteries can fall into disrepair, especially private memorials, families having moved away or become extinct. The CWGC, therefore, as explained in this book, relies heavily on the eyes and ears of the public to monitor the overall situation.

Brookwood Military Cemetery is, of course, perfectly kept, containing the graves of 5,627 casualties from both world wars – including certain of 'The Missing Few' recovered since 1972 (see Chapter Six). This fascinating and moving place is situated at Brookwood, 30 miles from London, the main entrance being found on the A324 from Pirbright (postcode GU24 0JB). Admission is free, the site only being closed for Christmas and New Year's Days, but seasonal opening times apply and there are frequent guided tours by CWGC staff and volunteers.

Kent Battle of Britain Museum

The KBoBM, situated on a part of what was once the forward airfield at Hawkinge, near Folkestone, and accommodates the world's largest

The replica 32 Squadron Hurricanes. *(KBoBM)*

Plan view of the Kent Battle of Britain Museum at Hawkinge. *(KBoBM)*

collection of Battle of Britain artefacts, including artefacts from over 700 aircraft, from both sides, shot down during the conflict. Indeed, a visit to Hawkinge is an assault on the senses, there being just too much for the brain to process; indeed, KBoBM volunteers consider it would take a visitor ten days to properly see everything! From a multitude of recovered aircraft engines to replica aircraft, including a Defiant, the museum is also now displaying and conserving a Blenheim, which is a re-build project involving four Canadian-built Bolingbrokes, a He 111H-16 and a Ju 52.

The hard work and passion of the volunteers is inspirational, and exhibits also now feature the 'Spirit of The Few' Monument (described in

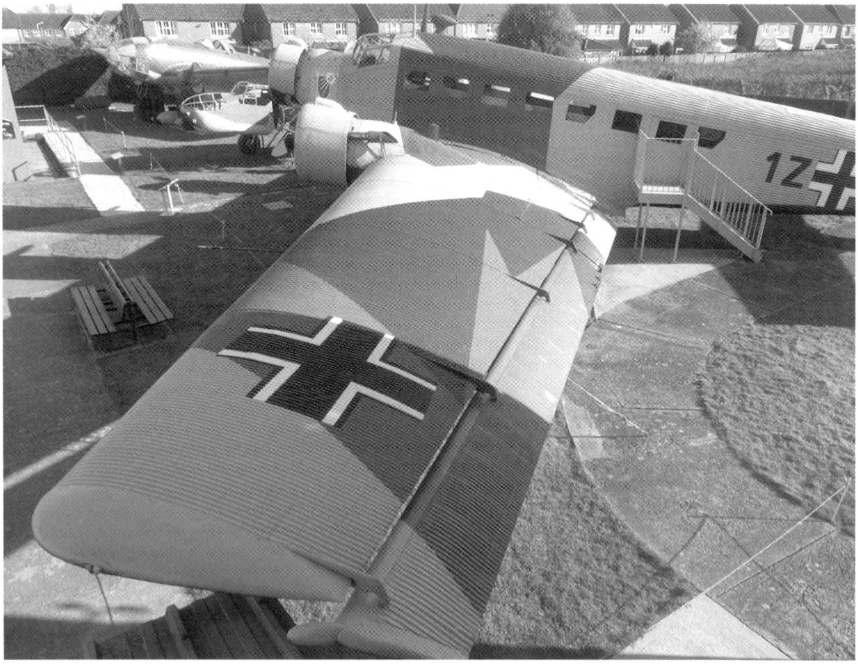

The Ju 52, and Blenheim and He 111 re-build projects. *(KBoBM)*

The Spirit of 'The Few' Monument. *(KBoBM)*

Above: The well-known photo taken of 32 Squadron pilots relaxing at Hawkinge between sorties, inspiring the monument.

Right: 'The Last of "The Few"' – detail of the Group Captain John Hemmingway statue.

Chapter Three), and statue of 'The Last of "The Few"', Group Captain John Hemmingway. Displays are comprehensive, covering both sides, the Home Front, and Hawkinge airfield's wider history. The Museum hosts educational visits and volunteers provide outreach work through delivering talks upon request, and the museum shop is, without a doubt, the best stocked enthusiast shop around.

Close to the National Battle of Britain Memorial at Capel-le-Ferne, the two sites perfectly compliment each other, being very different. The memorial's visitor centre provides the 'Scramble' experience, through modern technology, but is not a museum, the idea being to provide both a place of remembrance and quiet reflection, and an introduction to the Battle of Britain. Conversely, Hawkinge is overflowing with genuine artefacts, telling individual and personal stories of those who fought in the Battle of Britain – including many who died.

Above, opposite above and opposite below: Internal views of the museum's displays – which include artefacts from over 700 aircraft shot down during the Battle of Britain. *(KBoBM)*

THE ONE THAT GOT AWAY
HARDY KRUGER

Donations gratefully accepted

Across the road from KBoBM is Hawkinge cemetery, wherein lie various of 'The Few' and German Battle of Britain aircrew casualties, so visitors can always stop of pay their respects there too.

The museum opens annually from Easter through to Remembrance weekend in November. Opening times and admission charge applies, parking is free. Visitors also need to be aware that mobile phones, cameras and photography are not allowed on site, for security reasons, and so must either be left in cars or handed in at reception for collection upon conclusion of the visit.

RAF Museum, Hendon

Situated on the former airfield at Hendon in north-west London, it is a great shame that the former Battle of Britain Hall has recently been demolished. Nonetheless, the museum accommodates the Me 109E-3 of 2/JG 51, which was converted to the *Jabo* roll and shot down on 27 November 1940. The pilot, *Leutnant* Wolfgang Teumer was attacked

Leutnant Wolfgang Teumer's 2/JG 51 Me 109E-3 at Hendon.

Spitfire Mk IA X4590 of 609 Squadron at Hendon.

by Spitfires over the Thames Estuary, dropped his bomb in an attempt to escape – but was hit in the cooling system, so made a wheels-up forced-landing at Manston. The aircraft is exhibited in an approximation of its Battle of Britain colour scheme. Also at Hendon is another Battle of Britain airframe, namely Spitfire Mk IA X4590, which saw action with 609 Squadron in October 1940.

Opening times apply; admission is free but parking is charged.

RAF Museum, Cosford

Situated on the site of RAF Cosford in the West Midlands, the site accommodates the oldest surviving Spitfire, Mk I K9942; although with 57 OTU and not a fighter squadron during the Battle of Britain, the aircraft is of interest because it was flown when with 72 Squadron by Flight Lieutenant James Brindley Nicolson, the Battle of Britain VC.

Also at Cosford is the RAF Museum's restoration facility, The Michael Beetham Conservation Centre, the current projects of which include

Above: The oldest surviving Spitfire, K9942, once flown by the Battle of Britain VC, at Cosford.

Left and opposite above: Conserved parts of the Goodwin Sands Do 17 at Cosford.

preservation of the remains of the Do 17 recovered from the Goodwin Sands in 2013. Although nothing has been found to identify the aircraft, it is believed to be WN1160 of 7/KG 3, shot down on 26 August 1940 by a Boulton Paul Defiant turret-fighter of 264 Squadron. Perhaps appropriately, the sole surviving Defiant, N1671, can also be seen at the Cosford site. Although delivered to the RAF in August 1940, the aircraft saw no action, being taken on charge by 307 (Polish) Squadron, which was working up as a night-fighter unit, becoming operational in December 1940. The aircraft has been restored in its all-black 307 Squadron night-fighter colours.

Like the RAF Museum, Hendon, admission is free, opening times and parking charges apply.

The RAF Battle of Britain Memorial Flight

The BBMF is based at RAF Coningsby in Lincolnshire, amongst the aircraft of which, is, of course, a Battle of Britain combat veteran, Spitfire MK IIA, P7350, which can be seen, along with the Flight's other historic aircraft, at numerous air displays and flypasts annually.

Inspired: an 8-year-old Dilip Sarkar and Spitfire P7350.

At Dogdyke Road, Coningsby LN4 4SY, within the confines of RAF Coningsby, is the BBMF Visitor Centre, run by Lincolnshire County Council in partnership with the RAF, provides public access to the BBMF. Access to the hangar is by guided tour only, which can be booked online. Opening times and an entry charge apply, parking is free. Being on a military base, there are certain security constraints, including no bags allowed on the hangar tour.

Imperial War Museum London

The London branch of the IWM is situated at Lambeth Road, SE1 6HZ, and is open daily except between 24 and 26 December annually. Admission is

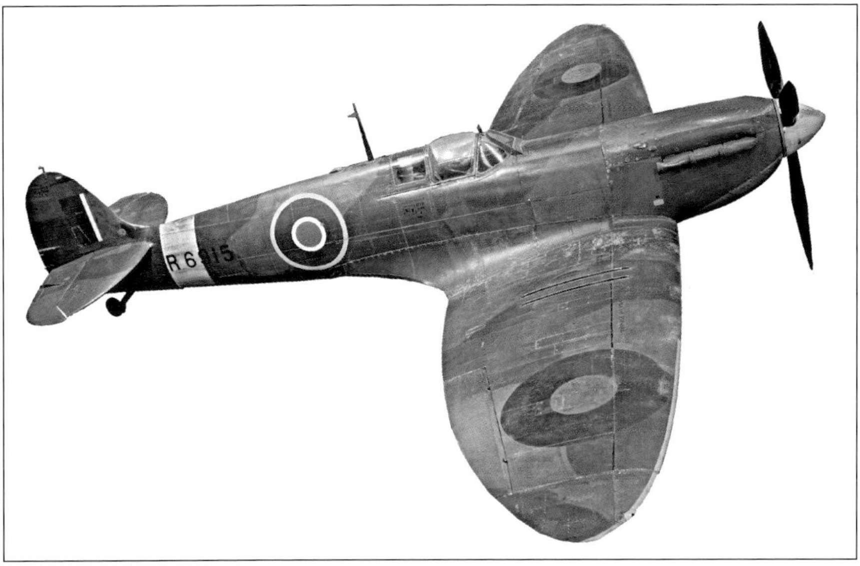

Spitfire R6915 at the IWM London. *(Historic Military Press)*

free; there is no parking but the museum is close to both Lambeth North and Elephant and Castle underground stations.

Amongst the museum's exhibits is Spitfire Mk IA, R6915, displayed suspended from the ceiling in its original wartime OTU colours – this aircraft, however, saw combat during the Battle of Britain and was flown by such pilots of 609 Squadron as Flying Officer John Dundas, Pilot Officer Noël le Chevalier Agazarian, and Flying Officer Rogers Freeman Garland Miller, all of whom recorded victories in this machine.

Imperial War Museum Duxford Airfield, Cambridge

Duxford, once a famous RAF fighter station, is now the IWM's working airfield, situated near Cambridge (CB22 2QR). This huge site accommodates various facilities, including vintage warbird restoration and operating companies, the American Air Museum, Airspace permanent display, a conservation hangar, Air and sea display, and land warfare. The Battle of Britain is well served at this one-time sector station from which the Hurricane squadrons of the controversial 12 Group 'Big Wing' once flew; it was also the station where 19 Squadron famously received the RAF's first

The East Dean Me 109E-3.

Spitfires, on 4 August 1938. It is also where some scenes of the 1969 *Battle of Britain* film were shot – and where a hangar was famously blown up for the cameraman!

Fortunately, 19 Squadron's hangar survives and is now the 'Battle of Britain Hall', housing various associated exhibits, including the battered Merlin engine of the Hurricane Squadron Leader Tom Gleave was shot down in on 31 August 1940 and horrendously burned. A prime exhibit, of course, is the Me 109E-3 of II/JG 26 in which *Unteroffizier* Horst Perez was shot-up and forced-landed at East Dean, Beachy Head, on 30 September 1940. Returned to its Battle of Britain colour scheme, the aircraft is displayed in a diorama replicating photographs taken at East Dean.

Also at Duxford is the recently refurbished Operations Room, the scene of high drama in 1940, which includes a room displaying some personal items of certain 19 Squadron Battle of Britain pilots, including the flying log books of Flying Officer (later Air Commodore) James Coward, and the silver cigarette case of Squadron Leader Brian Lane DFC, donated by myself in 2019.

Above: The refurbished Sector Operations Room at Duxford.

Right: A display within the Operations Room including the silver cigarette case of Squadron Leader Brian Lane DFC.

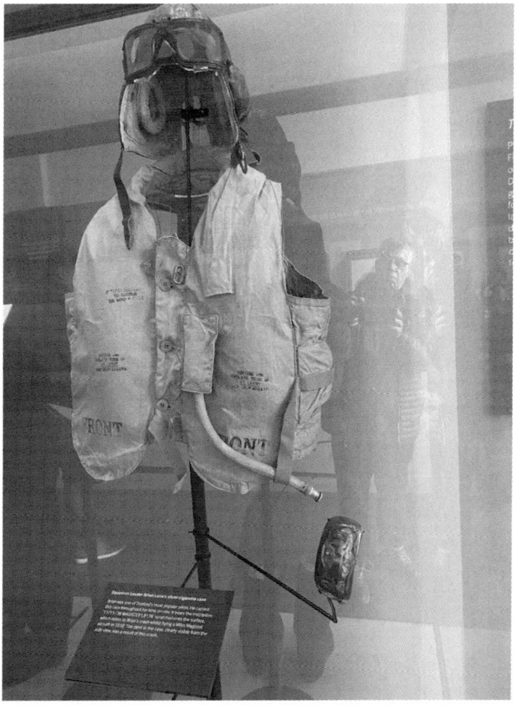

Duxford also hosts popular air shows, including the annual Battle of Britain show and various flying days at which visitors can marvel at the sight and sound of vintage warbirds.

Opening times and admission charges apply, and advanced booking online is recommended.

Fowlmere Airfield Museum

The airfield at Manor Farm, Fowlmere (SG8 7SH), just a few miles from Duxford, became that sector station's satellite, and during the Battle of Britain accommodated the Spitfires of 19 Squadron and, temporarily, the other Spitfire squadrons which flew with the 'Big Wing'. It is also where Flying Officer Stanley Devon took his iconic photographs of 19 and 616 Squadrons on 21 September 1940, including the haunting image of an exhausted-looking Squadron Leader Brian Lane. The grass area where that photograph, and others, were taken survives, as do the bases of the Nissen huts which appear in various images. A farm building also has a large-scale

Fowlmere Airfield Museum.

The 19 Squadron Memorial at Manor Farm, Fowlmere.

pair of wings painted on an internal wall by an RAF airman during the war, which has been preserved. Fowlmere, which is still an airfield with various businesses operating from premises there, was home to American fighters, the whole story being admirably recorded and told by the Fowlmere Airfield Museum, located in an original Nissen hut. Run by a team of just three volunteers, the museum opens to the public one Sunday monthly, although tours can be arranged by appointment. Also on site are various memorials, including one to pilots of 19 Squadron killed flying from Fowlmere during the Battle of Britain.

Nearby, at Whittlesford, is St Mary and St Andrew's church where several 19 Squadron Battle of Britain casualties are buried, including 19-year-old Pilot Officer Ray Aeberhardt; the 19 Squadron standard was laid up in the church, where it can be seen today.

Spitfire and Hurricane Memorial Museum, Manston

RAF Manston was hammered during the Battle of Britain because it was only ten minutes flying time from France and on the East Kent coast; it also has a much wider wartime and post-war RAF history.

The fiftieth Battle of Britain anniversary memorial outside the Spitfire and Hurricane Memorial Museum, Manston.

The Spitfire P9337 re-build project.

Manston's memorial to those who flew and served at this station.

Situated on the former RAF Manston site is the Spitfire and Hurricane Memorial Museum, and central to the displays there are a Spitfire Mk XVI and a Hurricane Mk IIC, neither of which, of course, are Battle of Britain survivors. There are, however, many exhibits relating to the summer and autumn of 1940, including artefacts recovered from crash sites. Of particular interest, for example, is the Spitfire Mk IA P9337 re-build project, this aircraft having been involved in both Dunkirk and the Battle of Britain, and now in the process of being returned to the air 'as a lasting tribute to all those who fought in the Battle of Britain'. Commendable too is the memorial plaque to the 600 Squadron Blenheim crew killed on 8 August 1940; shot-up, the pilot, Flying Officer Dennis Neve Grice DFC deliberately steered his burning aircraft away from the town of Ramsgate, thus avoiding civilian deaths, crashing into the sea off Royal Harbour. In 1979, a fishing trawler recovered a propeller assembly off Ramsgate believed to be from this aircraft, which is also on display.

This museum also has a Spitfire flight simulator, and a most impressive Lancaster cockpit section flight simulator.

Outside the museum is a memorial to those who flew from Manston, and the Allied Aircrew Memorial Garden.

The Museum is open daily from 10.00 hrs until 16.00 hrs, and admission and parking are free.

Kenley Airfield

Although a gliding club still operates from the former Kenley Sector Station near Caterham in Surrey, the aerodrome is now largely a common, providing an essential recreational facility for the local community. Visitors accessing the common from Hayes Lane will find the Kenley Airfield Memorial, and thanks to the admirable Kenley Revival Project are various infographics and trails relating the airfield's history and telling the stories of some who served there. Some of the blast pens remain, including that famously photographed from a low-flying Do 17 during the audacious raid on 18 August 1940. Unfortunately, however, the Operations Room has long been demolished, as have many other buildings, and part pf the airfield has become a housing estate – thankfully, like Hawkinge, with roads named after Kenley's pilots. The RAFA has a presence on site with its famous 'Portcullis Club', and the local Air Training Corps squadron is also based at Kenley. Personally, I find Kenley a most atmospheric place, it not being

The information marker welcoming visitors to Kenley Common.

The RAF Kenley Memorial, situated off Hayes Lane in an original blast pen.

The blast pen famously photographed during the low-level raid on 18 August 1940.

difficult to imagine the dawn chorus of Merlins being warmed up, squadrons scrambling to action, and fighters returning from combat. Kenley is best visited on a summer's day – have a walk around the perimeter, soak it all up – and take a picnic.

St George's RAF Chapel of Remembrance, Biggin Hill

In 1943, personnel at RAF Biggin Hill – known as 'The Strongest Link' – determined to create a memorial commemorating the airmen killed on operations whilst flying from this important sector station in the borough of Bromley, south-east of London and to the east of Kenley, not least those killed in the Battle of Britain. The intention was to commemorate that victory and the Station's 1,000th aerial victory, jointly shared in June 1943 between the Canadian Squadron Leader Jack Charles and Free Frenchman Commandant René Mouchotte. Three huts were converted to create a single chapel, the first commemorative service being held on Sunday, 19 September 1943. On this 'Battle of Britain Sunday' the reredos memorial was unveiled and the book of remembrance dedicated. Unfortunately, this original chapel was destroyed by fire in 1946, the current St George Chapel being a replacement built in 1951; there is also an adjacent and long-established Garden of Remembrance. St George's is a living chapel at which Anglican services are held at 09.30 hrs every Sunday.

St George's can be found at Main Road, Biggin Hill, TN16 3EJ.

The memorial window at St George's.

The reredos memorial at St George's Chapel, Biggin Hill.

Opening times apply – please refer to website and consider becoming a 'Friend'.

RAF Biggin Hill Museum

Situated on the same site as St George's RAF Chapel, which is owned by the London Borough of Bromley and controlled by the Biggin Hill Memorial Trust, is the RAF Biggin Hill Museum. Very much focused on the human experience, the Museum seeks to 'tell the story of Britain's most famous fighter station through the personal experiences of those who served there and the community that supported them.' Currently, in April 2024, the 'Women at War: Hidden Heroes of WWII' is running, and the museum also provides a Spitfire virtual reality experience.

St George's Chapel and RAF Biggin Hill Museum are open Tuesday to Sunday inclusive; an admission charge applies.

The somewhat austere Biggin Hill Museum's external appearance belies a warm welcome and interesting displays within.

Biggin Hill Heritage Hangar

Located at Biggin Hill Airport, 'Fly A Spitfire' operates a fleet of two-seater Spitfires and other two-seat warbirds, all of which are available for passenger experience throughout the year. Tours of the aircraft, hangar and restoration facilities can be booked, and of especial interest is Battle of Britain veteran Me 109E WN3579.

This aircraft was built in 1939 by Arado as an E-1, being upgraded to E-4 specification in early 1940. In April 1940 the machine was flying with LG2, and moved to the Pas-de-Calais in July 1940. On 24 August 1940, one of the most famous of all German fighter pilots recorded his first aerial victory, a Spitfire, flying this machine, namely *Fähnrich* Hans-Joachim Marseilles, the legend that became 'The Star of Africa'. On his second operation that day, Marseilles was shot-up over Sheerness by Spitfires and crash-landed

'White 14' at the Biggin Hill Heritage Hangar.

his damaged aircraft, WN3579, back at Calais-Marck. After repair the 109 later saw action in Russia where it was again damaged in combat and forced-landed by its pilot on the frontline; it was not recovered until 1992, by the Russian Aircraft Recovery Group. Acquired by Charleston Aviation that year, the aircraft was returned to airworthiness following a six-year re-build, making its first flight on 29 September 1999, in California. After a period of time in Canada the machine came to England, and can now be seen at Biggin Hill resplendent in the colours it wore when flown by Marseilles as 'White 14'.

RAF Northolt Sector Operations Room

RAF Northolt, to the west of London on the A40, is the only former Battle of Britain airfield to remain operational. In recent times, the Northolt Sector Operations Room in Building 27 – the 'Sir Keith Park Building' – has been painstakingly restored to its 1940 configuration by volunteers of the 'Sir Keith Park Heritage Project'. A 'Force Development Asset',

The excellent refurbished sector operations room at Northolt – where every effort, and more, has been made to achieve authenticity.

visits can be arranged to what is actually the birthplace of the Integrated Air Defence System.

RAF Hornchurch Heritage Centre

Another former London Sector Station now lost the development, the RAF Hornchurch Heritage Centre – another volunteer-run project – is located in two buildings of what were cottages used by the RAF from 1939–1946. After the RAF departed the buildings went over to the NHS, closing in 2013, before taken over by a developer, Bellway Homes, which gifted the buildings to the Hornchurch Aerodrome Historical Trust which opened the RAF Hornchurch Heritage Centre in 2019. The Centre can be found on Suttons Lane (RM12 6RU).

Firmly focusing on the stories of people, a series of themed rooms walks the visitor through the history of RAF Hornchurch, the Battle of Britain Room being the largest, accommodating numerous artefacts from aircraft recoveries and much more besides. The whole place is overflowing with

The RAF Hornchurch Heritage Centre.

Above and overleaf pages: Various displays at Hornchurch – another treasure trove of unique artefacts run by passionate volunteers.

Fred Barker & Ted Thorn
The Boulton Paul Defiant was a two seater British fighter fitted with a Rolls Royce Merlin engine. It had no forward firing armament but was fitted with a gun turret featuring 4 Browning 0.303 machine guns. During the Battle of Britain, the top scoring crew were Sergeant F J Barker and his Pilot Sergeant E R Thorn of 264 Squadron based at RAF Hornchurch who successfully downed 12 enemy aircraft. The Luftwaffe however quickly identified the Defiant's weakness in having no forward firing armament and poor manoeuvrability which resulted in its early withdrawal from the Battle due to high losses.
On 28th May 1940, Barker and Thorn shot down 3 Bf 109's and a Bf 110. The following day, they shot down 2 Ju 87's and a He 111 on the 31st May. Both men were promoted to Flight Sergeant and awarded the DFM for their actions.
Boulton Paul Defiant L7005 (PS-B) of 264 Squadron based RAF Hornchurch flown by Sgt E R Thorn & Sgt F J Barker
On 24th August 1940 they shot down a Ju 88 and on 26th August they engaged and shot down 2 Do17s and a Bf 109, but their Defiant L7005 (coded PS-B) was damaged and they crash landed in a field at Marshside near Chislet injuring both Barker and Thorn. The relic on display is part of Defiant L7005 (PS-B) recovered from the crash site and has been kindly loaned for display by Trevor Williams.
BATTLE of
AIR MINISTRY · PAMPHLET
Boulton Paul Defiant
264 Sqdn
Hornchurch, Essex
Sgts. E.R.Thorn & F.J.Barker.
HORNCHURCH MODEL CLUB

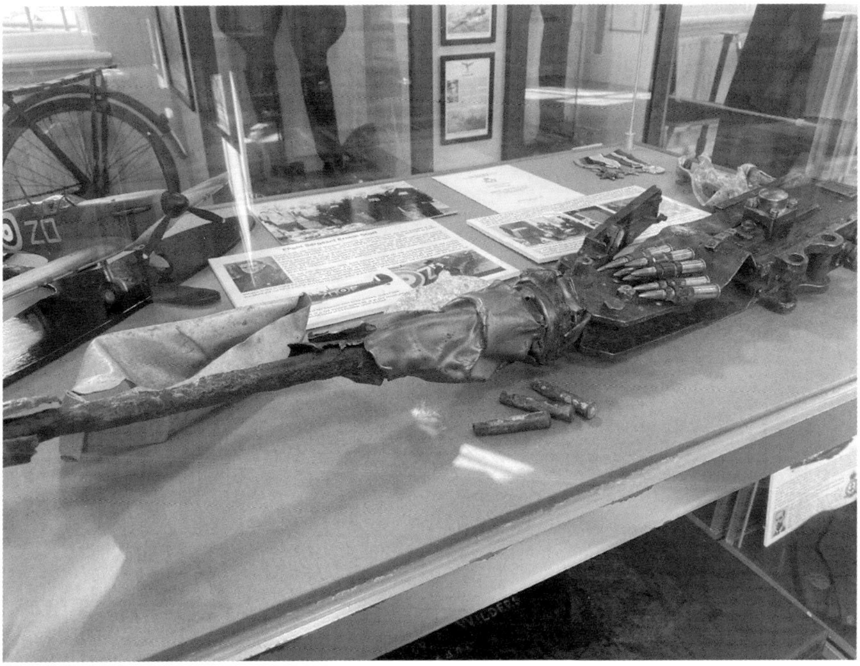

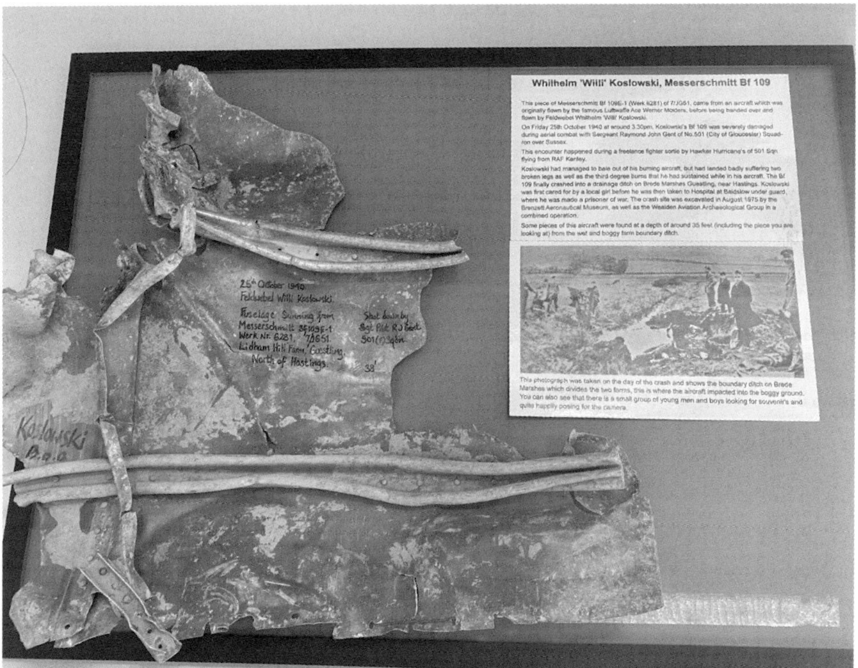
Whilhelm 'Willi' Koslowski, Messerschmitt Bf 109
On Friday 25th October 1940 at around 3.30pm, Koslowski's Bf 109 was severely damaged during aerial combat with Sergeant Raymond John Gent of No.501 (City of Gloucester) Squadron over Sussex.
This encounter happened during a freelance fighter sortie by Hawker Hurricane's of 501 Sqn flying from RAF Kenley.
Koslowski had managed to bale out of his burning aircraft, but had landed badly suffering two broken legs as well as the third degree burns that he had sustained while in his aircraft. The Bf 109 finally crashed into a drainage ditch on Brede Marshes Guestling, near Hastings. Koslowski was first cared for by a local girl before he was then taken to Hospital at Baldslow under guard, where he was made a prisoner of war. The crash site was excavated in August 1975 by the Brenzett Aeronautical Museum, as well as the Wealden Aviation Archaeological Group in a combined operation.
Some pieces of this aircraft were found at a depth of around 35 feet (including the piece you are looking at) from the wet and boggy farm boundary ditch.
This photograph was taken on the day of the crash and shows the boundary ditch on Brede Marshes which divides the two farms, this is where the aircraft impacted into the boggy ground. You can also see that there is a small group of young men and boys looking for souvenir's and quite happily posing for the camera.

treasures, inside and out, and encourages visits from all age groups. An asset for school visits is the Ted Exall Education Suite, named in honour of this inspirational man, a driving force behind recording the history of Hornchurch. It is impossible to be anything other than impressed by the quality of displays and passion of the volunteers involved.

Monday through to Friday are devoted to school and group bookings, the centre being open to the general public between 11.00 hrs and 16.00 hrs at weekends; an admission charge applies.

North Weald Airfield Museum

This former sector station to the north-east of London, at Epping, is still an airfield, although no longer an RAF station. Nonetheless, the airfield still reverberates to the sound of Merlins, given that Aero Legends operates from there (and Headcorn), providing 'vintage flying experiences' in aircraft including two-seater Spitfires. The museum is situated in a former airfield building, 'Ad Astra House', showcasing 'vintage aircraft, artefacts, and exhibits, preserving the rich heritage of aviation' – including North Weald's rich Battle of Britain history.

Open on weekend afternoons and most bank holidays, a small admission charge applies and parking free.

Tangmere Military Aviation Museum

The Tangmere Military Aviation Museum (TMAM) is located in a corner of this former sector station and most famous fighter aerodrome on the south coast, near Chichester in West Sussex. Opened by enthusiasts in 1982, the museum has grown considerably over the years, and now accommodates various static aircraft, exhibited indoors and outdoors, a memorial garden, and five halls, one of which is the Battle of Britain Hall.

Most impressively, Tangmere's Battle of Britain Hall showcases the tattered uniform worn by Flight Lieutenant James Brindley Nicolson during his VC-winning action on 16 August 1940, and other connected artefacts. The substantial wreckage of Sergeant Dennis Noble's Hurricane (see Chapter Six) provides a striking centrepiece.

Mainly staffed by volunteers, TMAM, which also encourages and accommodates school visits, is open seven days a week; an admission charge applies.

The display dedicated to Wing Commander James Brindley Nicolson VC DFC at Tangmere.

The substantial wreckage of Sergeant Dennis Noble's Hurricane.

Douglas Bader Statue, Goodwood

Tangmere's satellite airfield was at nearby Westhampnett, on the Goodwood Estate, owned by the Duke of Richmond. Now known simply as 'Goodwood' and famous as a motor racing circuit and civilian airfield, during the Battle of Britain the Spitfires of 602 Squadron flew from here. The following year, when Fighter Command was re-organised so that every sector station operated a three-squadron-strong Spitfire wing, Wing Commander Douglas Bader, the legless fighter ace, was appointed to command the Tangmere Wing – and based himself here, at Goodwood, with 616 Squadron. Indeed, it was from this grass airfield on 9 August 1941 that Wing Commander Bader made that fateful flight resulting in him being brought down and captured over France. Sixty-years later, on 9 August 2001, Bader's widow, Lady Bader, unveiled a life-size bronze statue of her late husband at Goodwood, created by the sculptor Kenneth Potts and based upon photographs in my archive. Today, the statue can be seen outside Goodwood Flying Club.

The Douglas Bader Statue as it appears today outside Goodwood Flying Club.

Rochester Memorial: Slaughter of the Innocents

A poignant memorial is the free-standing plaque at Rochester Airport, Maidstone (ME1 3QY), essentially commemorating the role played by Kentish airfields in the Battle of Britain whilst specifically remembering

Rochester Airfield Memorial.

the tragic events of 19 July 1940: the 'Slaughter of the Innocents'. On that day, when the Defiant equipped 141 Squadron was virtually annihilated. Appropriately, the memorial was unveiled by the Lord Lieutenant of Kent on 19 July 2010.

The Airfields of Britain Conservation Trust has marked many former Battle of Britain airfields with free-standing memorials, including Hawkinge, Gravesend, Eastchurch, Hornchurch, and even Bibury in the Cotswolds.

The Shoreham Aircraft Museum

Situated at the village of Shoreham near Sevenoaks in Kent (TN14 7TB), The Shoreham Aircraft Museum very much focuses on the Battle of Britain, accommodating countless artefacts from aircraft recovered by the museum

Replica Ju 88 cockpit at Shoreham. *(SAM)*

Display concerning 303 (Polish) Squadron at Shoreham. *(SAM)*

and items donated by the public. As with other museums in this selective guide, the concept is to tell the story of the human experience behind these distressed pieces of metal. As explained previously, the museum currently has an ongoing initiative to erect memorials to every one of 'The Few' who crashed and were killed within a ten-mile radius of the museum. As the museum's website explains, 'the list is not a short one'. So far, twelve such memorials have been erected close to where those commemorated died. This really is what it's all about: commemoration, remembrance and raising awareness, and donations towards the project are always gratefully received.

The museum is open from Easter to Remembrance Sunday annually, a small admission charge applies.

The South West Airfields Heritage Exeter Airport Memorial

RAF Exeter in Devon was an important 10 Group Sector Station, accommodating 87 and variously other Hurricane squadrons during the Battle of Britain. It was here that 'Widge' Gleed was based when he wrote

The Exeter airfield memorial. *(Chris Wiseman)*

his memoir *Arise to Conquer* (see Chapter Four), and from where Wing Commander Johnny Dewar took off but failed to return on 11 September 1940, becoming the highest-ranking RAF officer to die in the Battle of Britain. Indeed, twenty-two of 'The Few' lost their lives flying from Exeter during the Battle of Britain.

Today, Exeter International is a civilian airport, where The South West Airfields Heritage Exeter Airport Memorial was unveiled on 27 March 2012, commemorating those who died flying from Exeter throughout the Second World War, and detailing the various squadrons based there between 1940 – 1945. Sculpted by Devonian Frances Margaret, the statue depicts an RAF fighter pilot, who has safely returned from action, anxiously scanning the sky for his missing comrades, inspired by the heavy fighting with which Exeter squadrons were engaged in over Portland in August 1940.

Aerospace Bristol

In 1940, the aircraft and aero-engine manufacturing plants at Filton aerodrome, near Bristol, made it the largest aircraft manufacturing site in the world. This fact was well-known to the Germans – but what Luftwaffe intelligence did not appreciate was that Filton accommodated a 10 Group

The bomb-damaged girder at Filton from No. 2 Shop.

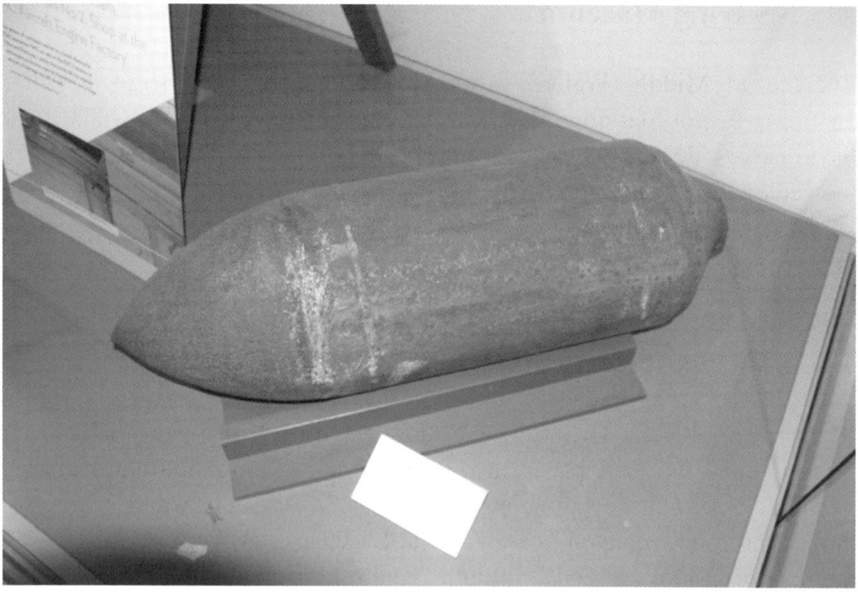

An SC250KG UXB at Filton.

Sector Operations Room, controlling fighters at Pembrey in South Wales, and Bibury in the nearby Cotswolds. Initially, there were no fighters based at Filton, however, which was heavily and accurately bombed by KG 55's He 111s on 25 September 1940, with great loss of civilian life and damage arising. Consequently, the Hurricanes of 504 Squadron were moved from Hendon to Bristol – a wise move, because on 27 September 1940 the newly arrived fighters routed a raid bound for Parnall Aircraft at Yate, in full view of Bristolians. Today, Filton no longer has an RAF presence but remains an aircraft production centre, having famously once produced the supersonic airliner Concorde.

The Aerospace Bristol Museum conserves Bristol Aerospace's heritage and celebrates the company's world-class innovations over the years. Naturally the site is of interest to Battle of Britain enthusiasts, having been a sector station and active airfield – and Luftwaffe target. Amongst the museum's exhibits are a bomb-damaged girder from a factory roof damaged in the big raid, and an unexploded SC250KG bomb (since made safe!) dropped by KG 55 that fateful day.

Aerospace Bristol can be found at Hayes Way, Patchway, BS34 5BZ, and is open seven days a week, except 24 to 26 December inclusive, annually, and for special events – please see website; an admission charge applies.

Army Flying Museum

Located at Middle Wallop, near Stockbridge in Hampshire, another 10 Group Sector Station and Operations Room during the Battle of Britain, the museum does not concern the Battle of Britain, but nonetheless is located on a site with a heritage link to 'The Few'.

The museum is open seven days a week, excluding the Christmas bank holidays; an admission charge applies.

The Southwest Battle of Britain Memorial

Remaining with 10 Group, the Southwest Battle of Britain Memorial was unveiled on 20 September 2020, marking the eightieth anniversary, paying tribute to those squadrons based in the West Country and, of course, those who died. Situated at Beachside, Bowleaze, Weymouth DT3 6PW, the memorial looks over Weymouth Bay and Portland, the scene of fierce fighting and many casualties during the Battle of Britain.

Bentley Priory Museum

The RAF has long been gone from Bentley Priory, the mansion in Stanmore, Middlesex (HA7 3FB), which was Fighter Command's HQ during the Battle of Britain, accommodating the Command Operations Room, Air

Replica aircraft outside Bentley Priory.

The replicated Fighter Command Operations Room at Bentley Priory.

Chief Marshal Hugh Dowding and his staff. Appropriately, prior to the RAF quitting the site in 2008, for many years the BoBFA held its annual reunions at Bentley Priory – and as at the time of writing, April 2024, only one known member of 'The Few' remains alive, it is bitter-sweet to reflect upon reunion dinners I personally attended back in the 1990s with up to 120 Battle of Britain aircrew present. Having since been sold by the MOD and developed as luxury apartments, fortunately the site is not lost to the Battle of Britain's heritage: in 2013, after eight years of planning and fundraising, Bentley Priory Museum opened its doors.

The museum includes stained glass Spitfire, Hurricane and a Royal Observer Corps window, and outside Spitfire and Hurricane replicas stand silent sentinel. The light, airy and very well-presented displays includes a collection of memorabilia relating to 'The Few', and Air Chief Marshal Hugh Dowding's office accommodates an educational film and has been restored to its 1940 appearance. To the mansion's east is the concrete and steel entrance to the RAF Bentley Priory Bunker, built in 1939 and which, in 1940, accommodated the vital Fighter Command Filter and Operations Rooms deep underground. Able to withstand a direct hit by both a 500lb HE and 250lb semi-armour-piercing bomb, most of the Bunker is now filled in, just leaving the imposing entrance.

Certain scenes of the 1969 film Battle of Britain were shot here, in Dowding's office, and when Laurence Olivier (Dowding) and Trevor Howard (Park) walk down the external stairs in a closing scene – the final take being over the Priory's formal gardens and fountain, looking towards London, and these remain, lovingly tended by green-fingered volunteers.

Bentley Priory Museum is only open of certain days of the week, times varying with the season, so please check website for details; an admission charge applies.

The Battle of Britain Bunker and Visitor Centre, Uxbridge

This underground bunker accommodated Air Vice-Marshal Keith Park's 11 Group Operations Room, from where the air component of the Dunkirk evacuation was controlled, along with 11 Group's operations during the Battle of Britain, in addition to Operations Jubilee and Overlord. It is also

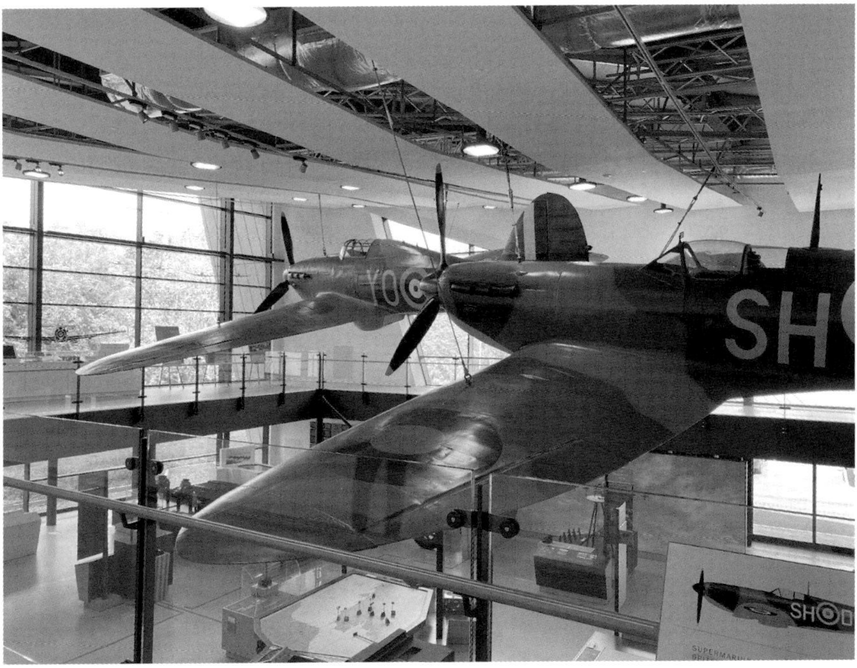

Interior of the Battle of Britain Bunker's state of the art visitor centre.

where Churchill was inspired, after witnessing high drama, to say 'Never in the field of human conflict was so much owed by so many to so few', and was present in the gallery on 15 September 1940: Battle of Britain Day. The Operations Room, deep underground and accessed via seventy-six steps, has been restored to represent how it appeared on that historic day. Owned by Hillingdon Council, visits to the actual Operations Room are via guided tours only, which must be pre-booked. For those unable to negotiate the steps, a virtual Bunker tour is hosted on the facility's website.

The site also includes a modern, state of the art, visitor centre on two floors, focused upon the aircraft and people involved, including an exhibition detailing the development of Britain's air defence system. Various artefacts are displayed, which, along with modern technology, bring the Bunker's story to life. With nearby RAF Northolt being synonymous with Polish fighter squadrons, including the famous 303, the Visitor Centre promotes that link very well, with many Polish Air Force related artefacts, a replica Polish Hurricane being outside, and displays the medals of Group Captain Ronald Kellett, who led 303 Squadron in the Battle of Britain. The Centre also benefits from a top-class lecture theatre.

No. 11 Group Operations Room.

No. 11 Group Operations Room gallery – where Churchill famously watched the dramatic events of 15 September 1940.

The bunker and visitor centre are open seven days a week; admission charge is variable, depending upon whether both the bunker and centre are visited, or just one or the other.

East Grinstead Museum

Throughout the six volumes of this series devoted to a day-by-day narrative of the Battle of Britain's sixteen weeks, we have learned of the visionary reconstructive surgery, of body and soul, undertaken at East Grinstead's Royal Victoria Hospital by the plastic surgeon Archibald McIndoe. Together with certain of his patients, McIndoe became a founder member of the 'Guinea Pig Club', and a section of East Grinstead Museum is devoted to these remarkable men. Just a few minutes from the town's historic High Street (RH19 3BJ), the museum's permanent 'Rebuilding Bodies and Souls' exhibition provides a lasting legacy for the Guinea Pig Club, telling the story of the unconventional burns unit on Ward III. Although

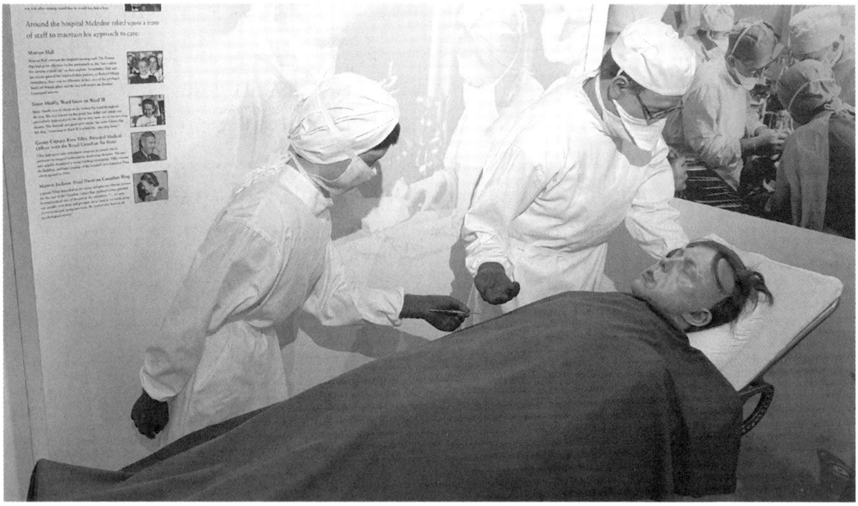

One of the hard-hitting displays at East Grinstead.

not specifically focused on 'The Few', there were no shortage of Battle of Britain aircrew treated at East Grinstead, and to witness this exhibition, and to have some comprehension of the agony they must have endured, through countless operations and ongoing treatment, is humbling indeed.

Supermarine Bombing Memorial

The vulnerable Supermarine factory, on the banks of the river Itchen at Woolston, Southampton, was a vulnerable target, being so close to the

Supermarine Memorial, Southampton.

coast – and also a priority one, given that it produced the all-important Spitfire. The factory was hit a number of times, most notably on 24 and 26 September 1940, with great loss of life and devastating damage. Although the factory is long-gone, making way for a health centre and flats, a plaque commemorates the Woolston workers killed and injured in these raids. The plaque can be found on the Itchen's eastern bank, just south of the Itchen Bridge, on the west side of Hazel Road, and on the site of the former Itchen Ferry and Supermarine works.

Surviving Fortifications

Pill boxes and other bunkers sprang up all over the country, ready to defend beaches, arterial roads, waterways and other key sites, many of which remain – and are a study all of their own. Interestingly, anti-tank defences and pill boxes can still be seen today at Kimmeridge Bay in Dorset, and Cuckmere

Beach defences at Kimmeridge Bay in Dorset – which was one place at which the Germans intended to land.

Cuckmere Haven in East Sussex – another landing site chosen for Operation *Seelöwe*.

One of many surviving pill boxes at Cuckmere Haven.

Haven in East Sussex, both beaches having been selected as landing grounds by the Germans in the event of Operation *Seelöwe* going ahead.

The MECO bombing memorial, Worcester

On 3 October 1940, Worcester, a provincial city in the West Midlands and of little military significance, was mistaken for Coventry by Ju 88 pilot

After the unveiling of the MECO Memorial by survivor Irene Allen (with trolly), Dilip Sarkar, having delivered the keynote, pictured with councillors Karen Lewing (extreme left) and Richard Udall (obscured), and families of survivors.

Leutnant Otto Bischoff, who attacked the Mining and Engineering Company premises in Bromyard Road, St John's, from low-level (see Volume 7, *The Final Curtain*). Seven workers were killed and fifty more civilians injured in what was the only time loss of life was caused through bombing in 'The Faithful City'. On 26 July 2023, a survivor, 95-year-old Irene Allen, unveiled a sculpture commemorating the victims in the new MECO Memorial Nature Park off Sanctuary Close, St John's. Jointly funded by Worcester City Council, Platform Housing and Worcestershire County Council, this is the latest memorial to civilian war dead from the Battle of Britain but, at the time of writing, June 2025, the memorial has been temporarily removed for repair following mindless vandalism.

Hangar 42, Spitfire Visitor Centre

Located at Blackpool Airport, Squire's Gate, 'Hangar 42' was built in 1939 to accommodate night fighters. The Spitfire Visitor Centre in Hangar 42 now comprises five Spitfire replicas, a Hawker Hurricane MK I, and a superb Me 109E replica in JG 51 Battle of Britain colours. With flight simulators, artefacts from locally recovered crashed aircraft and many more displays besides, the Centre also has a collection of wartime RAF airfield vehicles, and is very much about recreating the atmosphere and times of 1940, both at Hangar 42 and via outreach work. An important aviation museum in the north-west, Hangar 42 is volunteer-run, and like most independent museums relies upon donations and entrance fees to continue its work.

Guided hangar tours can be booked online; admission charge applies.

The Armstrong and Aviation Museum, Bamburgh Castle

The north-east was heavily attacked during the Battle of Britain, when on 15 August 1940, He 111s, escorted by Me 110s, sallied forth from Norway – but were decimated by RAF fighters from 12 and 13 Groups. Indeed, the Norway-based *Luftflotte* 5 was defeated in that single day, and played no further substantial part in the assault on Britain. Bamburgh Castle, that huge and ancient coastal fortress in Northumberland was not somewhere I expected to find traces of the Battle of Britain – but artefacts from that fateful day are on display there.

The Me 110-tyres at Bamburgh Castle.

Bamburgh Castle is owned by and remains the private residence of the Armstrong family, of Armstrong-Whitworth aviation manufacturing fame – and the Castle also accommodates The Armstrong and Aviation Museum, devoted to telling the remarkable story of inventor William Armstrong, and includes artefacts from both world wars. Amongst these are the substantial remains of Spitfire L1037, which saw action with 610 Squadron at Dunkirk and the Battle of Britain before being lost in a mid-air collision on 30 September 1940, after 610 had been withdrawn from Biggin Hill to Acklington. Most unexpected, though, was the pair of tyres washed up on Seahouses Beach in 1988, from one of the Me 110s shot down in the great north-east air battle of 15 August 1940.

Access to the Armstrong and Aviation Museum is on the general Bamburgh Castle admission ticket, which can be booked online.

Yorkshire Air Museum and Allied Air Forces Memorial

According to its website, the Yorkshire Air Musuem is 'the UK's largest independent aviation museum' and located on the site of the former RAF Elvington, a bomber base. Of interest to Battle of Britain enthusiasts will be the area devoted to 609 'West Riding' Squadron, which operated from Middle Wallop and Warmwell in 10 Group throughout the summer and autumn of 1940.

Open seven days a week, excluding Christmas and New Year holidays, an admission charge applies.

Other Commemorations

In this necessarily selective guide, over fifty sites of interest are covered, which includes the primary memorials and museums; there are literally hundreds of smaller commemorations, such as the many plaques erected at schools attended by 'The Few', and it would be virtually impossible to list them all. Nonetheless, this guide will hopefully be of help and interest to anyone wishing to reach out and do some time travelling back to those dark days of 1940.

Reflections

So there we have it: *The Battle of Britain Remembered.* Whilst the world has changed beyond recognition since 1940 and the early post-war period, there can be no doubt that the Battle of Britain is actually in no danger of being forgotten.

From imposing, permanent, official memorials and monuments to individual tributes, from museums great and small to independent film makers, commemoration of the Battle of Britain is very much alive and well. It may not attract the same media interest that once it did, but the demonstrable fact is there are many people and organisations still working tirelessly to keep the memory of the Battle of Britain alive.

As explored in Chapter One, the Battle of Britain remains relevant, and always will be: for without it there would have been no other battles and the world would undoubtedly have slid into a fascist dominated abyss – from which democracy may never have recovered. It is right, then, that those who fought in, or in some other way contributed to this victory, are remembered. That some involved were fighting alone, in their aircraft 5 miles high, and were still teenagers, is something which remains incomprehensible, to me, anyway: unsurpassed and inspirational courage indeed.

Social media, of course, can be a great tool for raising awareness, and the Battle of Britain is far from neglected across platforms such as Facebook and Twitter. Computer games, flight simulators, virtual reality, all reach out to attract and interest youthful minds. Times continue to change as technology rockets ever forward – and with it so too must be how we think about how best to encourage and maintain commemoration and remembrance. By that, what I mean is, without glorifying war, the Battle of Britain has to be presented in such a way, on modern communication platforms and innovatively reach out and appeal to the young. To that end, then, the 'Scramble' experience at the National Battle of Britain Memorial Visitor Centre, using modern audio-visual technology, is very much sign-posting the future.

This book, whilst a stand-alone one, is also the last in my eight-volume series, written as an official history for The Battle of Britain Memorial Trust. It is an unprecedented narrative of virtually a million words, and, I can say with some certainty, is never likely to be repeated. Returning to primary sources, as the narrative progressed it was clear that in some respects history was being re-written, new facts discovered and evidence assembled. The Battle of Britain is a huge story, a diverse range of human experience, which I have tried my best to also capture. Furthermore, it was not just about fighter pilots, and nor was it only fought over London and the south-east. Bomber Command and Coastal Command, and the FAA, all played their part, and those stories are vitally important too. This collectively enormous story is, I hope the reader agrees, now well-covered by this 8-volume, 360 narrative.

Martin Mace, my close friend and commissioning editor at Pen & Sword, and I first mooted the production of this series back in 2020. By early 2022 certain other projects were concluded, and discussions began with the Battle of Britain Memorial Trust and Pen & Sword, both of which were immediately enthusiastic. The series was planned out and commissioned, and I recall walking with friends in the Cotswolds at the time, mulling things over and, I must admit, feeling a little intimidated as reality set in regarding the enormity of my self-imposed task. For the next two years the project dominated my life, day in, day out; sleepless nights, even, as I worked out how best to cover and present certain stories or sections of the narrative.

My brief was to produce a readable and accessible narrative, unfettered by notes and references, hence why I opted for simple in-text referencing and not reams of footnotes, in a similar style, I suppose, to that great British narrative historian Martin Middlebrook, and my old mentor, the late Dr Alfred Price. Rather than simply provide boxes of facts and flashy graphics, the intention was to create a readable and coherent, chronological, narrative. That process posed no challenge, but what was surprising was just how much of the long-accepted and heavily myth-laden narrative was at odds with the actual evidence – leading in certain cases to new interpretations.

Time consuming, it was, to check every single combat report, verify every fact from primary sources, and even that was fraught with danger given the haste with which the records of the time were completed and are often found to be either contradictory or wholly inaccurate, not least in respect of dates, times, locations and aircraft types engaged. There has been, it seems, an almost irrebuttable presumption amongst historians of the period, for example, that Luftwaffe casualty and combat records are entirely accurate. The fact is this investigation and narrative proves they are not. The same is true of RAF records, especially those of the 'Big Wing', which demonstrably over-claimed on occasions by as much as 7:1. What many still do not appear to fully grasp is the huge gulf of difference between a combat claim and an actual confirmed kill, which there was insufficient time and information available in 1940 to cross-reference and corroborate. Indeed, as former Chief Supermarine Test Pilot Jeffrey Quill, himself one of 'The Few', once said to me many years ago, 'Dear boy … In 1940 our minds were not focussed [*sic*] on either records or posterity!'

Another demonstrable fact is that the more numerous Hurricane did not execute substantially greater damage on the enemy than all other defences combined as has previously been believed. The fact is that the Hurricane and, much smaller, Spitfire forces destroyed, in reality, virtually the same amount of enemy aircraft – which makes the less numerous Spitfire, therefore, more successful per capita. Moreover, the altitude at which the lethal Me 109 intruded significantly increased as the battle progressed, and by late October 1940 we are talking about 31,000ft – or even up to 34,000ft. Only the Spitfire could take on the Me 109 at that height. The fact is, we desperately needed the Camm's Hurricane – but could not have done without the Spitfire and its high-altitude capacity. Again, the evidence is at odds with the long-accepted narrative. All of this, and more, is explained, in forensic detail, in these eight volumes.

The project became a tangible entity in 2023 when Volume 1, *The Gathering Storm*, was published, and now, with publication of this book the whole series has now been realised in print. I could leave no greater legacy after a lifetime's obsession with and study of the Battle of Britain, fulfilling what I have always felt was a moral obligation to continue telling the story of 'The Few', so many of whom I knew as personal friends. None have lived to see this project, but I am sure a number of ghosts have joined me at my desk during many an early hour spent writing.

Further words would be superfluous.

COMMONWEALTH
WAR GRAVES

Remembering the Battle of Britain

In the annals of human history, there exist moments that transcend time, etching themselves into the collective consciousness of nations and generations. The Battle of Britain is one such moment – a pivotal chapter in the crucible of the Second World War, it stands as a testament to the resilience, sacrifice, and indomitable spirit of the men and women of the Royal Air Force and her Allies during this country's darkest hours.

This series, researched and written by the historian Dilip Sarkar MBE, has explored the fascinating facts of how the Battle was fought and won, but equally compelling is the way the Battle, and those who took part in it, have been portrayed or remembered – either in official histories, popular culture, and even physical memorialisation. In many ways, that narrative has been greatly influenced by Churchill's famous words… "Never in the field of human conflict has so much, been owed by so many, to so few." This book will explore both the reality and the myth.

For the Commonwealth War Graves Commission, the task is perhaps clearer. Those who died are commemorated in graves marked and cared for by the Commission across the United Kingdom. Those who by the very nature of air warfare have no known grave, are commemorated on the magnificent CWGC Air Forces Memorial at Runnymede, near Windsor. As Her Late Majesty, The Queen remarked when she unveiled the memorial in 1953… "As only free men can, they knew the value of that for which they fought, and that price was worth paying."

The Battle of Britain was not merely a clash of arms, but a testament to the resilience of the human spirit. It was a struggle for the very soul of civilisation, where ordinary men and women rose to extraordinary heights – both literally and metaphorically – to defend hearth and home against the forces of tyranny. In the pages that follow, we explore how the Battle has been remembered but we also pay homage to those who gave their all so that we may live in a world free from oppression.

As we remember the Battle of Britain, let us never forget the lessons it imparts – the importance of unity in the face of adversity, the resilience of the human spirit, and the enduring power of hope. May this book serve as a tribute to all those who fought and died for freedom, and may their legacy continue to inspire future generations to strive for a better world.

Lest we forget

Claire Horton CBE, Director General,
Commonwealth War Graves Commission

Bibliography

Unpublished Sources

Dilip Sarkar Archive

Published Sources

Allen, H. and Forbes, A. (eds.), *Ten Fighter Boys*, Collins, London, 1942
Ashworth, C., *RAF Coastal Command 1936–1969*, PSL, Sparkford, 1992
Bekker, C., *The Luftwaffe War Diaries*, Corgi, London, 1967
Brickhill, P., *Reach for the Sky: Douglas Bader, His Life Story*, Collins, London, 1954
Burt, K. and Leasor, J., *The One That Got Away*, Collins with Michael Joseph, London, 1956
Calder, A., *The Myth of The Blitz*, Pimlico, London, 2008
Campion, G., *The Battle of Britain 1945–1965: The Air Ministry and The Few*, Palgrave MacMillan, Basingstoke, 2015
Campion, G., *The Battle of Britain in the Modern Age, 1965–2020: The State's Retreat and Popular Enchantment*, Palgrave MacMillan, Basingstoke, 2019
Cannadine, D. (ed.), *The Speeches of Winston Churchill*, Penguin Books, London, 1989
Clapson, M., *The Routledge Companion to Britain in the Twentieth Century*, Routledge, Abingdon, 2009
Corbin, J., *Last of The Ten Fighter Boys*, History Press, Stroud, 2007
Dando-Collins, S., *The Hero Maker: A Biography of Paul Brickhill*, Vintage Books, Sydney, 2016
Deere, A.C., *Nine Lives*, Hodder Paperbacks Limited, London, 1959
Dezarrois, A. (ed.), translated from the French by Stead, P.J., *The Mouchotte Diaries, 1940–1943*, Staples Press Limited, London, 1956

Dickson, L., *Richard Hillary: A Life*, MacMillan & Co. Limited, London, 1950

Donahue, A.G., *Tally-Ho! Yankee in a Spitfire*, MacMillan & Co. Limited, London, 1941

Douglas, S. MRAF and Wright, R., *Years of Command: A Personal Story of War in the Air*, Collins, London, 1966

Dundas, Sir H.S.L., *Flying Start*, Stanley Paul, London, 1988

Forrester, L., *Fly For Your Life: The Story of R.R. Stanford Tuck, DSO, DFC and Two Bars*, The Companion Book Club, London

Francis, M., *The Flyer: British Culture and the Royal Air Force 1939–1945*, Oxford University Press, Oxford, 2008

Galland, A., *The First and The Last: Germany's Fighter Force in the Second World War*, Corgi, London, 1957

Gleave, T.P., *I Had a Row With a German*, MacMillan & Co. Limited, London, 1941

Harrison, T., *Remembrance Today: Poppies, Grief and Heroism*, Reaktion Books Limited, London, 2012

Hillary, R., *The Last Enemy*, MacMillan & Co. Limited, London, 1942

Johnson, J.E., *Wing Leader*, Chatto & Windus, London, 1956

Kent, J., *One of The Few*, Corgi, London, 1977

Kesselring, A., *The Memoirs of Field-Marshal Kesselring*, William Kimber, London, 1953

Longworth, P., *The Unending Vigil: The History of the Commonwealth War Graves Commission*, Pen & Sword, Barnslcy, 2010

MacDonell, A.R.D. and MacDonell, L.E.F., *From Dogfight to Diplomacy: A Spitfire Pilot's Log, 1932–1958*, Pen & Sword Books, Barnsley, 2005

Milne-Day, K., 'The 35th Anniversary of the Unveiling of the Lord Dowding Statue' in Oranges & Lemons: The Friends of St Clement Danes, Issue 56, Autumn 2023, Central Church of the RAF, London, 2023

Orange, V., *Sir Keith Park*, Methuen, London, 1984

Orange, V., *Dowding of Fighter Command: Victor of the Battle of Britain*, Grub Street, London, 2008

Ramsey, W. (ed.), *The Battle of Britain: Then & Now, Mk V*, After the Battle Magazine, London, 1989

Rawnsley, C.F. and Wright, R., *Night Fighter*, William Collins Sons & Co. Limited, London, 1957

Riley, G. and Trant, G., *Spitfire Survivors Round the World*, Aston Publications, Bourne End, 1986

Sarkar, D., *The Last of The Few: Eighteen Battle of Britain Fighter Pilots Tell Their Extraordinary Stories*, Amberley Publishing, Stroud, 2010

Sarkar, D., *The Final Few: The Last Surviving Battle of Britain Pilots Tell Their Stories*, Amberley Publishing, 2015

Sarkar, D., *The Battle of Britain on the Big Screen: The Finest Hour Through British Cinema*, Pen & Sword, Barnsley, 2022

Simpson, A. and Simpson, G. (eds.), *Aircrew Casualties of the Battle of Britain 1940*, Battle of Britain Memorial Trust, Capel-le-Ferne, 2014

Simpson, G., *A History of the Battle of Britain Fighter Association: Commemorating The Few*, Pen & Sword, Barnsley, 2015

Smith, M., *Britain and 1940: History, Myth and Popular Memory*, Routledge, London and New York, 2000

Wellum, G.H.A., *First Light*, Penguin, London, 2002

Winter, J. and Sivan, E., *War & Remembrance in the Twentieth Century*, Cambridge University Press, Cambridge, 1999

Wright, R., *Dowding and the Battle of Britain*, MacDonald & Co. (Publishers) Limited, London, 1969

Zumbach, J., *On Wings of War: My Life as a Pilot Adventurer*, Corgi, London, 1977

Books Referenced

Hitler, Adolf, *Mein Kampf*

Films Referenced

303 Squadron, directed by Denis Delic (Art Fiction, 2018)

A Yank in the RAF, directed by Henry King (20th Century Fox, 1941)

Albert RN, directed by Lewis Gilbert (Angel Productions, 1953)

Angels One Five, directed by George More O'Farrall (Templar Film Studios, 1952)

Battle of Britain, directed by Guy Hamilton (Spitfire Productions, 1969)

Dangerous Moonlight, directed by Brian Desmond Hurst (RKO, 1941)

Dark Blue World, directed by Jan Sverák (Sony Pictures, 2001)

Malta Story, directed by Brian Desmond Hurst (Theta Film Productions, 1953)

Mrs Miniver, directed by William Wyle (Metro-Goldwyn-Mayer, 1942)

Reach for the Sky, directed by Lewis Gilbert (The Rank Organisation, 1956)

Target for Tonight, directed by Harry Watt (Crown Film Unit, 1941)

Tawny Pipet, directed by Bernard Miles and Charles Saunders (General Film Distributors, 1944)
The Dam Busters, directed by Michael Anderson (Associated British Picture Corporation, 1955)
The Flemish Farm, directed by Jeffrey Dell (Two Cities Films, 1943)
The First of The Few, directed by Leslie Howard (British Aviation Pictures, 1942)
The Gap, directed by Donald Carter (Gaumont-British Instructional, 1937)
The Lion Has Wings, directed by Michael Powell, Adrian Brunel and Brian Desmond Hurst (London Films 1939)
The One That Got Away, directed by Roy Ward Baker (Julian Wintle Productions, 1957)
The Purple Plain, directed by Robert Parrish (Two Cities Films, 1954)
The Sea Shall Not Have Them, directed by Lewis Gilbert (Angel Productions, 1954)
The Warning, edited by R.Q. McNaughton (British National Films, 1939)
The Way to the Stars, directed by Anthony Asquith (Two Cities Films, 1945)
Things to Come, directed by William Cameron Menzies (London Films, 1936)
Triumph Des Willens ('Triumph of the Will'), directed by Leni Riefenstahl (Universum Film AG, 1935)
Twelve O'Clock High, directed by Henry King (20th Century Fox, 1949)

Television Programmes Referenced

A Piece of Cake, directed by Ian Toynton (Holmes Associates, 1988)
A Perfect Hero, directed by James Cellan Jones (Havahall Pictures, 1991)
First Light, directed by Matthew Whiteman (Lion Television, 2010)
Forgotten, directed by Julian Austwick (Independently produced, 2023)

Newspapers Referenced

Daily Express
Daily Mail
Daily Mirror
Daily Telegraph
Evening News

Evening Standard
Folkestone Herald
Kent Today
London Gazette
News Chronicle
Sunday Chronicle
Sunday Times
The Financial Times
The New York Times
The Scotsman
The Sun (Sydney)
The Times Literary Supplement

Magazines Referenced

Jägerblatt
Life
Look
The Tatler
Time

Websites

Aerospace Bristol: https://aerospacebristol.org/vision
Airfields of Britain Conservation Trust: https://www.abct.org.uk
Army Flying Museum: https://armyflying.com
Auckland War Memorial Museum: https://www.aucklandmuseum.com
Bamburgh Castle: https://www.bamburghcastle.com
Battle of Britain Bunker: https://battleofbritainbunker.co.uk/#the_bunker
Battle of Britain London Monument: www.bbm.org.uk
Battle of Britain Memorial Trust: www.battleofbritainmemorial.org
Battle of Britain – The People's Project: www.battleofbritainthepeoplesproject.com
BBMF Visitor Centre: https://www.lincolnshire.gov.uk/history-heritage/battle-britain-memorial-flight-visitor-centre
Bentley Priory Museum: https://bentleypriorymuseum.org.uk
Biggin Hill Heritage Hangar: https://flyaspitfire.com/tours/

Billy Fiske Foundation: https://billyfiskefoundation.org
Brookwood Military Cemetery: https://www.cwgc.org/visit-us/find-cemeteries-memorials/cemetery-details/44400/brookwood-military-cemetery/
Commonwealth War Graves Commission: www.cwgc.org
Dilip Sarkar: www.dilipsarkarauthor.com
Douglas Bader Foundation: https://www.douglasbaderfoundation.com
East Grinstead Museum: https://www.eastgrinsteadmuseum.org.uk
Fowlmere Airfield Museum: https://www.fowlmere-airfield-museum.uk/en/
Hangar 42, Spitfire Visitor Centre: https://spitfirevisitorcentre.co.uk
Hunter Fighter Collection: https://hfcscone.org.au/
IWM: https://www.iwm.org.uk
Kenley Revival Project: www.kenleyrevival.org
Kent Battle of Britain Museum: https://www.kbobm.org
Laguna's Spitfire Legacy: https://lagunasspitfirelegacy.org/what-we-do/
Lee-on-the-Solent Memorial: https://www.cwgc.org/our-war-graves-your-history/explore-great-britain/south-region/lee-on-solent-memorial/
Manston Spitfire and Hurricane Memorial Museum: https://www.spitfiremuseum.org.uk
Museum of Transport and Technology: https://www.motat.nz
North Weald Airfield Museum: https://www.nwamuseum.co.uk/index.htm
Polish Air Force Memorial Committee: www.polishairforcememorialcommittee.org
Polish Airmen's Association UK: http://www.polishairmensassociation.org.uk
RAF Battle of Britain Memorial Flight: https://www.raf.mod.uk/display-teams/battle-of-britain-memorial-flight/
RAF Biggin Hill Museum and St George's RAF Chapel of Remembrance: https://bigginhillmuseum.com/visit/chapel/
RAF Chapel, Westminster Abbey: https://www.westminster-abbey.org/history/explore-our-history/raf-chapel#:~:text=At%20the%20eastern%20end%20of,between%20July%20and%20October%201940.
RAF Hornchurch Heritage Centre: https://rafhornchurch.com/heritage-centre/
RAF Museum: https://www.rafmuseum.org.uk/london/
Runnymede Memorial: https://www.cwgc.org/visit-us/find-cemeteries-memorials/cemetery-details/109600/runnymede-memorial/
Shoreham Aircraft Museum: https://www.shoreham-aircraft-museum.co.uk
Sir Keith Park Memorial Project: https://www.sirkeithparkmemorial.org.nz
Sir Keith Park Operations Building: https://www.facebook.com/groups/1058592944214890/

South West Airfields Heritage Exeter Airport Memorial: https://southwestairfields.co.uk/page25.html
Southern Locomotives, 'Sir Keith Park': https://www.southern-locomotives.co.uk/34053/34053_Restoration.html
Spitfire and Hurricane Memorial Museum: https://www.spitfiremuseum.org.uk
Spitfire Association: https://www.spitfireassociation.com
St Clement Danes, Central Church of The RAF: https://stclementdanesraf.org
Tangmere Military Aviation Museum: https://tangmere-museum.org.uk
The Pat Hughes Spitfire Restoration: https://hfcscone.org.au/supermarine-spitfire-mk1a-x4009/the-pat-hughes-spitfire/
The Sir Keith Park Memorial Campaign: http://www.sirkeithpark.com/index.aspx
Yorkshire Air Museum: https://yorkshireairmuseum.org

YouTube

Dilip Sarkar's Battle of Britain Channel: http://www.youtube.com/@battleofbritain_DilipSarkar
Jan Leeming – Searching for Rene Mouchotte DFC, Free French WW2 Pilot: https://youtu.be/oVNwEZ8KriM?si=Uy-c-ago902uW3D0

Images

All photos Dilip Sarkar Archive unless otherwise accredited.

Other Books by Dilip Sarkar

Spitfire Squadron: No. 19 Squadron at War, 1939–41

The Invisible Thread: A Spitfire's Tale

Through Peril to the Stars: RAF Fighter Pilots Who Failed to Return, 1939–45

Angriff Westland: Three Battle of Britain Air Raids Through the Looking Glass

A Few of the Many: Air War 1939–45, A Kaleidoscope of Memories

Bader's Tangmere Spitfires: The Untold Story, 1941

Bader's Duxford Fighters: The Big Wing Controversy

Missing in Action: Resting in Peace?

Guards VC: Blitzkrieg 1940

Battle of Britain: The Photographic Kaleidoscope, Volumes I–IV

Fighter Pilot: The Photographic Kaleidoscope

Group Captain Sir Douglas Bader: An Inspiration in Photographs

Johnnie Johnson: Spitfire Top Gun, Part I

Johnnie Johnson: Spitfire Top Gun, Part II

Battle of Britain: Last Look Back

Spitfire! Courage & Sacrifice

Spitfire Voices: Heroes Remember

The Battle of Powick Bridge: Ambush a Fore-thought

Duxford 1940: A Battle of Britain Base at War

The Few: The Battle of Britain in the Words of the Pilots

OTHER BOOKS BY DILIP SARKAR

Spitfire Manual 1940

The Sinking of HMS Royal Oak *in the Words of the Survivors* (re-print of Hearts of Oak)

The Last of The Few: Eighteen Battle of Britain Pilots Tell Their Extraordinary Stories

Hearts of Oak: The Human Tragedy of HMS Royal Oak

Spitfire Voices: Life as a Spitfire Pilot in the Words of the Veterans

How the Spitfire Won the Battle of Britain

Spitfire Ace of Aces: The True Wartime Story of Johnnie Johnson Douglas Bader

Fighter Ace: The Extraordinary Life of Douglas Bader, Battle of Britain Hero (re-print of above)

Spitfire: The Photographic Biography

Hurricane Manual 1940

River Pike

The Final Few: The Last Surviving Pilots of the Battle of Britain Tell Their Stories

Arnhem 1944: The Human Tragedy of the Bridge Too Far

Spitfire! The Full Story of a Unique Battle of Britain Fighter Squadron

Battle of Britain 1940: The Finest Hour's Human Cost

Letters from The Few: Unique Memories of the Battle of Britain

Johnnie Johnson's 1942 Diary: The War Diary of the Spitfire Ace of Aces

Johnnie Johnson's Great Adventure: The Spitfire Ace of Ace's Last Look Back

Sailor Malan – Freedom Fighter: The Inspirational Story of a Spitfire Ace

Spitfire Ace of Aces – The Album: The Photographs of Johnnie Johnson

The Real Spitfire Pilot, being the previously unpublished original manuscript of Spitfire Pilot by Flight Lieutenant David Crook, with introduction, commentary and photographs by Dilip Sarkar

Bader's Big Wing Controversy: Duxford 1940

Bader's Spitfire Wing: Tangmere 1941

Spitfire Down: Fighter Boys Who Failed to Return

Forgotten Heroes of The Battle of Britain

Faces of The Few

Spitfire Faces

Arise to Conquer: The Real Hurricane Pilot by Wing Commander Ian Gleed, introduction, commentary and photographs by Dilip Sarkar

Free French Spitfire Hero: The Diaries of and Search for René Mouchotte (with Jan Leeming)

I Had A Row With a German by Group Captain Tom Gleave, introduction by Dilip Sarkar

Battle of Britain: The Finest Hour in Cinema

Battle of Britain: The Movie (contributor to and publisher of the now late Robert Rudhall's original edition (2000), and editor and substantial contributor to 2022 revised edition)

Faces of HMS Royal Oak*: The 'Mighty Oak' Disaster at Scapa Flow*

Battle of Britain, Volume 1:
The Gathering Storm – Prelude to the Spitfire Summer of 1940

Battle of Britain, Volume 2:
The Breaking Storm – 10 July 1940–12 August 1940

Battle of Britain, Volume 3:
Attack of the Eagles – 13 August 1940–18 August 1940

Battle of Britain, Volume 4:
Airfields Under Attack – 19 August 1940–6 September 1940

Battle of Britain, Volume 5:
Target London – 7 September 1940–17 September 1940

Battle of Britain, Volume 6:
Daylight Defeat – 18 September 1940–30 September 1940

Battle of Britain, Volume 7:
The Final Curtain – 1 October 1940–31 October 1940

Index